THE FORGOTTEN FAITHFUL

A Window into the Life and Witness
of Christians in the Holy Land

Front cover photo: The Church of the Resurrection
(Holy Sepulchre), Jerusalem.

THE FORGOTTEN FAITHFUL

A Window into the Life and Witness of Christians in the Holy Land

editors
NAIM ATEEK, CEDAR DUAYBIS
AND MAURINE TOBIN

SABEEL ECUMENICAL LIBERATION
THEOLOGY CENTER

The Forgotten Faithful
First published 2007

ISBN 978-965-7409-00-8

Published by Sabeel Ecumenical Liberation Theology Center, Jerusalem, 2007
Printed and bound by Emerezian Est., Jerusalem

TABLE OF CONTENTS

THE DISAPPEARING LANDSCAPE

CHRISTIAN-MUSLIM RELATIONS

ARAB IDENTITY IN A JEWISH STATE

THE POLITICAL SITUATION AND STRATEGIES
TO END THE OCCUPATION

EDITORS' NOTE

Sabeel is grateful to the many contributors to this book, the vast majority of whom presented their papers to the Conference in English. Although space has necessitated abbreviating some of the papers, we have endeavored to keep intact the central message of each presenter.

We have sought to preserve their distinctive voices and styles in this volume, maintaining differing conventions of spelling and syntax as well as of bibliographic form. We have included all footnote and source information provided to us by the authors.

The content and point of view of each paper is that of the author and does not necessarily reflect the position of the Sabeel Liberation Theology Center of Jerusalem.

ACKNOWLEDGMENTS

Sabeel Ecumenical Liberation Theology Center, wishes to express its deepest gratitude to all those who contributed to the success of the Sixth International Conference held 2 – 9 November 2006. The Conference, entitled "The Forgotten Faithful: A Window into the Life and Witness of Christians in the Holy Land" was a traveling conference with sessions held at the Notre Dame Center of Jerusalem, the Bethlehem University, the Cultural Palace of Ramallah, and the Baptist Church of Nazareth, enabling international participants to interact with Palestinian Christians from the West Bank and the Galilee as well as from Jerusalem. Participants stayed in hotels in Jerusalem, Jericho, and Nazareth and in small groups worshipped in a total of seven Christian communities in the West Bank and visited seven additional Christian villages in the Galilee.

A traveling conference of this sort required extraordinary planning and logistical coordination on the part of many people. We are especially grateful to the Coordinator of the Conference, Dr. Lynn Holmes, who, along with Staff Conference Coordinator Dr. Catherine Nichols, was responsible for bringing the Conference into being. As always, the Sabeel Board of Directors in Jerusalem, especially the Executive Committee, and the Sabeel Nazareth Committee provided invaluable guidance throughout the planning and implementation of the Conference.

Staff and volunteers of both Sabeel Jerusalem and Sabeel Nazareth gave countless hours in preparing for and making possible the many lectures, panels, worship services, and special events of the Conference. Although they are too many to name individually, we express our heartfelt thanks to each and every one of them.

Finally, the Conference would not have been possible without the generosity of our funding partners who underwrote many aspects of the Conference. Norwegian Church Aid provided funding for Conference scholarships for local participants as well as for a series of pre- and post-conferences in several Palestinian Christian communities. Diakonia, the Christian development agency funded by five Swedish churches, underwrote publication of this book as well as The Sabeel Survey on Palestinian Christians in the West Bank and Israel. This groundbreaking study by Dr. Bernard Sabella and Mr. Romell Soudah and their research associates at Bethlehem University was the centerpiece of the Conference. The findings of the Survey are available in print in both English and Arabic from Sabeel Jerusalem (www.sabeel.org) as well as electronically on the same website.

CONTRIBUTORS

Dr. Hanna Abu-Hanna has published more than 20 books of poetry, autobiography, and research on the Palestinian cultural heritage as well as a series of stories for children. Dr. Abu-Hanna won the Prize of Palestine for Literature in 1999.

Dr. Mamdouh Aker is a urologist and was a member of the Palestinian delegation for peace talks in Madrid and for bilateral negotiations in Washington, 1991-1993. He is Commissioner General for the Palestinian Independent Commission for Citizen's Rights.

Archbishop Dr. Anba Abraham is the Orthodox Coptic Bishop in Jerusalem and the Near East. He holds degrees in Medicine and Aromatic Plants as well as an M.A. degree in theology from Cairo University.

Archbishop of Constantina Aristarchos is the Chief Secretary and Librarian of the Greek Orthodox Patriarchate of Jerusalem and is a member of the Central Committee of the World Council of Churches.

The Rev. Dr. Naim Ateek is the Founder and Director of Sabeel Ecumenical Liberation Theology Center Jerusalem, which emerged from a Palestinian theology of liberation articulated in his 1989 book *Justice, and only Justice, a Palestinian Theology of Liberation.*

The Rev. Dr. Kenneth Bailey, Presbyterian minister and distinguished New Testament theologian, spent 40 years living and teaching in the Middle East. He has written extensively on the cultural context of the scriptures and what the Gospels meant to their original audiences.

Ms. Suhad Bishara, is an Advocate and Coordinator of the Legal Department of Adalah, the Legal Center for Arab Minority Rights in Israel, with a degree in Public Service Law from New York University School of Law (USA) and a law degree from Hebrew University.

Ms. Terry Boullata is the Coordinator for the Lobbying and Advocacy Department at the Palestinian Agricultural Relief Committees (PARC) in Palestine. She was a participant in the Geneva Accord initiative for peace, is an activist against the Wall, and is assistant producer for the film *The Iron Wall*.

Father Frans Bouwen is a Roman Catholic priest and member of the Society of Missionaries of Africa (the "White Fathers"). He specializes in history, theology, liturgy and the present life of the churches in the Middle East, with a particular emphasis on inter-religious relations.

Dr. Henry Ralph Carse is Director of Special Programs at St. George's College, Jerusalem, and Founder and Director of "Kids4Peace," an interfaith education-for-peace initiative. He teaches experiential study programs on such diverse subjects as Desert Spirituality, the Art of Pilgrimage, and Interfaith Dialogue.

Bishop Dr. Kenneth Cragg has had a long and impressive career as one of the world's foremost Christian scholars on Islam, Qur'anic studies, and Muslim-Christian dialogue. He is the author of innumerable articles and books including the seminal volume, *The Call of the Minaret*, and *The Qur'an and the West* (2006).

Mr. Jafar Farah is the Founder and Director of Mossawa Center: the Advocacy Center for Arab Citizens in Israel, which supports capacity building for NGO's, conflict prevention, and equal socio-economic status for Arab Israelis. He has written many articles on issues of concern for the Arab minority in Israel.

Mr. Kevork (George) Hintlian is a local historian specializing in 19th century Jerusalem. He frequently organizes conferences on the Christian heritage of the Holy Land and is author of a number of books and articles on this topic.

Dr. Y. Lynn Holmes is a professor and university administrator with a theological degree as well as degrees in Ancient History. He has published articles in the areas of religion, ancient history, and the modern Middle East.

Dr. Jad Isaac is the Director General of the Applied Research Institute-Jerusalem (ARIJ), a leading Palestinian institute that conducts research on agriculture, environment, land use and water. He advises the Palestinian negotiating team on final status issues.

Dr. Ali Khashan is the founder and former Dean of the College of Law at Al Quds University. He was a prominent member as well as secretary of the Constitution Committee for developing the draft of the Palestinian Constitution in 2001.

Mr. Ghassan Khatib is co-founder and co-editor of the *bitterlemons* family of internet publications. He is the former Palestinian Authority Minister of Planning, has been a political analyst and media contact for many years, and currently is Lecturer of Cultural Studies and Vice-President for Community Outreach at Birzeit University.

Father Dr. Rafik Khoury is a priest in Palestine's Latin Patriarchate and Secretary General of the Pastoral Catholic Committee in the Holy Land. He has written numerous books in Arabic and is a scholar of the long history of Christians and Muslims living together in the Holy Land.

Mr. Jonathan Kuttab is a Palestinian lawyer, advocate for Human Rights, and renowned Christian speaker. He is on the Executive Committee of Sabeel and often represents Sabeel in local and international gatherings.

Bishop Giacinto-Boulos Marcuzzo is Auxiliary Bishop and Patriarchal Vicar General for Israel, serving in Haifa. He was ordained priest in 1969, and in 1993 he was ordained Bishop and appointed Titular Bishop of Emmaus.

Archbishop Mar Sewerios Malki Murad is Patriarchal Vicar of Jerusalem, Jordan, and the Holy Land in the Syrian Orthodox Patriarchate.

Dr. Khalil Nakhleh is a Palestinian socio-cultural anthropologist whose research focuses on Palestinian society, history and education, its internal transformation and development and its regional and international interactions. His latest book is *In Search of Palestinian Identity: A Personal Odyssey* (2005).

Dr. Yousef Nasser was born in Palestine and raised in the United States. He has taught at Birzeit University since 1980, acted as economic advisor to UNRWA and as senior water economist for UNDP, serves on many research and development boards and is Mayor of Birzeit.

Dr. Ilan Pappe, an Israeli-born professor at Haifa University, is well-known as a revisionist or "post-Zionist" Israeli historian. Chair of the Emil Touma Institute for Palestinian Studies and Academic Director of the Research Institute for Peace, he is the author of many books, the most recent being *The Ethnic Cleansing of Palestine* (2006).

Patriarch Michel Sabbah is the Latin Patriarch and Archbishop of Jerusalem. In 1987, Pope John Paul II named him the first Palestinian to serve as Patriarch in Jerusalem; he has been a strong spokesman on behalf of Palestinian rights and often serves as the voice of Christians of all denominations in the Holy Land.

Leila Sansour is the founder and Chief Executive of Open Bethlehem. She returned to her hometown in 2005 to set up the Bethlehem campaign after a long career in film and TV production abroad.

Archbishop Paul Sayah is Archbishop of Haifa and the Holy Land and the Patriarchal Exarch for Jerusalem and Palestine. As the titular of the Maronite Church in the Holy Land, he has brought a renaissance to the Maronite community and is well-known for his rich ecumenical experience.

Dr. Irfan Shahid is the Oman Professor of Arabic and Islamic Studies at Georgetown University. His research and publications include three themes: the intersection of the Greco-Roman world and the Arabic and Islamic worlds in late antique and medieval times; Classical and Medieval Arabic poetry; and Islamic studies, especially the Qur'an.

Archbishop Aris Shirvanian is Director of Ecumenical and Foreign Relations of the Armenian Patriarchate in Jerusalem. A graduate of the Armenian Seminary in Jerusalem, he was ordained in 1957 and has served Armenian communities in Paris, California, Canada and India.

Patriarch Theophilos III of Jerusalem and All Palestine was enthroned as 141st primate of the Orthodox church of Jerusalem in November, 2005. From Messina, Greece, he served in Cana of Galilee, where he created the society of "Nour al Masih" ("Light of Christ"), and was Archbishop of Tabor before his enthronement.

Mr. Alain Epp Weaver, a doctoral student in theology, served in the Occupied Territories and Jordan for the Mennonite Central Committee and is the editor of the forthcoming *Under Vine and Fig Tree: Biblical Theologies of Land and the Palestinian-Israeli Conflict* and of *Borders and Bridges: Mennonite Witness in a Religiously Diverse World*.

Bishop Munib A. Younan is Bishop of the Evangelical Lutheran Church in Jordan and the Holy Land (ELCJHL) and President of the Board of Managers of the International Christian Committee of Jerusalem. A leader in ecumenical and interfaith groups, he has received many awards for his work on behalf of human rights and justice.

Ms. Jean Zaru is Presiding Clerk of the Ramallah Friends Meeting in Palestine, a founding member of Sabeel and Vice-chair of its Board of Directors. As a Palestinian woman living in a traditional culture under Israeli military rule, she is a renowned spokesperson for liberation for her own people, for women, and for all humanity.

FOREWORD

Palestinian Christians are the offspring of those first disciples and apostles whom Jesus called and who followed him. They are the descendants of those who, on the Day of Pentecost 2000 years ago, experienced the empowerment of the Holy Spirit and responded to the Gospel, the good news of Jesus Christ. Yet Palestinian Christians of today's Holy Land are painfully aware of their declining numbers. Virtually all Palestinian Christian families have one or more members living abroad. In 1949, according to the Statistical Abstract of Israel, Christians made up 21.3% of the total number of Palestinians (Arab Israelis) who remained in that part of Mandatory Palestine that became the state of Israel. They constituted 3% of the total population then. Today (2007) they comprise 9% of the Arab Israeli population and less than 2% of the total population.

According to the census of the Israeli military in 1967, the number of Christians on the West Bank including East Jerusalem and the Gaza Strip was 42,494. If we assume a 2% annual growth, by 2007 their number should have been over 90,000, whereas in fact, even a generous estimate of the total number of Christians in these areas does not exceed 50,000.[i]

Another example is that of the city of Jerusalem itself. In 1945, the Christian population of Jerusalem was 31,330.[ii] If we assume a growth rate of

---

i See *The Sabeel Survey on Palestinian Christians in the West Bank and Israel*: Sabeel Ecumenical Liberation Theology Center. Summer, 2006, p. 50.

ii Ibid, p. 43.

2%, then the Christian population of Jerusalem by 1980 should have been 62,000 and in 2007 over 100,000[iii] whereas the actual estimate is 8,000.[iv] Tragically, worsening economic, political, educational, and social conditions are prompting many Christians to consider joining those who have already fled their homeland.

In light of this reality, Sabeel entitled its Sixth International Conference held November 2 - 9, 2006, "The Forgotten Faithful: A Window into the Life and Witness of Christians in the Holy Land."

Prior to the Conference, Sabeel received a generous grant from Diakonia, a Swedish development organization to commission a sample survey of 1500 Christian families representing the approximately 50,000 Palestinian Christians living in East Jerusalem and the West Bank as well as the approximately 110,000 Palestinian Christians living in Israel. Unfortunately, conditions in Gaza prevented including in the Survey the approximately 2,500 Christians there.

The Sabeel Survey on Palestinian Christians in the West Bank and Israel was supervised by Dr. Bernard Sabella, a Palestinian sociologist and a long time friend and supporter of Sabeel. University Lecturers Romell Soudah, Walid Atallah, and Father Jamal Khader, all of Bethlehem University, supervised the graduate students from Bethlehem University who gathered the data, which was analyzed by Dr. Sabella and Mr. Soudah. The results of the Survey were presented at the Sabeel Conference in November, 2006, and are available from Sabeel in print form both in Arabic and English as well as electronically on the Sabeel website: www.sabeel.org

The conference itself had two goals:

1. To give an opportunity for international Christians to share in the lives of Palestinian Christians by visiting their churches and communities and by interacting in various locales during the Conference. Thus, the Conference held sessions in Jerusalem, Ramallah, Bethlehem, and Nazareth enabling participation by many Palestinian Christians.

---

iii Ibid, p. 44.
iv Ibid, p. 43.

2. To educate participants about the history and current realities of Christians and Christianity in the Holy Land and clarify the role of Palestinian Christians in peacemaking and in seeking to shape a just and sustainable society in the future. Conference worship services, lectures, panel discussions, and cultural presentations thus conveyed:

- The rich diversity of Christianity both historically and currently through the participation of all the Leaders of the Churches in the Holy Land.
- The differing experiences of Christians who are Israeli citizens from the experiences of those who live under the Israeli occupation.

- The impact of Occupation in the West Bank including East Jerusalem and the Gaza Strip on all Palestinians and the relationship of Christians and Muslims who share these difficult conditions.

- The tradition of pilgrimage and the importance of cultural context in Biblical interpretation and worship in sustaining the faith of local Christians.

Presentations on these and related topics are collected in the present volume.

Many fear the time when there will be pilgrimages to the "dead stones" of the traditional Holy Sites but no "living stones" witnessing to the message of Jesus in the place of his birth, ministry, death, and resurrection. However, Palestinian Christians of all denominations are called to live out Jesus' message of peace in his homeland, not a false peace based on militarism and power but a true peace based on non-violence, justice and equity for all the peoples of the land. As we Palestinian Christians struggle to remain in our homeland and to witness to our faith, may we be strengthened not only by our hope in God but by the prayers, support, and advocacy of Christians throughout the world.

Naim Ateek
Sabeel Jerusalem
August 2007

GREETINGS TO THE SIXTH INTERNATIONAL SABEEL CONFERENCE

Patriarch Theophilos III, Greek Orthodox Church

It is an honor as the Patriarch of Jerusalem to be amongst you and to address Sabeel's sixth International Conference on the subject, "The Forgotten Faithful: A Window into the Life and Witness of Christians in the Holy Land." This Conference provides a unique opportunity to encounter the realities faced by Christians in the Middle East in general and in Israel and Palestine in particular. Jerusalem, as the host city of the three monotheistic religions, Judaism, Christianity and Islam, undoubtedly constitutes a window into the life and witness of Christians who are part and parcel of the sacred history, that is, the history of salvation, which is inextricably associated with the history of the Holy Land, the land that has been blessed with the sacrificial blood and the burial of our Lord, Jesus Christ.

Christian witness throughout the 2,000 years of Christianity in the Holy Land has been manifested in and through the very establishment by our Lord Jesus Christ of the Apostolic Church of Jerusalem and its elevation to the well-known Greek Orthodox Patriarchate of Jerusalem. The Church as the Body of Christ and the Christian faithful as the members of the Body of Christ serve with and participate in the birth, the passion and crucifixion, and the resurrection of our Lord, Jesus Christ, who is the Head of His Body, the Head of the Church, and the leader of our life in faith. The ultimate purpose of the Church is to help us attain transformation, that is, deification or unity with God, in and through the process of healing and sanctification. Attainment of our transformation implies deliverance from our sinful human predicament and is conditioned on the emptying of oneself as Christ emptied Himself. The Christian community as a whole, and Christian churches in particular, have been assigned an apostolic mission that is both local and ecumenical. This local and ecumenical mission aims at maintaining Christian presence in the Holy Land as well as facing challenges, aspirations, and encounters with real life: political, social, and economical situations as well as religious conditions and relationships between persons of different religious affiliations. The presence, therefore, of this international Christian ingathering in Jerusalem gives hope that the voice of the "forgotten faithful" is no longer the voice of one crying in the wilderness, but the way of awareness of Christian fellowship. In seeking the grace of the Holy Spirit, the Spirit of our Lord Jesus Christ, to come upon you, we prayerfully wish you success in your Holy Land Christian mission. God bless you.

FORGOTTEN CHRISTIANS
OF THE HOLY LAND

Patriarch Michel Sabbah

Who are we Christians of the Holy Land? We are thirteen traditional churches: five Orthodox (Greek, Armenian, Copt, Syrian and Ethiopian), six Catholic (Roman [Latin] Catholic, Greek Catholic, Maronite, Armenian, Syrian, and Chaldean), and two Protestant (Anglican and Lutheran). As churches, we all have ecclesiastical jurisdiction over the same three countries: Israel, Palestine and Jordan. In these three countries, the total number of Christians is about 400,000, half of whom live in Jordan, the other half in Palestine-Israel. A larger number of Christians, who have been emigrating from the 19th century until today, live in the Diaspora. All of them are Arabs, Palestinians or Jordanians.

Besides this basic traditional Arab Christian presence in the Holy Land (Israel, Palestine, and Jordan), there is in Israel a Christian Hebrew-speaking community, both Catholic and Protestant. To that must be added a large Russian presence which increased with successive waves of Jewish immigration to Israel. According to various estimates given by Israeli sources, non-Jewish Russians in Israel number between four and five hundred thousand people. Non-Jewish means that they are either Christians or they have Christian roots. Varied, but limited, pastoral work is carried out among this population by monasteries in Israel or by a few priests exclusively dedicated to their pastoral care. At the same time, Jewish religious organizations are very active in "Judaizing" these non-Jewish Russians.

Additionally, there is a third Christian presence in the Holy Land, an international one made up of workers and business people. It is approximately as large as the indigenous Christian presence, particularly in Israel. This paper is limited to the Arab Palestinian Christians in the Holy Land.

The reality in which we Palestinian Christians are presently living has the following characteristics:

First, we are **an integral part of the Arab world** and hence of the Arab Muslim world. We are a part of it, and we are sent to it by God. As Arab Christians in the Holy Land, we are called to be witnesses to Jesus in His land and in our Arab Muslim society as well as in the Israeli Jewish society. In order to do that, we dialogue with both Muslims and Jews. In the last few years, a Council of Religious Leaders in the Holy Land, comprising Christians, Jews and Muslims, was created. It is functioning, though very hesitatingly. Nevertheless, it is an effort that will continue because all three religions are in need of it.

Second, as Christians in the Holy Land, we live in a **situation of conflict**, the Israeli-Palestinian conflict; we live under a military occupation imposed by the Israelis on the Palestinians and within a Palestinian resistance to this occupation which pursues both violent and non-violent means.

Within this conflict, we are at the same time Palestinians and Christians. As Palestinians and Christians, we say three complementary things. First, occupation is an injustice that must stop. Therefore, resistance to occupation is a right and a duty. Second, resistance can be violent or non-violent. We, as Christians, call for non-violent resistance. Third, our position is based on the following fundamentally Christian and human principles: all human beings are equal in dignity before God. They all have the same rights and the same duties. No one, for religious or political reasons, should be subjugated by the other. All people have the right to live in security and to choose their own type of independent government, Israelis and Palestinians alike. Therefore, in this conflict, we call for an end to the occupation, declaring at the same time that we care for the well-being and for the security and peace of both peoples, Israelis and Palestinians.

Are we Christian Palestinians in the Holy Land forgotten? The answer is both yes and no.

We are not forgotten by ever so many Christians who belong to various churches around the world. Indeed, we receive a lot of attention from many Catholic, Protestant and Orthodox churches. The important presence of pilgrims, in response to our frequent invitations, is a sign that we are not forgotten. Moreover, we receive many messages of solidarity from churches all around the world, and we are morally and materially supported by the great generosity of many people and by numerous donations that allow our institutions and many of our individual Christians to keep functioning. We cannot forget, either, the advocacy conducted by the churches, by the WCC and its accompaniment program, and by the divestment initiative adopted by some churches, although it is strongly opposed by others despite the fact that it is an effort to limit war and bring peace and reconciliation. There is also the voice and the presence of the Holy See in Rome and of so many other churches, with a special mention of the churches of the United States and Great Britain.

Taking all this into consideration, we can say that we are not forgotten. But the fate and future of Palestinian Christians do not depend only on messages of solidarity, on generous charity, and on limited advocacy. The present and future of Christians depend on the conflict itself: the longer it continues, the more endangered is their presence. The greatest contribution that can be made to Christians in the Holy Land is to help put an end to the conflict and to ask the churches to intervene by calling for an end to the conflict. We are speaking of a contribution to reconciliation, which is the proper action for all churches. As St. Paul says: "He reconciled us to himself through Christ and he gave us the ministry of reconciliation" (2 Cor 5:18).

The churches are called to exercise this ministry of reconciliation in the midst of this conflict here in the Holy Land between Israelis and Palestinians because the conflict is taking place here where the holy places are located, where the roots of Christianity itself are found, and where the conflict seriously endangers the Christian presence and its future.

Despite all the signs of solidarity mentioned above, it seems that not all the churches are sufficiently aware of this ministry and of this obligation, either because of negligence or because they fear involving themselves in a conflict that concerns Judaism and the Jewish people. Christians of the Holy Land, the Land of the Redemption itself, wait for more awareness, more courage, and more concerted and decisive action on the part of the churches in order to bring reconciliation to all in this Land of the Redemption.

We are forgotten when it comes to the political leaders and to the **political agendas** for the region. We can say that the political agendas are indifferent to the survival or disappearance of Christians. Some political leaders have occasionally visited church authorities in Jerusalem and paid attention to their existence and concerns. Some US Congressmen, these days, show interest in our survival and believe we are endangered by our Muslim society. Others think we can be a disincarnated and purely religious community, belonging to nothing, to no place. They offer to help us, to protect us, as a special community, independent of the conflict, while the overall occupation, oppression and injustices are taking place. We say: uprooting us from our Palestinian society is not the way to help us. **It is the way to kill us.** We keep saying: we are human beings; we are part of our society, of those who die, of those who go to prison, and of those whose houses are demolished. All these people are part of us, and we are part of every human being, of Muslims and Jews alike. We are part of this land. We are part of the conflict because it is not a conflict between Muslims and Jews; it is a conflict about the dignity of the human person, and about human rights and freedom. Christians cannot and must not be set apart as mere spectators entitled to enjoy an "inhuman, disembodied" life, while others are paying the price of freedom by their lives or their daily suffering.

Again we say to those political leaders interested in helping Christians: you must understand that the best support you can offer us is to get involved in the process of reconciliation between the two peoples because this is the true and real condition for our survival, and this is our vocation and our mission in this land.

Moreover, we Christians of the Holy Land must know that our survival is first in our own hands and depends upon our awareness of our own faith lived in all the aspects of our political and social life. We must have a vision, and act accordingly. Then all support that comes to us from all the other churches can truly help us.

The question of emigration, the question of our survival and of our future, involves our own re-education. It is a question of a coordinated catechesis so that all of us become equally aware of our vocation and mission in this land. This means a catechesis that teaches our faithful that a truly authentic Christian life begins with worship in the presence of God. It begins with a presence before God, a presence that sends us out from the church to our society, to the heart of the conflict. It requires that we see ourselves as partners in all of the suffering that is taking place, in all of the heavy sacrifices that are being made. This also means a catechesis that teaches all those among us who are involved in direct political activity that their actions must be intimately linked to moments of worship and of presence before God, inside or outside the church. To belong to the church does not mean having denominational, sectarian, negative, or fanatical attitudes and behaviors. It means having love and strength similar to God's own love for all his creatures of all religions and nationalities. It means a more decided contribution to and sharing in all aspects of the life of our society.

For that, we need more coordination among the churches in the Holy Land. It is true: we meet often as Heads of Churches in Jerusalem. We talk about our situation, but we still need a clearer agenda that takes into consideration the roots of our life and the meaning of our witness to Jesus in His land. We need to know that, though we are a small number, we are not lost between two majorities. We have our own vocation and mission, we have our full place in our society, and we share in the general obligation to establish peace and justice within it.

Perhaps we need an ecumenical Christian synod in the Holy Land to call for deep and serious reflection to put together the mode of Christian living in this Holy Land, a mode that clearly states how we relate to each other in terms of our basic Christian commandment of love, how we relate to all our brothers and sisters of different religions here in the land, and how we relate to our Christian brothers and sisters throughout the world, as we ask them to support us in our vocation and in our mission to our own society.

What is our future? Many books have been published about us Christians in the Holy Land or in the Middle East. Almost all these studies made by westerners are pessimistic about our future. They see us as disappearing in a few generations. For them, the Christian presence is in the final stage of its struggle for survival within the Muslim Arab world.

As for us, we say: a Christian vision of the future is essentially a vision of hope, a hope based on trust in the goodness of God as well as in the basic goodness of all human beings who are God's creatures and children, "since it is in him that we live, and move, and exist" (Acts 17:28). Therefore, it is also a hope based on the daily efforts and struggles of men and women, as well as on our own efforts to foster, among all Christians in this holy and difficult land, more unity, love and faithfulness to our vocation and mission here.

With this, we will live and develop as best as we can. Some of us will leave. But those who remain will live and grow in love for each other and for all of our society.

THE CHALLENGES AND WITNESS OF PALESTINIAN CHRISTIANS

Jean Zaru

Ahlan wa Sahlan bikom. Welcome to each and every one of you gathered for the 6th International Sabeel Conference. Some of you traveled across oceans and continents to be present. We are grateful for your efforts and enriched by your solidarity. Please feel the breadth of our hospitality and know that you are at home.

For some of you, Jerusalem is your home and Palestine is your native land. We appreciate the sacrifices you made, the risks you took, the checkpoints you crossed to be here and to share your witness. We are thankful for your steadfastness and know very well that this conference is only meaningful with your presence.

For others, to be here today is impossible, for the Palestinian right of return is a right long denied.

And finally, my friends, there are those who wanted to be here but could not. There are those of us indigenous Palestinians who live fragmented and separated in our own homeland. We especially grieve the absence of these sisters and brothers. Yet, we acknowledge and honor their presence with us in Spirit. For we know that the dividing Wall of hostility will not last. Rather it is the abiding and just love of our One Creator that will see us through and have the final word.

This conference, this shared journey, will surely demand all our resources: physical, psychological, emotional, and spiritual. And, my friends, it will do so as we find ourselves in one of the most discouraging, distressful and dangerous points in history. These are very hard days in Palestine. The settlement expansion and the construction of the Wall continue unabated. International law and UN resolutions sit collecting dust. While the political landscape has changed dramatically and global powers maneuver a response, humanitarian aid and military violence against civilians are used like playing cards without regard to ordinary families struggling to secure their daily bread. During such times as these, it is necessary to name the atrocities, to name our individual and collective pain. For it often goes unheard. Voicing it always includes risk but is nonetheless crucial, for with the cry of pain begins the formation of a counter community around an alternative perception of reality. Thus, the act of crying out and groaning is at once an act of subversion and an act of hope. In fact, for the prophet Jeremiah, grief is a radical form of criticism and de-legitimizing. As he publicly mourns over Judah, Jeremiah exclaims:

> My anguish, my anguish! I writhe in pain!
> Oh, the walls of my heart!
> My heart is beating wildly;
> I cannot keep silent,
> for I hear the sound of the trumpet, the alarm of war.
> Disaster follows hard on disaster,
> The whole land is laid waste (4:19-20).

My friends, we have been working for a long time to end oppression and occupation and have, thus far, not secured our rights. It is discouraging. Fear and loss surround us, and many forces are at work to make us feel marginalized and disempowered. At best the work ahead seems overwhelming.

What do we do? What actions do we take? Without a doubt, the way of transformation calls us to stand against the forces of death and evil, both within us and around us. It challenges us to resist the temptation simply to re-arrange the furniture, whether that re-arrangement is in the structures of our psyches or those of our planet.

What is that inner force that drives us, that provides regeneration and perseverance to speak the truth that so desperately needs to be spoken in this moment in history? I am older, my health poor, my body fragile and yet, as do so many others, I believe that I have no choice but to bear witness to what is happening in my land, to expose the structures of violence and domination, to bring them out into the light, and thereby to undercut their power. If I deserve credit for courage, it is only for continuing the struggle under occupation on so many fronts, for remaining *samida* (steadfast) and, all the while, open to love of neighbor, to the beauty of the earth, and to contributing to its healing when it is violated.

My friends, struggle changes us in profound ways. For the essence of struggle is neither endurance nor denial. Rather, the essence of struggle is the decision to become NEW rather than simply to become older. That is, within the essence of struggle lies the opportunity to grow either smaller or larger, to become more than what we already are or to retreat into becoming less. Indeed, the process of life itself may be found within this opportunity. **For life is about movement.** And everyday we either become more or we diminish. In the struggle, and especially in this particular struggle, we cannot give up.

Some of my people have opted to withdraw, either to withdraw internally or to withdraw both internally and externally, that is, to leave Palestine. In fact, many have responded in this manner because they truly perceive their situation as intolerable. Regardless of the motivation, withdrawal cushions us from feeling the full impact of our situation, and it also cuts us off from information and observations vital to our survival as a people. When we withdraw, our gifts and our perceptions often get buried. The realities of domination go unchallenged, leading neither to inner nor outer transformation.

Other people have chosen to accommodate, comply or manipulate. When we manipulate, we have the illusion of being in control. We can reap some rewards, but in doing so we are accepting the system's terms, its unspoken rules and values, including the often negative values it assigns to us. Furthermore, manipulation does not challenge the low value the system places on individuals. In order to manipulate, we cannot be ourselves, express our true feelings, or share our real perceptions; we literally mask ourselves. Manipulation may get us some of the system's rewards, but it neither liberates us individually nor transforms the structures of domination.

The alternative is to **resist**. Resistance challenges the system's values and categories. Resistance speaks its own truth to power and shifts the ground of struggle to its own terrain. Resistance is often thought of as negative. However, resistance is the **refusal to be neglected**. Today, Palestinians find themselves embedded in structures that neglect their humanity and human rights; only acts of resistance can transform these structures. And I, along with many others, have opted for the path of active nonviolent resistance. To resist is to be human, and yet resistance is not easy. It requires constant hard work. Indeed, it is not easy to sustain the path of nonviolent resistance for years and years over many issues. None of us can resist all the time, in every area of life.

We must choose our battles, meaning we must choose the priorities of struggle. But the question remains: where do we find sustenance? How are we re-energized, how are we empowered to continue to go forward on the path of resisting structures of domination and establishing the reign of God, indeed establishing a household of life?

I believe that we continue because something is so sacred to us, so sacred that it means more than our comfort and convenience. It might be God, or the Spirit, or the sacredness of life, or Mother Earth, or equality and freedom, or human rights and human dignity. Whatever it is and whatever we call it, it can nurture us. To be nurtured personally empowers and sustains us as individuals. But in the struggle we need community. We need each other and we need to build together a local and global movement for peace with justice, for the struggle is one.

I have found that times of grief and anguish can actually strengthen our bonds. And now, in such times in this movement in Palestine and Israel and beyond, we need each other as never before. We need to treat each other well, to cherish and care for and support each other to become the community we imagine. Our solidarity must go deeper than we've ever known before. At its best, solidarity means strengthening our openness and communication with each other, our willingness to bring everyone to the table, our practice of direct democracy, as well as our commitment to build broad-based alliances and to network with like-minded people.

It is now more necessary than ever to move from statements to direct non-violent action, like divesting from structures that enable the Occupation. Such action gives hope to the people in the forefront of the struggle. To advocate vociferously for the implementation of international law and the protection of human rights gives hope, as well.

Clearly, involvement in any just action has a price. Thus the question then becomes, "Am I ready to pay the price and share the suffering of others?" Suffering for me is bearable if it is for the cause of liberation. For we not only move closer to liberation but within the very process itself we may find a new beloved community with others and with God. We are called to conversion, to be converted to the struggle of women and men everywhere who have no way to escape the unending fatigue of their labor and the daily denial of their human rights and human worth. We must let our hearts be moved by the anguish and suffering of our sisters and brothers here in Palestine, in Iraq and throughout the world. But how can we bear the pain, and where do we look for hope? Is there anything meaningful we can do to solve the political chaos and crisis in the world? Is there anything significant we can do to stop wars of all kinds?

Those of us committed to peace and justice, whether with respect to the Palestinian experience or to any other issue, should not give up, for to give up is to give in and allow injustice to prevail. Rather, we must continue to fan the embers into flames of light, no matter how small they are, because these embers of light give hope to those in the forefront of struggle. And they will keep the work for justice and peace in the Middle East alive.

The words of II Corinthians 4: 8-9 seem to echo our predicament and the promise with which we are blessed: "We are pressed on every side by troubles, but we are not crushed and broken. We are perplexed, but we don't give up and quit. We are hunted down, but God never abandons us."

May God's solidarity and promise be mirrored in our words and actions now and in the future!

THE CHRISTIAN VOCATION
IN CONTEMPORARY PALESTINE

Bishop Kenneth Cragg

Who could presume to address himself to such a topic, least of all one who comes from the nation that orchestrated in 1917 that famous "Balfour Declaration"? If I am saddened by that nexus in my ancestry, it is transcended here in the unity we have in Christ and in the common human compassion which makes us all kin. But it is well to begin here for reasons that will appear.

First I must apologize for my English connection with that Arthur Balfour–though I was a mere four-year old at the time and helpless to intervene. The point is that the "Declaration" enshrined three conspicuous factors which beset the situation to the present day and have bedeviled it too long. The first and most grievous of them was its deliberate ambiguity. It talked about a national home **in**, when it meant a national state **of**. This was a quite deliberate ambivalence for fear, as Balfour remarked in a letter to his son, "We did not wish to disturb the ultimate authorities." It is this factor of inconclusiveness, some would even call it chicanery, of having a hidden agenda, in the context of the creation of facts, which being deliberately pursued, in the absence of genuine negotiation, made possible the long story of subterfuge and frustration.

You are all acquainted in your sense of oppression and humiliation with this situation. How do we resolve it unless somehow we can reach for an integrity in both directions? The theme and the influence of Sabeel has long been part of this concern and in our hearts. All we have time for on this occasion is to try to pursue two main areas of Christian faith and witness, because they deeply concern the second and third dimensions of Balfour which I have in mind. The second, so obvious from the outset, was the involvement of the international situation. The British imperial concern was for what might well be a secure base in the vicinity of the Suez Canal. There were other vested interests on the part of the international community in what was then the great First World War. This international factor is one that has to be always kept in mind in relation to the policy, attitude and philosophy of any resistance movement needing and recruiting sympathy now.

The third ingredient was a rather vague Biblicism, a sentimental interest in the situation of the Jewish dispersion. Balfour, the nominal author of the Declaration, was deeply fascinated for several years by Chaim Weizmann, who later became the first president of Israel. He was the main diplomatic aegis behind the Declaration. He had very little English when the two men first met, and he talked in broken English about the plight of his community. The heart of a rather aristocratic Englishman went out to him on the basis of the rootlessness, as Weizmann presented it, of the Jewish people, and the aura of their Biblical tradition. The Prime Minister Lloyd George also was reared in the piety of the Welsh Chapels. This sense of something via the Bible enjoying and requiring a deep emotional sympathy for the Jewish people has since then found deep and more tragic aspects in the genesis of Christian Zionism.

So these three factors continually beset the situation. In view of them, let us here pursue just two clues about the spiritual vocation of Christian Palestinians in the present situation. Let nobody think that the word "spiritual" here is a kind of evasive or a non-political term. We have first to begin by discerning how the themes of Christian faith must always determine the practice of Christian living and the goals of Christian politics. The first of these two themes is the one addressed by the Christian conscience to the state and people of Israel since these people, their mentality, and indeed their conscience, as well as their long prophetic tradition, will always be vital ingredients of our relationship.

It would be fair to say, in paradox, that there are no more anti-Semitic voices than those of prophets like Amos, Hosea and Jeremiah. Hosea could think, the Lord speaking through him and saying "I am not the I Am you think I am" (Hosea 1:9). "You are not my people in the way you think you are." And there was Isaiah, "Woe unto them that join house to house and field to field that they may dwell alone in the midst of the earth until there be no room." How opposite that is in Isaiah 5:8 to the current scene with the illegal settlements so behaving.

What, then, is the Christian witness to the people of Jewry in their political concentration in this territory, in their ancient land-love and in their wide dispersion? Just as some have said that the vital hope of the Palestinians lies in the good and decent conscience of the United States, so it is also in the recovery of "the fear of God before their eyes" on the part of the Jewish people in their Zionist enterprise. We must argue from the Biblical doctrine of creation for which the Other in deed and truth is not **an** other, but shares one undifferentiated humanity. The Lord made of one kindred all nations of men to dwell on the face of the whole earth. Jewish particularity is not exempt from this universality. When you analyze the Jewish love of the land and the fundamental theological logic of Zionism, you find a triad of land, people and memory. Or, in an alliteration, people, place and past, or tribe, territory and time. It is entirely obvious both in the Bible and in the Qur'an that this triad of identity belongs alike to all people so that, in this sense, there are not and cannot be in the meaning and the ultimate doctrine of creation one exceptional people. France and the French, Finland and the Finns, Africa and Africans, you have it everywhere in the junction between where we are and who we are and therefore whence we came.[1]

The Christian faith in its biblical tradition emphasizes and consecrates all human identity. Mother-land, mother-tongue, mother's milk...these are the definitive constituents of every human identity. As the Creator of us all, the Lord has only Chosen Peoples, in the plural. Thus surely it is part of our witness, in the memorable phrase of John Donne, to say "I am involved in mankind." Whether we see it and allow it or not, this is the reality of the current situation. We cannot alienate one another from this same fundamental humanism whereby our humanity is one. It seems to me that this realization has to be at the heart of the spiritual vocation across this territory so that somehow, in spite of all the difficulty within the soul, creating and affirming this irrefragable human single, mortal community in Christ is our bounden duty. It is important to realize that this basic land-love, people-love, is common and proper to all.

One of our English poets, who was deeply fond of the south of England, wrote these words as his reading and vision of the meaning of creation:

> God gave all men all earth to love, but since man's heart is small,
> Ordained for each one place should prove beloved above all.

---

[1] See the illuminating study of this inkling in: Heribert Adam and Kogila Moodley: *Seeking Mandela, Peace-making Between Israelis and Palestinians.* Philadelphia, 2005.

That as He watched creation's birth, so we in Godlike mood,
Might of our love create our earth and see that it is good.[2]

This cannot be an argument for the return, without being known as an argument for those who were already here if we make our love a concrete aspect of the good earth of God alone. You might say to me, "If this is the case, we're all equally entrusted, man the peasant, man the farmer, woman the family maker, if you see it that way." [We are using 'man' in no masculine sense, but as we Christians must need to do, in non-gender terms by the very nature of our creed, "and was made man."] This one mankind, to which we all belong, is the good earth's skilled and divinely-willed tenant and custodian. In the Holy Qur'an Surah 2 verse 30, the Lord says to the assembled angels, "I am appointing a dominion-holder in the earth." The very amenability of nature to the mind of man seems manifestly to argue a certain intentionality about all that is. The Lord has "let us be." What might have been nothingness was taken away and here we are. This is the truth of us, here in a managerial capacity which is at the heart of our dominion and of our liability under God. This is a common truth of all the Semitic faiths.

Let me remind you of that marvelous vision in Surah 7, verse 172, which visualizes the whole of humanity in every generation from the start of time, of all races and languages and habitations. Can you imagine a single human community all assembled together? And they are faced with this question from the Almighty Himself: ". . . ". ". . . وأَشْهَدَهُم على أَنفُسِهم أَلستُ بِربكُم قالوا بلى" ([God] made them testify concerning themselves, "Am I not your lord?" They replied: "We bear witness [that you are]."') Negative questions expect the answer "yes." ["Haven't you heard?" "Don't you know?"] Here, then, is Omnipotence waiting for an answer. What does that tell you about Allah within Islam? No tyrant but somehow seeking our consent to be the God He is. Why is it important to keep reiterating "Allahu Akbar"? Why does it urgently need to be said? Only because the reality of God is forever waiting on the human confession, the God who has let us be, seeks to be "let be" by us in our custody of His creation.

It is in this context that we have to transcend a particularity which thinks only of itself or somehow regards with a unique singularity the identity

---

[2] Rudyard Kipling: *Definitive Edition of His Verse*. London, 1943, pp. 215-16, the poem "Sussex."

it possesses. And, in turn, of course, this truth has been wonderfully corroborated in the whole meaning of redemption, "to make of both one, so making peace," so that the doctrine of redemption fulfills the significance of creation. But in the present context I stay with the first. Here is the Biblical scenario, as in the parable of the husbandmen in the three Gospels: creation, creaturehood, prophethood.

Our dignity is so great and so fraught with potential disaster that we need guidance, we need reminders, we need exhortation, we need a structure of conformity, all of which the pillars of Islam intend to provide. There is no doubt about the human reality in the Biblical world. That audience in Surah 7.172 was pre-Abraham, pre-Sinai, pre-Melchizedek, pre-everybody, but did those conspirators heed it on their way to the cockpits of those planes on Sept. 11, 2001?

Was that not occasion for what William Temple once called "the dreadful astonishment of God"?[3] "What is this you are doing in My Name and on My behalf? Have you become your own lords?" For that was the whole logic of the husbandmen parable. If they could somehow demonstrate possession as nine-tenths of the law, they might get rid of the original ownership, and usurp the real owner. Such has always been the potential conspiracy of humankind against the sovereignty of God. Let me say there is no doubt about this central foundational theme in the Biblical and in the Qur'anic tradition. We are not talking here about "creationism". Maybe in some senses the evolutionary hypothesis, duly tested scientifically, can be seen in this context as the procedure of creation. What we are talking about is an intendedness behind all things and what that had in mind as entrusted to humankind.

Twice comes the reminder in the Qur'an: "We did not create the heavens and the earth and all that is between them as if in jest."[4] God is not "a jesting Creator." There is this deep seriousness about our human being, a seriousness

---

[3] William Temple: *The Church Looks Forward.* London, 1944, p. 71. He is referring to how far humans will go in defiance of the divine mind and will, how they will do so in deliberate repudiation of ethical duty and precept.

[4] Surahs 21.16 and 44.38. *La'ibin* is the operative word as a frivolous "player with a plaything." The doctrine of creation has at its heart this truth of a divine "intendedness" about the world and about its human custody in trust and care. "Let there be." "Let us make…" "Have thou dominion"–these are its watchwords. Its "impartiality" as between races–and, indeed, between religions, is strikingly evident in how the sciences and their technological applications are equally available to each and all. One does not have to be a Buddhist to practice medicine, nor a Christian to fly a plane, nor a Muslim to manage a laboratory. Nor, we might add, do you have to be a "Gentile" to drop cluster bombs.

which is only theologically defined as being under God, and here is where particularity, Israeli, Palestinian, French, whatever, has to find its place. This is not to say that particularity is no part of the situation. We cannot disinherit our origins. We may learn another mother tongue, but unless we are long, long exiles, we cannot forfeit our own. All we have been exploring underscores the bitterness and pain of exile and being absent from land. So, let me say this is a very difficult hurdle for the Jewish mind to take, in conceding the "other" particularity in aggressively asserting its own.

Those who are American know their good old Walt Whitman. He has a poem about himself, sitting on the shore of the Pacific Ocean – or any other – and saying: "All this is rolling in for me," as if he is the only mortal in the world. And he is right! He has the whole of the ocean, and the whole of the ocean is his. But that deep particularity which he senses for his own does not isolate him from a neighbor alongside who also has, unimpeded, the same whole and entire ocean. Our possessions in creation do not require isolation or admit an attitude of exceptionality. The "other's right legitimates mine."[5]

Can we, then, let our particularities belong? Anti-Semitism has long been a disavowal of a Jewry's very articulate longstanding and deeply entrenched particularity. It is important for us to recognize how that particularity, with its intense emotion, has its origins in history. It is fair to say that Palestinian Christians, and all of us who would be your colleagues, are facing in the whole Zionist enterprise – what shall I call it? – a vote of non-confidence, a vote of non-confidence in the humanity of humankind. We are, they say, an unwanted people. This was the thesis of Hertzl. The "Gentile" world is incorrigibly inhospitable. It will never genuinely accommodate us. The enlightenment wooed us out of the ghetto and then betrayed us when we began to circulate. This "Gentile" world offers us only two impossible alternatives. One is assimilation whereby we lose our identity. There is what many Jewish rabbis are calling a hemorrhage from inter-marriage, secularization, and a drift away from authentic Judaism. The other alternative offered was pogroms in Russia, and this was long before the Holocaust and Nazi Germany, the horror of the genocide and elimination.

---

[5] How, one might ask, does this analogy of the shoreline and the ocean fit the context of a very small, competitively loved and wanted territory? Only that either's case for legitimacy is mutual to the other's. If neither's case is a pseudo-thing–and the necessity for sovereignty via statehood is parallel– then either's claim ipso facto concedes the other's. That one party should think theirs exclusive denies even the most "sacrilised logic" with which it claims to move.

We should understand where the Zionist is coming from in this vote of non-confidence about the genuine participation of Jews in the world, although so many in the U.S., in Europe and in the Diaspora give the lie to this philosophy. But it runs deep and it remains a basic prerogative justifying the existence of Israel. It argues that we can only be safe in our own land, under our own state, with our own power, on our own behalf. Then, if this deep radical distrust of the rest of humankind remains, surely part of our vocation is to try to nourish and wean this mentality into a better assurance about basic humanity being expressed to what is Jewish as well as non-Jewish. You will find, if you remember your Shakespeare, from the mouth of a Jew himself, the best statement of this identity with world humanity. Shylock says: "I am a Jew. Hath not a Jew hands, organs, dimensions, appetites, warmed and cooled by the same summer and winter as a Gentile is? If you prick us do we not bleed? If you poison us, do we not die? And if you will revenge, I will better you in that." Shylock knows all too well that in John Donne's classic phrase "he belongs with mankind." Indeed, he has no other option. In spite of his beginning affirmation, so violent, so exclamatory, "I am a Jew!" he makes his plaintive appeal, "Hath not a Jew eyes?" So particularity, in which we must rejoice, has to belong with the universal humanity of which we are inextricably a part. Christian witness to this truth has to take into love's redemption all the misgiving Jewry has concerning it and the latent bitterness of heart.

There was an occasion some years back when Menachim Begin was offered an international guarantee, to which he replied, "There is no guarantee that can guarantee an international guarantee. We are on our own; we will not be beholden to anybody. For the moment we start to be, they will let us down." Such is the guarded reservation about the world seen through Zionist eyes, at least in its traditional form, so part of the Christian calling, surely, the spiritual vocation, is to learn what to do with our particularity, and serve others in doing likewise.

There are two other points here. You may well say, in the light of this argument, what happens to Jewish identity? Are we asking them, as it were, somehow to suppress it in an international self-forfeiture? No. It will always have historically the Biblical role it played, just as Greece and its Greeks will always be the territory of Plato and Aristotle. Remember that haunting line about human bitterness, "Sophocles heard it long ago"? History does not undo the enormous legacies which it creates. So this dealing with Jewish particularity does not require a repudiation of the history. All it requires is consent to belong with mankind and in that context most strenuously to belong with the Palestinian presence. And the other answer, the clue we all need to understand, would be – as I indicated about Whitman and the ocean – that what we think is exceptional, indeed what we experience as exceptional in all validity has to be internalized. In interiority we can fully possess our identity, knowing that, by the same human token, it is only ours as the incidence in us of that in which all humanity consists.

Thus to internalize the mystery does not require that we disqualify the meaning that others find in identical experience whereby all in this internal sense are the children of God. This must be the necessary text of any Zionism via Judaism, ready to belong with where it is, and with where it chose to be. Whatever that might mean in terms of two states or of one state, it tells the fundamental condition of either. It is the sure ground, the irrefutable case, for Palestinianism and its one inherent warrant under God.

Thus in respect of Zion and Zionism, it is surely our spiritual vocation in the present context, land love, people love, time love, as the God-given denominators of all of us in both our solidarity and our particularity. We have to hasten on because a Christian Palestinian role or task in the present situation is inevitably involved with Islam, the majority religion, the dominant factor. It has always been both a need and a problem of Christian Palestinianism, as I understood it, to make its number authentically with the rest of its people, to accept to be minoritized, though hopefully without further reduction of that situation. Necessarily the fundamentals of its response to the Zionist situation will be cooperative with the world of Islam. We have already seen that this same vision of humankind is deeply rooted in the Qur'an, though it is sadly true that in the context of the prophet's mission, there came a deep asperity against unbelievers, especially in the Medinan period. However, it was not so in the Meccan origins. This is a theme that would take greater space to explore. But being together with Islam in the understanding of the task requires that we, as it were, as far as possible, theologize together.

You may have wondered why once or twice I have cited the Qur'an in its own language. This was in part out of deference to Muslim susceptibility when they decry translation. The heart of the situation here, surely, is that we can share this fundamental doctrine of the community of humankind and somehow let it be extended even across all barriers that otherwise would inhibit it. I want to say in this context that the heart of the Christian message to Islam lies in the abrogation, the rescinding by Jesus of the law of retaliation, what they call in Latin *lex taliones*, "an eye for an eye, a tooth for a tooth." This law of retaliation is very dire and deep in contemporary history. Muslims read the invasion of Iraq in these terms. We could say that the Crusades were a long delayed retaliation against the invasion of North Africa and Spain and even part way into France, that the Western penetration into the Arab East in the latter days of the Ottoman Empire was a kind of retaliation for its dark incursions as Ottomans into the Balkans. The pattern is perennial in human history and really it is no palliative, no solution, to say "one eye for one eye." You still have another life forfeit or another limb. It is a false notion that there is something benign about limiting it. Why not let it go altogether? That would be the logic even of the proviso about limitation. A life is a life and part of our witness these days across the world is to the abolition in Christ of the law of retaliation. Jesus said, "I say unto you." Or that marvelous phrase taken from Jesus in Ephesians, "Let not the sun go down upon your wrath." I don't find this message in the Qur'an. "Sufficient unto the day is the evil thereof. Be not overcome with evil, but overcome evil with good." That first clause does not mean that there is no place for something like a policing of the world, but can it be, as Lincoln had it, "with malice towards none"?

There is a point in the discipline, as it were, of resistance in that sense. Hitler needed to be disavowed. By the way, did not those who died on the Normandy beaches contribute to the end of the Holocaust? How can Jewish people think or argue that they were never in debt to anyone, never involved in debt to mankind. Would there ever have been a State of Israel if Rommel had broken through at Al Alamein? We are all deeply indebted in the many vicissitudes of history. The siege of Stalingrad had its role in the ending of the Holocaust.

But, back to the Islamic situation. "Let not the sun go down upon your wrath." We need to resist evil as a corrective to it, but without therein becoming vindictive against it. Part of the legacy of the First World War was the vindictiveness of the Versailles Treaty and it was this which provoked and nurtured the Nazi regime at long length. "Let not the sun go down upon your wrath." How shall we learn this lesson? How shall we commend it? This was the pattern of our Lord, and it has to be ours also. The world surely is calling very tentatively to the United Nations for some kind of world policing so that we do not say that what's happening beyond somebody's borders is only their concern. Peace and its sinews become everywhere a single world concern. [My late friend in Lebanon, Charles Malik, was the author of the Declaration of

Human Rights, along with yeoman help from Eleanor Roosevelt.]

So, it does matter what is happening inside any state anywhere, but not by actions of an army that represents a national interest and is bound to be suspect of vested interests in the way it deploys itself. Can the world come to organize something like a policing of mankind on behalf of all? This needs to be a global vision. So, we are not arguing that there is no necessity for patterns of control and resistance in these terms. But how can those mechanisms, with all our human frailties, avoid being vindictive and be withheld from what is retaliatory, harsh and victimizing, as well as victim-making? Power has to be sacred as the arbiter of justice. Can traditional Islam reconcile its cult of power with this duly non-retaliatory role?

This is the message I want to leave with you. A spiritual vocation of Palestinian Christians has to have its origin and take its impetus from the theme of "God in Christ reconciling the world." And nowhere else, nowhere else can it find the energy and the authority for which its mission yearns, or right the wrongs and wipe the tears or serve the hopes of their beloved Palestine.

Let us finish with one further point out of these two considerations vis-à-vis Zionism and Islam which have left aside much that ought to have been said. It is that there has to be a theology of hope. It has been said among some Zionists that there is an adage totally applicable to Palestinians. It runs: "We are only defeated when we think we are." So we have to keep this high courage, this suffering hope, as part of the dimension of the love of God. Or, as the old writer had it, we wait "Verily to see the goodness of the Lord in the land of the living." Sometimes, you know, it is good to play on words a little. What of the notion of "compatibility"? How can people find the capacity to be compatible? But when you think further, what is at the heart of this word except "pathos," the Greek "pathos" which sadly gives us the minimized "pathetic." Pathos, fellow feeling, in another analogy, has also the double meaning of a single word, namely "suffer." We suffer each other. The word "suffer" has an archaic meaning which is like "allow." "Suffer the little children to come unto me." To suffer is to be compatible in the old sense that you allow the other. But when you do so, inherently you suffer in the mainline sense of the word. Why? Because you do not get your own back. You do not get your own back, but if thus you win your neighbor, you have saved your soul.

There is, finally, in the heart of the Qur'an that saying that you also have among the Jewish rabbis and in their Talmud which runs: "Whoever kills a single soul, saving for the cause of manslaughter or in relation to corruption in the earth, it is as if he slew all mankind. And he who saves a single soul, it is as if he saved all mankind" (Surah 5, 32). Such, in Christ, is our solidarity and this solidarity has to be the heart theme, the life desire, the steady mission of our particularity. It is one which, out of the core of the Gospel, tames and arrests the exclusive exceptionality of Israeli Zion and the instinctive retaliatory habit of Islam. It is only where the witness of a theology concludes that the onus of policy and polity can begin to find both plan and hope.

ARAB CHRISTIANITY IN BYZANTINE PALESTINE

Irfan Shahîd

In Byzantine times, Palestine extended geographically from Mount Hermon in the north to the Gulf of Clysma in the south and was divided administratively into three smaller units: Prima, Secunda and Tertia. Chronologically, the Byzantine period spanned three centuries from the reign of Constantine in the fourth to that of Heraclius in the seventh. The Arab Christian presence in Byzantine Palestine will thus be traced diachronously in the three Palestines in the course of these three centuries, based almost entirely on contemporary Greek and Syriac sources. [1]

This presence-it should be pointed out at the outset-was not uniform; it was bi-morphic in many ways: (1)In legal status; some Arabs were *Rhomaioi*, citizens to whom *civitas* was extended after the edict of Caracalla in AD 211; such were the Nabataean Arabs of Palaestina Tertia in Sinai and the Negev. Others were not citizens but were *foederati*, that is, allies with a treaty relationship, a *foedus*, to Byzantium, which enabled them to settle on Byzantine territory in return for military service; such were the Christian *foederati* settled

---

[1] I should like to thank Dr. Shafiq Abou Zayd for organizing the ARAM Sixteenth International Conference on the topic of Palestinian Christianity, which took place 16-18 July in Oxford. In five of my volumes in the series, *Byzantium and the Arabs*, the theme of Arab Christianity before the rise of Islam has been treated in each of these volumes, in the three centuries of the Byzantine presence in Palestine. The ARAM Conference provided me with an opportunity to put together for the first time my researches on the theme of the Conference in the form of a short synthesis presented in this article. As this synthesis has drawn on researches distributed among five volumes,there is continual reference to these volumes as an aid to the reader, who may care to go into the multitude of relevant details and to be acquainted with the critique of the sources involved. The published text is substantially that of the paper orally delivered at the Conference within the constraints of time allotted to each participant. Hence, its retention of some features peculiar to oral delivery.

in the Desert of Juda in Palaestina Prima in the fifth century. (2)The Arab presence was bi-morphic in another sense; some of them were pastoralists, such as those who roamed the wastes and the desert spaces of Sinai and the Negev, while others were sedentary. (3)These, too, were bi-morphic in a third sense: some were urban, as the Arab *Rhomaioi* were, the former Nabataeans of towns in the Negev such as: Elusa, Sbaita, Oboda Nessana, Mampsis, and Rouhaiba, which might be termed the Hexapolis of the Negev; while others were rural as the foederati mostly were, an important distinction, which our colleagues at the symposium have reminded us to keep in mind. (4)Finally, they were bi-morphic confessionally: Some were Chalcedonians and others Monophysites: such were the Arabs of Palaestina Prima in the Judaean Desert and Palaestina Secunda in the Golan, respectively.

THE FOURTH CENTURY

The great turning point in the history of Christianity in Palestine as a Holy Land was the reign of Constantine and, so, this presentation of Arab Christianity in Pre-Islamic Byzantine times begins in the fourth century, dominated by a large Arab religious figure, a Holy Man by the name of Moses. According to the fifth century ecclesiastical author, Theodoret, he lived between Egypt and Palestine and so must have belonged to Sinai in Palaestina Tertia.[2] And if he can be identified with the Monk of Rhaithou in the oasis of Phārān, the one mentioned in the *Ammonii Monachi Relatio,* his Sinaitic provenance can be clinched.[3] He stood for the Nicene Creed during the reign of the Arian Emperor, Valens. The mailed fist behind his stance was the Arab Queen, Mavia, who also stood for the same Creed and warred the Arian Emperor down, as recounted fully in the ecclesiastical sources, Socrates and Sozomen.

By the terms of the treaty with Valens, Moses became the bishop of the Arab *foederati* of Queen Mavia.[4] He must have performed both as a Holy Man and as a Christian hierarch some significant services to the Faith, the record of which has not survived in the extant sources. Otherwise, it is difficult to understand

---

[2] For all that pertains to the holy man, Moses, see the present writer in *Byzantium and the Arabs in the Fourth Century,* (Dumbarton Oaks,Washington, D,C., 1984), pp. 152-158, 184-187; henceforth referred to as *BAFOC.*

[3] *Ibid.,* pp. 296-319, 327-328.

[4] For Mavia, see *ibid.,* pp. 138-202.

why he was canonized, becoming a saint of the Universal Church whose feast falls on February 7th. His fame apparently spread to the Roman Occident. In the eighth century, four centuries after his *floruit,* Pope Gregory III, had an encounter with St. Willibald, the nephew of St. Boniface, the Apostle of Germany. The latter was unwilling to join his uncle in his German mission and the Pope tried to persuade him to join his uncle, and presented the Arab Saint Moses as a model for St. Willibald in his prospective evangelizing activity.[5]

In addition to this Bishop Saint of the Arab *foederati* of Palaestina Tertia, the sources speak of two other bishops, in this century, who were Arab *Rhomaioi* of the same Tertia, bishops of the urban centers of Elusa in the Negev and of Phārān, the oasis in the south of the Sinai Peninsula. The bishop of Phārān is attested around AD 400 with the name Nathyr, probably Arabic Naḍīr, of Naḍīr.[6] The history of Christianity in Byzantine Palaestina Tertia, which comprised the Sinai and the Negev, was the history of Arab Christianity since these regions have been Nabataean territories with a strong Arab ethnic complexion. I leave its detailed history to other scholars, especially in Israel, who have been excavating Sinai and the Hexapolis of the Negev such as Professor Pau Figueras.

THE FIFTH CENTURY

The Orthodox tradition of Arab Federate Christianity started by Queen Mavia and Moses continued in the fifth century in both Palaestina Prima and Secunda. In the latter, the new group of Arab *foederati,* the Salīhids, had their headquarters in Gaulanitis in Secunda. The sources have preserved their strong attachment to the monastic way of life which began with their very conversion at the hands of a monk/holy man and ended with the renunciation of the world by their last king, who became a monk and founded a monastery, Dayr Dāwūd, in the vicinity of that famous pilgrimage center near the Euphrates, Sergiopolis, and which remained an important locality well into Islamic times. What monasteries he built in Gaulanitis is not known since the sources for this period are scant and whatever sources there were on Salīhid monastic foundations in Gaulanitis have not survived.[7]

---

[5] For Pope Gregory III and St.Willibald, see *ibid.,* pp. 186-187.

[6] *Ibid.,* p. 303 and n. 73.

[7] For all that pertains to the Salīhids, see the present writer in *Byzantium and the Arabs in the Fifth Century,* (Dumbarton Oaks,Washington, D.C.,1989), pp. 233-271 and 297-300; hence-forth referred to as *BAFIC* .

More important is the Christian Arab presence in Palaestina Prima in the Desert of Juda. The region witnessed the rise of a diminutive Arab church of *foederati*. These had left the service of Sāsānid Persia and became the allies, *foederati* of Byzantium, where they were settled in the Jordan Valley and were later converted by St. Euthymius.[8]

Their chiefs, the phylarchs, became zealous Christians, and one of them, the first, was the most distinguished member of this Federate Arab group, who brought from Persia his name, which was Persian, (Pahlevi), his military title Aspebetos, Sepahbad. On conversion he assumed the name Peter. He built for the monastery of St. Euthymius two cisterns, a bakery (*a mancipium*), and three cells. He was thought fit by Euthymius to be consecrated bishop.[9]

Aspebetos/Peter walked into ecclesiastical history when he not only participated in the Council of Ephesus in AD 431 but also was selected as one of the three delegates whom the Council sent to negotiate with Nestorius and John of Antioch in order to return them to Orthodoxy. His successors in the episcopate took part in the Second Council of Ephesus in 449, and in the Council of Chalcedon in 451.[10]

In addition to their contribution to the fortunes of orthodoxy at home and at the Ecumenical Councils, these Federate Arabs of the Desert of Juda contributed to the Christian monastic life. Two of them became *hegoumenoi,* abbots of the monasteries in the Jordan Valley. Such were Maris, the brother-in-law of Aspebetos/Peter, who became the *hegoumenos* of the monastery of Theoctistus. Stephanus, another Arab, not federate but a *Rhomaic* became the *hegoumenos* of the monastery of Euthymius. In addition to these two monasteries in the Jordan Valley, there was another Arab monastery in Prima by the name of Dayr ʿAmr, which may have been built by the Salīḥid *foederati* but it could equally well have been a Ghassānid foundation; the name recurs in the genealogies of both federate groups. The monastery lay in the vicinity of Jerusalem to its north.[11]

---

[8] The Arab *foederati* of the desert of Juda are often referred to as those of the Parembole, the Greek equivalent of the Arabic military term, *ḥīra*. For their history, secular and religious, see *ibid.*, pp. 181-207.

[9] On Aspebetos, see *ibid.*, pp. 40-49, 181-184.

[10] For Aspebetos and the participation of Arab Federate bishops in Ecumenical Councils, see *ibid.*, pp. 214-224.

[11] For these monasteries, see *ibid.*, pp. 191-192, 255.

THE SIXTH CENTURY

The sixth century is the best documented period in the history of Arab Christianity in Oriens, Bilād al-Shām. The sources, especially the Syriac, are abundant. It was the century that witnessed the rise of the third and last group of Arab *foederati* of Byzantium, the Ghassānids, the most powerful and most zealous in their attachment to Christianity. Unlike their predecessors, the Tanūkhids and the Salīḥids, these were not Orthodox Chalcedonians but Monophysites. They played a major role in the resuscitation of the Monophysite movement in Oriens after it was disestablished by the advent of the Chalcedonies House or Justin in AD 518. Their relation to Palestine was quite close since their headquarters were in Palaestina Secunda in Gaulanitis, where their capital Jābiya was located [12], the see of their chief hierarch.

The most active period of their contribution to Christianity began around AD 540 when their King, the celebrated Arethas, with the help of Empress Theodora, had a monk by the name of Theodore, consecrated the Bishop of the Ghassānid *foederati* with a mandate to propagate the Faith in the whole of the Limitrophe from the Euphrates to Eilat and beyond. What this chief Ghassānid hierarch with his extraordinary powers and jurisdiction achieved in the service of Christianity is not known because of the problem of source survival, but it can be inferred from the duration of his episcopate, which was long, more than thirty years, at the end of which he was still active and well remembered in the Syriac documents *à propos* of the Tritheistic heresy which around 570 rocked the Monophysite movement, and in which he played a major role. As the sources on what he had done in the course of the previous thirty years that antedated his involvement in the Tritheistic movement have not survived, his activity in the strictly Arab area in Oriens is a matter of inference. [13] Fortunately, there are data to suggest that the mandate for the resuscitation of the Monophysite church

---

[12] For the Ghassānids, see the present writer in *Byzantium and the Arabs in the Sixth Century*, (Dumbarton Oaks, Washington, D.C., 1995) in two parts, the second of which is exclusively devoted to ecclesiastical history; henceforth referred to as *BASIC*.

[13] For Theodore, the Bishop of the Ghassānids, see *ibid.*, pp. 771-774; 806-808; 850-860.

in Oriens, including its Arab component, was implemented by him.[14] The Ghassānids had no power-base in Palaestina Prima, which was strongly Chalcedonian. Besides, they were unlucky in that the ecclesiastical historian of Palestine in that century was Cyril of Skythopolis, who was violently anti-Monophysite, witness his thundering against a distinguished churchman such as Severus of Antioch, the moderate Monophysite Patriarch[15], to whom some sober and objective scholars have done justice.[16]

The result of Cyril's antipathies was the elimination of any reference to Ghassānid religious activity in Palaestina Prima[17], with the exception of a faint trace that may be recovered from toponymy. Two place-names which still exist in the region in our day may reflect the Ghassānid presence: such as Dayr ͨAmr which, as the word *dayr* indicates was originally a monastery before it became a little village located to the southwest of Jerusalem. This monastery in Palaestina Prima may be Salāḥid not Ghassānid, but it is Arab Federate.[18] A second toponym, namely Dayr Ghassāni, can only have been a Ghassānid monastery. [19] Its appearance in strongly Chalcedonian and anti-Monophysite Palaestina Prima may be explained by the concession made by the Orthodox Church and the

---

[14] Around the year 570, the *provincia* Arabia alone (with portions of the two neighboring provinces, Palaestina and Phonice Libanensis) had 137 monasteries, the abbots of which wrote a letter to Arethas, the Ghassānid king, on their rejection of the Tritheistic heresy and the letter has survived. It is difficult to believe that Theodore, originally a monk before his elevation to the episcopate, and after an episcopate of some thirty years,was not responsible for the foundation of some of these monasteries; These were in the very province, Arabia, which was the headquarters of the chief Ghassānid phylarch, Arethas, his protector and the *fidei defensor* of the Monophysite confession. For the letter of these abbots, see *ibid.*, pp. 824-838.

[15] For his anti-Monophysite sentiments, see Cynthia Jean Stallman-Pacitti, *Cyril of Skythopolis: A Study in Hagiography as Apology*, (Hellenic College Press, Brookline, Mass., 1991), pp. 79-89.

[16] For example, see J. Lebon, *Le Monophysisme*, sévérien, (Louvain, 1909).

[17] His anti-Ghassānid antipathies are reflected in one passage in his work, which refers to a military encounter between the Ghassānid Arethas and another phylarch, by the name of al-Aswad. Cyril says anarchy spread in the region of this encounter. The reference is clearly meant to be uncomplimentary to the reputation of the famous Ghassānid king, a Monophysite,who is presented merely as a Saracen spreading evil in the Holy Land! Arethas, however, spent a life-time as a *miles Christianus* in the service of his Faith and the Empire for whom, see *BASIC* I, pp. 62-338, 734-860. Contrast the image of another phylarch,a Chalcedonian, in the work of Cyril, a diminutive one compared to Arethas, namely Terebon II, one of the phylarchs of the Parembole, who is referred to by Cyril as "the renowned phylarch in this region" for whom, see *BAFIC*, p.190 and *BASIC*, I, p. 652.On this inter-phylarch strife referred to by Cyril, see *BASIC* I, pp. 251-255.

[18] For Dayr 'Amr, see *BASIC*, 996, 997, 966, 997 and supra, p. 3.

[19] On Dayr Ghassāni, see *ibid.*, pp. 654-55, 996.

Government to the power of the Ghassānids or possibly to the fact that some of them become Chalcedonians as a contemporary Syriac source testifies.[20]

The Greek literary source, Cyril of Skythopolis, records the existence of two localities which might have been Arab or had an Arab component in their populations, namely, Bethabudison and Lazarium: both very close to Jerusalem and they still exist.[21] The modern pronunciation of the village Bēth-Abū-Dis intrudes a tecnonymic, Abū-Dis, which makes no sense, while a different syllabication Ābūdi plus the Greek final sigma is more meaningful as it extrudes the tecnonymic and relates the toponym to the word "worship," an etymology that is culturally suitable and is supported by the existence of a village called ᶜĀbūd, which lies nowadays to the northwest of Jerusalem.[22] But this could be Aramaic as well as Arabic. Lazarion, on the other hand, is mentioned in Cyril as the village associated with Christian figures with recognizable Arab names such as Thaᶜlaba and ᶜUrqūb. The relevant passages in Cyril of Skythopolis, involving these toponyms and individuals date to the years 543-553.

If the Ghassānids had no presence to speak of in Prima, they had a strong one in Secunda and Tertia, where two Ghassānid phylarchs/kings reigned. The sources, Greek and Syriac, present them as doughty warriors in the defense of the Byzantine frontier against the pastoralists of the Arabian Peninsula but also as firebrands in the service of Christianity, albeit in its Monophysite version. What they achieved in Palaestina Secunda and Tertia may be traced from what has survived in the sources in references to their religious architecture, which may be divided into monasteries and churches. [23]

THE MONASTERIES

A precious Syriac document of the year AD 569 involving the Ghassānid King Arethas, the protector of the Monophysite Confession and arbiter in the Tritheistic controversy, has preserved the names of no less than 137 monasteries, mostly in the *provincia* Arabia, but including a few in the neighboring provinces, one of which was Palaestina Secunda. About 30 of these are associated with

---

[20] For this, see *ibid.*, p. 845-850.

[21] For Lazarium, see *BAFIC*, pp. 200-202 and *BASIC*, 656.

[22] On the etymology of Bethabudis, see *BASIC*, p. 655, n. 70 and *BAFIC*, 202.

[23] These have been treated in the latest volume, *Byzantium and the Arabs in the Sixth Century*, (Dumbarton Oaks, Washington, D.C.,2000), *BASIC*, II. i.

the Ghassānids. [24] The letter was written by the archmandrites of these monasteries, the 137 in the *provincia* Arabia and it is not fanciful to assume that the other provinces must have also had monasteries, not far behind the number of those recorded for Arabia.

As far as this list of 137 monasteries in the letter is concerned, the following monasteries may be picked up from the list located in Palaestina Secunda: (1)The monastery of Abbot Marcellinus on Mt. Arethas, Jabal Ḥārith in Gaulanitis, named after the Ghassānid King, which survives till the present day as Tall-Ḥāra; (2)The monastery of Bēth Ar^c, apparently another monastery on Mt. Arethas; (3) The monastery of Kefer Shemesh in the Eastern Golan; and (4)the monastery of Bēth-Mar-Sergius in Jābiya, the Ghassānid capital in the Golan. [25]

THE CHURCHES

The Syriac document that has preserved the list of the monasteries has also preserved the name of the Ghassānid church dedicated to the patron saint of the Ghassānids, Sergius, in the capital, Jābiya. [26] If another letter referred to in the Syriac sources and written to the *churches,* not the monasteries of the Oriens had survived, it would have revealed the names of many churches in Palaestina Secunda and elsewhere, but unfortunately it has not. The church of St. Sergius at the Ghassānid capital, Jābiya, also referred to in the Syriac Document, served some two decades later as the venue where the two warring Monophysite Patriarchs, Damian of Alexandra and Peter of Callinicus met under the patronage of the Ghassānid phylarch, Jafna, in AD 587, who acted as an arbiter in order to compose inter-Monophysite differences [27]; such was the prestige of this secular Ghassānid in the world of the Monophysite *ecclesia.*

That Palaestina Secunda, in Gaulanitis, must have witnessed a large number of religious foundations, churches and monasteries, is reflected in the fact that in the Islamic period immediately following the Muslim Conquest of the region, Secunda/Gaulanitis was considered one of the Holy Mountains of

---

[24] *BASIC,* I, 2, pp. 824-838. For the detailed study of Ghassānid monasticism and monasteries in Oriens,see *BASIC,* II. i.

[25] For these four monasteries in the Golan,in Palaestina Secunda, see *BASIC,* II. i., pp. 183-184, and their footnotes.

[26] *BASIC,* II. i., pp. 149-150.

[27] For this, see *BASIC,* I, 2, pp. 925-935.

the region, Arabic <u>al-Jibāl al-Sharīfa</u>, an appellation that surely derived from the pre-Islamic period of Byzantine Christian rule.[28] In that period, Secunda was considered a part, not only of the secular province of Palestine, but part of the Holy Land. It was the scene of some of Christ's miracles performed during his Gallilean Lakeside ministry and hallowed later by Byzantium[29], after the Christianization of the Empire in the fourth century, a process in which the Ghassānids participated together with the central Orthodox Church. The role of the Ghassānids as residents in the region, and consequently as ones who cared for it, bring to mind the similar role of the Herods of Judaea in the first century, and who, too, resided in Gaulanitis and for that reason revived it.[30]

They made pagan Paneas their capital, re-founded as Caesarea Philippi by one of them, the Herodian Tetrarch, Philip. As the Herods relieved the region of its pagan character by spreading monotheistic Judaism in it, so did the Ghassānids participate with the Orthodox Church and the Central Imperial Government in the spreading of monotheism in its Christian version in the same region. Thus, it was the succession of the two Abrahamic religions that relieved Gaulanitis of its pagan character by its sanctification with synagogues and churches.

PALAESTINA TERTIA

In Palaestina Tertia ruled the brother of the more famous Arethas, namely Abū -Karib, another Ghassānid Monophysite firebrand, who, too, was active in spreading the faith.[31] A Greek inscription and a Syriac literary source associate him with a church and a monastery respectively in the *provincia* Arabia and Phoenicia Libanensis, not his provinces.[32] It is easy to imagine how much he must have achieved in his own vast province, Tertia, which included Sinai, the Negev, the lower part of Trans-Jordan south of the Arnon river, and northern Ḥijāz. The Arabic sources document the existence of monasteries in this region, some with distinctly Arabic names, but whether they were founded by Abū-

[28] For the phrase al-Jibāl al-Sharīfa in Muqadassi's Ahsan al-*Taqāsīm*, see *BASIC*, II.i., p. 91.
[29] *Ibid.*, p. 90.
[30] As Benjamin Isaac has well argued; see *The Limits of Empire*, (Oxford,1992), pp. 370-371.
[31] For Abū-Karib, see *BASIC*, I, pp. 124-130, 167-168, 845-850, 981-984.
[32] For the association of Abū-Karib with the church of St. George at SammaChrSet2 15, a village in Auranitis in the provincia Arabia, see *BASIC*, p.153; and with the monastery at Nabk in Phonicia Libanennsis, see *BASIC*, I, p. 846-850.

Karib is impossible to tell. Whether the monophysitism preached by their chief hierarch, Theodore, and protected by the Ghassānid, Abū-Karib in Palaestina Tertia reached ultimately the Bishop of Phārān, a namesake of his, Theodore, of the reign of Heraclius, and apparently the spirit behind the new theology of Monoenergism and Monotheletism, remains to be shown. [33]

Elias, Patriarch of Jerusalem

If the Federate Arabs did not figure prominently in Palaestina Prima, the Rhomaic Arabs did. Elias had been a monk in one of the monasteries of St. Euthymius in the Jordan Valley, before he was elevated to the Patriarchate of Jerusalem, which he occupied from AD 494 to 516. He built a monastery in Jerusalem and others in the district of Jericho. He also laid the foundation of the Church of Theotokos in Jerusalem, the *Nea Ecclesia* which was completed by Justinian and was dedicated in AD 543. He died in exile in Eilat, whither he had been exiled by the Monophysite emperor Anastasius, for his unswerving loyalty to the Orthodox faith of Chalcedon. [34]

The Defence of the Holy Land

In addition to their direct contribution to Christianity in the Holy Land, the Ghassānids contributed indirectly as military *foederati* by the protection they afforded Palestine from the raids of the pastoralists of the Arabian Peninsula. As guardians of the Oriental Limes, especially its sector to the east of the Holy Land, and from their bases in Palaestina Secunda, *the provincia* Arabia, and Palaestina Tertia, they guarded the Holy Land and provided security, reflected *inter alia,* in the astounding number of religious structures that sprang up on both sides of the Jordan in the sixth century, and which the spade of the archaeologist has turned up in the course of the last fifty years on both sides of the Holy River.

---

[33] *Ibid.,* pp. 981-984.
[34] On Patriarch Elias, see *ibid.,* pp. 697-698.

After defending the Holy Land for some three centuries as watchmen over the Limes, the Arab Christian *foederati* represented by the last group, the Ghassānids, took part in its defence from their headquarters in Gaulanitis against the two historic invasions in the second and fourth decades of the seventh century. In the second decade, they had to face the entire imperial army of Sāsānid Persia, which outnumbered them greatly. The battle of Aḏriʿāt in AD 614 opened the way to the capture of the Holy City by the Persians in the same year. In the fourth decade, the defence of Oriens was repeated, this time against the forces of Islam advancing from the Arabian Peninsula. In AD 629, the Ghassānids defeated the first Muslim column at the battle of Muʾta in Palaestina Tertia, but they were finally beaten together with the Byzantine Imperial army in AD 636 at the fateful battle of Yarmūk, an affluent of the Jordan.

THE CAPTULATION OF JERUSALEM, A. D. 638
ABU AL-JUʾAYD

The sources are silent on Arab Christianity in Palaestina Prima after the death of Patriarch Elias[35], in AD 516. But a century later, one of them occupies the scene of Arab-Byzantine relations in an especially significant manner, namely, active participation in the negotiations that surrendered Jerusalem to the Caliph Omar in AD 638, by Patriarch Sophronius. Both the Syriac and the Arabic sources confirm his participation in the dramatic event. His name was Abū al-Juʿayd. He evidently was a well-known, influential figure of that period. The presumption is that his ethnic and linguistic background was essential in the process that transferred Jerusalem from the hands of a Greek- speaking Patriarch to an Arabic-speaking Caliph. And he must have been bilingual in Greek and Arabic, acting as interpreter between the Patriarch and the Caliph and he was possibly the one who translated the famous Covenant of Omar, written in Arabic, to the Greek Patriarch. The Syriac source explicitly says that he was a prominent Jerusalemite, who came with the Patriarch to meet the Caliph. [36] This is

---

[35] With the exception of a reference in Cyril of Skythopolis to the phylarch of the Parembole, for whom see *supra*, n. 17.

[36] For reference to him in the Syriac sources, see *BASIC* I, p. 656.

confirmed by one of the trustworthy sources on the Arab Conquests, namely the *History* of al-Azdī, which credits him with another important transaction that preceded the capitulation of Jerusalem, namely the one involving Abū-ᶜUbayda, the Commander-in-Chief of the Arab forces in charge of the campaign in Bilād al-Shām. Abū al-Juᶜayd negotiated with Abū ᶜUbayda the treaty regarding Urdunn, (Jordan), presumably the other side of the Jordan, Trans-Jordan, and Abū-ᶜUbayda wrote him a Covenant for Jordan.[37] This confirms the Syriac sources on the prominence of Abū-al Juᶜayd in Jerusalem and that it did not rest on his bilingualism, irrelevant in this transaction involving Jordan between two Arabic-speaking personages.

Abū al-Juᶜayd was the last representative of the Christian Arab community in Byzantine Palestine noticed by the sources, both Syriac and Arabic. While his Christian Arab predecessors who left their mark on Byzantine Palestine had been clerics, he was not. He was a secular who, by taking part in the negotiations that ended with the capitulation of Jerusalem, closed one important chapter in the long history of Arab Christianity in Palestine in this Proto-Byzantine period and opened another, namely, that of Arab Christian-Muslim relations in Bilād al-Shām. Abū al-Juᶜayd was, thus, the last of the four prominent figures of Arab Christianity in Byzantine Palestine: Moses, the holy man and saint of the fourth century; Aspebetos, the bishop of the Parembole and active participant in the Council of Ephesus in the fifth century; and Theodore, the chief hierarch and theologian of the Ghassānids in the sixth.

Although Islam was tolerant to other religions and accorded their adherents considerable autonomy, it terminated the Golden Period of Arab Christianity, which lasted for at least three centuries in Bilād al-Shām and elsewhere in the Arab Lebensraum, where and when the Christian Arabs contributed *inter alia* saints, martyrs, and theologians to the Universal Church. It also initiated a new long period during which the Christian Arabs acquired a new status in medieval times, namely, that of Covenanters or Scriptuaries, Ahl-al-Ḏimma, in the New Order that prevailed in Palestine and Bilād al-Shām in the seventh century.

---

[37] For this, see M. al-Azdi, Tārikh *Futūh al-Shām*, ed. A.ᶜAmir, (Cairo,1970), pp. 112-113. For his participation in the capitulation of Jerusalem, *ibid.*, p. 254.

CHRISTIAN ARABS BEFORE ISLAM

Hanna Abu-Hanna

LITERARY AND HISTORICAL SOURCES
FOR ARAB CHRISTIAN PRESENCE BEFORE ISLAM

Studying pre-Islamic Arabic literature at school opened new knowledge to us. Far from the heart of the Arab Peninsula in what we call nowadays Syria and Iraq, there were two Christian kingdoms: the kingdom of the Manadhirah in the north-east (Iraq) and the kingdom of the Ghasasinah in the northwest. Arab poets traveled on camels to these kingdoms to chant eulogies exalting their kings' bravery, generosity, wisdom and other attributes. The poets earned rewards and the kings had their praise chanted throughout the Arab world.

The famous poet an-Nabighah a-Dhubiani (d. 604 AD) was in both Christian courts: Hira, the capital of al-Manadhirah and Damascus, the capital of al-Ghasasinah, although they often fought each other. After a close relationship with the King An-Na'man ibn Al-Mundhir, this poet had to go to his opponent in Damascus to chant the opponent's praise, later apologizing upon return to Hira. He introduced a Christian aspect into his eulogy of the kings of the Ghasasinah: "Their Book is divine, their religion is sound and their aspiration is to achieve the most virtuous goals."

In another poem he mentions that children presented flowers to the kings in the festivities of Palm Sunday and "an-Na'man, King of Hira, used to process every Sunday and every feast day with his family and the dignitaries of the Al-Mundhir family, wearing garments of gilded silk and golden coronets and on their waists girdles bedecked with gold ornamented with jewels, carrying flags with golden Crosses." [1]

---

[1] Al-'Umary, *Masalik al-Absar,* vol.1 (Cairo, 1924), p.326.

Poet 'Adi ibn Zayd, born in Hira to Christian parents in the late sixth century, was well-versed in the Arabic and Persian languages and served at the court of Xerxes (Kisra Anu Shirwan). His poetry refers to incidents in the Bible and his biography describes Hind, the daughter of King an-Na'man, whom he saw in church during the Passover ceremony. Later he arranged with one of Hind's maids for a visit to the "Church of Tuma," where they were introduced. The whole story of asking her father for the hand of the princess appears in Al-Aghani 2, pp.106-109.

After the tragic murder of 'Adi in prison, Hind spent her last years as a nun in a monastery. In one of his poems composed in prison, 'Adi swears by "the God of Mecca and the Cross." This combination is strange. Mecca before Islam was a religious center where pilgrims from many different tribes came to pray at the Ka'ba. We are not told that "the god of Mecca" was the Christian god. Does 'Adi use this oath to assure his non-Christian listeners? Al-Azraqi, in the book *Akhbar Makka* (*The News of Mekka* vol.1, p.104),[2] describes the pictures painted on the walls of the Ka'ba: "On its pillars were pictures of the prophets , pictures of trees and pictures of the angels. There was a picture of Abraham, the favorite of God, as an old man revealing one's lot by the divining arrows, and the picture of Jesus, son of Miriam, and his mother and pictures of the angels – may God bless them all." When Mecca was occupied, the messenger of God (Muhammad) – may God have mercy upon him – entered the House (Ka'ba). He sent Al- Fadl ibn El-'Abbas ibn 'Abd El Muttaleb to bring water from the well of Zamzam:

> Then the prophet asked that a cloth be wetted… and that those pictures be erased. He put both palms of his hands on the picture of Jesus, son of Miriam, and his mother - peace be on them - and said: "Erase all the pictures except those under my hands." Then he raised his hands from Jesus, son of Miriam, and his mother. He looked at the picture of Abraham and said: "Woe unto them that made him seek to reveal the lot by the divining arrows. What is the relation of Abraham to those arrows?"

---

[2] Al-Azraqi, *Akhbar Makka* (Leipzig, 1858), p.104, quoted by George Anawati in *Al-Maseehiyyah wal-Hadarah al-'Arabiyyah* (Christianity and Arabic Culture), 2nd ed. (Cairo , 1992). Anawati refers to the opinion of L. Cheikho in *Shu'ara' an-Nasraniyyah* (*Christian Poets before Islam*) that the Ka'ba was a church built not long after Christ and that it was built by Christians who came to settle in Mekka. Yaqut in Mu'jam al-Buldan, vol. 4, p. 465 says: "The Christian Arabs made the pilgrimage to Mekka."

In his book *Shu'ara' An-Nasraniyya Qabl Al-Islam* (*Christian Poets before Islam,* Beirut 1890), Louis Cheikho lists more than two dozen prominent pre-Islamic poets as Christians; however, some researchers debate the number. One well-known poet, Hassan ibn Thabit (562-674 AD) traveled from Medina to Damascus to sing the praise of the Ghasasinah, receiving an annual salary; later he went to Hira. One of his poems says: "Passover is approaching, the children are hastily threading coral wreathes/They compete in reciting prayers to God and all imprecations to Satan/Prayers to Christ in that monastery and supplications of priests and monks." When the Prophet Muhammad declared his mission and was fought by some of the leaders of his Quraysh tribe, he was compelled to migrate to Medina in 622 AD, where Hassan was proclaimed his poet.

The famous and eloquent Yemenite orator, the Bishop of Najran, Qiss ibn Sa'eda, who died about the year 600, used to go to Suq 'Ukadh, where people gathered from far away places to trade and compete in poetry and to participate in different cultural activities. His sermons are famous for their appeal and distinguished rhetoric. Books on the history of Arabic literature regard him as a prominent representative of pre-Islamic prose.

This literature indicates that the sophisticated, poetic Arabic language was the language of the wide area from Yemen in the south to Syria and Iraq in the north before and during the expansion of Islam, while Persian remained the language of only one country after it adopted Islam. A map of the region of Arabic speakers from the first to the seventh centuries extends from Yemen through the Arab Peninsula to the Taurus Mountains in the north and from the Mediterranean coast to Mesopotamia in the east.

And how did Christianity make its way amongst the Arabs? In The Acts of the Apostles we read: "And when the day of Pentecost was fully come, they were all in one accord in the place" (2:1). "Cretans and Arabians, we do hear them speak in our tongues the wonderful works of God" (2:11). In the Epistle of Paul the Apostle to the Galatians (1:17), he notes "Neither went I up to Jerusalem to them which were apostles before me, but I went into Arabia, and returned again unto Damascus."[3] Clearly there were already Christian Arabs in the first century AD. Apostles and preachers were active in spite of persecution and pursuit. The number of monasteries and churches expanded, culminating in the fifth and sixth centuries as extensive research shows.

---

[3] "Arabia" here is the Province east of the Jordan River where major towns are Busra, Madaba and Philadelphia .

The Roman Empire was already in the region some time before Christ. Its presence expanded when Pompey conquered Palestine and entered Jerusalem (63 BC). The map of the region shows two major powers, the Roman Empire ruling the western part of the Fertile Crescent and the eastern coast of the Mediterranean and the Persian Empire in the eastern part.

Hellenic culture was also an influence in the region. Breasted says: "When Christianity issued from Palestine...it found itself but one among many other influences from the Orient that were passing westward. Thus, while Greek civilization, with its language, its art, its literature, its theaters and gymnasiums, was Hellenizing the Orient, the Orient in the same way was exercising a powerful influence on the West and orientalizing the Eastern Mediterranean world. In this way there was gradually an Eastern Mediterranean world of Hellenic-Oriental civilization." [4]

On the margin of each of the two major powers, two Christian Arab kingdoms emerged in the sixth century. On the western side was the kingdom of the Ghasasinah and on the eastern side the kingdom of the Manadhirah. How had Christianity come to power there? For various reasons, many Arab tribes had migrated from various parts of the Arab peninsula to the north, mainly to the Fertile Crescent. Many Yemenite tribes, including the Ghasasinah in the fourth century AD, settled in Syria while others settled along the shores of the Euphrates and the Tigris. The Nabateans had seized Petra from the Edomites at the beginning of the sixth century BC. Their rule flourished at the end of the fourth century BC and about 85 BC they occupied Damascus. Aretas was the Nabatean king Al- Hareth the Fourth, whose governor in Damascus persecuted Paul (2 Corinthians 11:32). The Nabateans were Arabs who spoke Arabic and wrote in Syriac letters.[5] There is extensive research about the migration of the Arab tribes northwards, their inter-relations and their relations with the surrounding major powers.

The information about the expansion of Christianity among the Arabs in the early stages is gathered from news, anecdotes and extracts from different sources. Missionaries and hermits were very active not only in prayers and preaching but in tending the sick. St. Hilarion (291-371 AD) devoted himself to preaching to the pagans in the Negev in the first half of the fourth century.

---

[4] James Henry Breasted. *Ancient Times – A History of The Ancient World, 2nd ed.* (Boston , 1935), p. 552.

[5] Philip K. Hitti. *History of the Arabs* (Arabic translation), p. 90.

Other hermits converted whole tribes in one coup. Zocomos, who was the head of the tribe Daj'am and who was a Phyllarc in the reign of Valens, was converted, along with his whole tribe, when God granted him a son in response to the prayers of a certain hermit.

Arab sources describe Daoud ibn Haboulah, another Christian king of this tribe who built a monastery near Madaba. The historian Ibn al-Kalbi says about him: "He hated blood, hated the world and killing and devoted himself to worship in his Christian creed."[6] Cyrille of Scythopolis in *The Life of Saint Euthyme the Great* tells the story of the conversion of another whole tribe. Spabedh, a tribal head who was a cavalry commander in the Persian regime fled from the tyranny of King Yazdajert (d. 420 AD) to Arabia. He had a paralyzed son who was healed by Euthyme, a Christian hermit who lived east of Jerusalem, leading the whole tribe to adopt Christianity. Euthyme renamed Spabedh "Peter" and appointed him bishop of his people in 427 AD. The tribe moved into houses instead of tents and built a church. Some of the bishops who succeeded Peter participated in the Christian Councils.[7]

Another reference is to Philip the Arab, who became Emperor of Rome between the years 244-249 AD. He was born in the Province of Arabia southeast of Damascus and married Marcia Otacilia Severa. We are told that as Emperor he did not deny the fact that he was Christian. On Holy Saturday night, while in Antioch, he went to the church with his wife to attend Mass. Bishop Babylas insisted that the Emperor could not participate without penitence and confessing his sins. The Emperor and his wife had to yield to the bishop's terms.[8]

A different story is that of Queen Mawiya, who ruled Arab tribes in the south of Syria during the reign of the Emperor Valens (364-378 AD). Mawiya attacked the Roman territory in southern Palestine and when the Romans could not defeat her, they had to negotiate an agreement with her. One of her conditions was to appoint in her territory a bishop called Moses (Musa), an Arab who was a pious hermit from Mawiya's tribe. He proved to be a worthy bishop who gathered many to his creed. In the sources he is called "The Bishop of the Saracens."[9]

---

[6] Ibn al-Kalbi. *Nasb Ma'add wal-Yaman al- Kabeer* (*The Genealogy of Ma'add And Yemen*), vol.2 (Damascus, 1986), p. 449.

[7] Al-'Ayeb, Salwa Balhaj Saleh. *Al- Maseehiyyah al-'Arabiyyah wa Tatawwuratuha* (*Arab Christianity and its Developments*), 2nd ed. (Beirut, 1998), p. 34.

[8] Anawati , op.cit. pp 60-61.

[9] Al-'Ayeb, op.cit. p. 32.

CHRISTIANITY IN THE ARAB PENINSULA

Missionaries from the Monophysite creed, coming from Edessa, Hira and other centers, spread throughout the Arab Peninsula. Some bishops lived with nomad tribes, migrating from one place to another. Other bishops participated in the Council of Nicaea. Some carried epithets like "Bishop of the Allied Eastern Tribes" or "Bishop of the Saracens." The Arab historian al-Ya'cuobi gives a list of Arab tribes in which people adopted Christianity, including the famous Quraysh tribe of Mecca.[10] Yaqout, another Arab historian, says that Eilat, "the furthest northern outskirt of Hijaz" was Christian and al-Mas'oudi says that the bishop of Eilat who discussed terms of surrender with the Prophet Muhammad in Tabuk is called Yuhanna Ru'ba.

There is also a list of Arab bishops whose centers were in Dumat el Jandal, Tayma, Tabuk, Wadi el-Qira and Yathrib, which was later called Medina. Nestorian sources mention appointing a bishop in Yathrib and tell how the monk Abd Yashua' preached Christianity in Bahrain at the end of the fourth century. He came from the south of Iraq, where he was head of some monasteries under the Catholicos Toumarsa (d. 392 or 410 AD). Christianity in what we now call the Arab Gulf began in Qatar. Sources name it as the center of a bishopric from 225 AD. Nestorian missionaries reached Oman in the first quarter of the fifth century and bishops from Oman were present at church councils of 424, 544, and 576.[11]

An anecdote by at-Tabari[12] testifies that Christianity was in Oman at the time of the Muslim occupation as Abu Tufayl related: "I was in the army which Ali ibn abu Talib sent to Bani Najiyah. When we reached them, we found three parties. Our leader said to one of the groups, 'Who are you?' They said, 'We are Christians who found no religion better than ours, so we stayed firm.' He said to them, 'Stay aside.' Then he said to the other group, 'Who are you?' They said, 'We are Christians who adopted Islam.' He said to them, 'Stay aside.' Then he said to the third group, 'Who are you?' They said, 'We are people who were Christians, then adopted Islam, but we found no religion better than our first religion.' He said to them, 'Adopt Islam.' But they refused."

The Nestorian Catholicus Echo'yab the Third (ordained in the year 650 AD) wrote to the people of Oman to adhere to their religion and accept

---

[10] Al-Ya'qubi. Tareekh … (History …), vol.1 (Beirut, 1960), p. 227.
[11] See Al-'Ayeb, chapter 1.
[12] Al-Tabari. Tareekh…(History …), vol.5 (Beirut, 1967), pp. 125-126 .

the conditions of the Muslims. In different references[13] we find a long list of tribes who adopted Christianity. Al-Jahiz says: "Christianity prevailed on the kings of the tribes of the Arabs...." Then he gives a list of those tribes.

CHRISTIANITY IN IRAQ

Iraq was under Persian rule until the Muslim occupation in the seventh century. It is interesting that the first missionaries to Iraq were Christian Greek prisoners, captured by Shapur the First in his wars against the Byzantines, 241-260 AD. Among the prisoners were bishops and patriarchs from Antioch who settled in special towns. The authorities treated them with tolerance. They spread Christianity and gradually established monasteries and churches. The increase of parishes required a common "administration" based in Ctesiphon under the chair of Antioch. The Catholicos was called the Catholicos of the East and Ctesiphon became the site of councils of the Eastern churches.

Christianity outlived the oppression of the reigns of Shapur the Second (340-379 AD) and Ardasheer the Second (379-383 AD). In the reign of Yezdejert the First, Christianity was recognized as legal in the empire. Churches expanded over many districts. In those days the Nicaean creed, adopted at the Council (Synod) of Nicaea brought Eastern and Western churches together. Later, after the Council of Dadiso in the year 424, the Eastern Church released itself from the custody of the Patriarch of Antioch. The schism that begot the Jacobite and Nestorian creeds was also reflected here.

After the expulsion of Nestorius from his patriarchate in the year 435, some patriarchs in Syria and most of the teachers in Edessa supported him. This creed flourished in Iraq and supplied missionaries to the Arab Peninsula. From the end of the fifth century, Nestorianism became the official religion of the Eastern Church.

However, the Jacobite church found its way to Iraq among the Arab tribes, and in some places it competed with Nestorianism. The Nestorian Synod in 484 disclaimed the Jacobite creed, leading to their persecution in Iraq by their Christian brothers. But the Jacobites survived and received reinforcement from the Syrian Jacobites, who fled persecution by the Emperor Justin the

---

[13] Al-Ya'qubi, op.cit. vol.1, p.298 and Al-Jahiz in *Ar-Radd 'ala an-Nasara (Answer to Christians)*, (Cairo, 1926), p.5.

First between 518 and 527 AD. In the beginning of the sixth century the Jacobites had bishops in Iraq, where a substantive role was played by Ya'coub el Barad'i. The most significant success of the Jacobite church in Iraq was Bishop Ahoudemmah (d. 575 AD), who was born in a Nestorian family, but changed his beliefs. He was very active among Bedouin tribes and built a church named after St Sergius near the town Balad as an alternative to the other church named after Sergius in Rusafah.

CHRISTIANITY IN YEMEN (SHEBA OF THE OLD TESTAMENT)

Judaism was already well established in Yemen when Christianity found its way there in the fourth century. Emperor Constantinos the Second sent a delegation headed by Bishop Theophile to the King of Himyar about 356 AD to establish Yemen as a trade link for the Roman Empire. Both emperor and bishop were Arian Christians. The historian Philostorge[14] says that the delegation was very successful: the king himself adopted the Christian faith and three churches were built in different towns. The Arab historian At-Tabari[15] gives another version of Christianity's introduction in Najran by the missionaries Phoemon, a Syrian, and Abdullah ibn Thamer, a nobleman from Najran.

The Abyssinians say that a saint called Azqir introduced the new faith in the second half of the fifth century, but by the beginning of the fifth century, the Monophysite missionaries were already active there. The Emperor Anastasius (491-518 AD) appointed Silvanus as a Monophysite bishop in Yemen.

However, in the year 523 AD, Christians suffered a tragic blow when a Himyarite Jew called Dhu-Nawas, in a *coup d'etat*, seized the throne from his king and revolted against the Abyssinians, who dominated the kingdoms of Himyar and Yemen. He captured the Ethiopian garrison at Zafar and burned the church. When he captured Najran, he massacred the Christians. Bishop Simeon of Beyh Arsham in Syria was sent to Yemen to interview eye -witnesses and wrote a report:

---

[14] Quoted by Anawati, op.cit. p.85.
[15] Al-Tabari, vol.2, op.cit. pp. 119-123.

The Jews amassed all the martyrs' bones and brought them into the church, where they heaped them up. They brought in the priests, deacons, sub-deacons, readers and sons and daughters of the convent....They filled the church from wall to wall, some 2000 persons – according to the men who came from Najran – then they piled wood all round the exterior of the church and set light to it, thus burning the church with everyone inside it.

During the next week, hundreds more were martyred, among them godly women who were killed with the most terrible tortures when they refused to renounce Christ. Deep pits were dug, filled with combustible material and set afire.

The Roman Emperor Justin (518-527 AD) asked the Abyssinians to avenge the Christians, and they sent a strong army which defeated Dhu Nawas and killed him. The Abyssinians ruled Yemen afterwards from 525-570 AD, during which Christianity revived. In San'a, the capital, a grand church called "Culais" (Greek: *ekklesia*) was built.

Under Persian rule, which succeeded the Abyssinian occupation, Christianity was tolerated and the building of churches continued, including the grand church called the "Ka'ba of Najran." Together with those of the Jacobite creed, there were the Melkite church and followers of a third creed called the Julianites (the Aphthartolates) who were Monophysites that believed that the body of Christ is immortal. We read in Ibn Hisham[16] that Bishop Haritha ibn`Alqamah al-Bakri received help from the Christian Roman kings to build Melkite churches.

CONTROVERSY AND SCHISMS

Christianity, in the early stages, had to answer many primary questions, including:

- How is Christ both divine and human?
- Are the divine and human combined or separate?
- How can the Trinity be explained?

---

[16] Ibn Hisham, Sirah ... (Beirut, 1975).

Schools and academies in Alexandria, Antioch, Jerusalem, Nisibin, and Edessa taught Greek philosophy and other channels of culture. Religious creeds were discussed and debated, but different interpretations resulted in controversy. Discussions in Alexandria echoed in Constantinople and Edessa. Christianity, which had suffered from oppression and persecution, had to deal now with internal struggles which were sometimes more painful than those against the authorities.

Gnostics claimed there were two gods: the Supreme Being and the lesser deity, the demiurge – the deity responsible for the creation of the physical aspect of humanity. They denied the reality of Christ's human nature, claiming He came from the good God alone. His human nature was only an appearance or phantom so He could move among men. They also denied the physical resurrection, viewing material as evil. In the middle of the second century, they were declared heretics.

Another "theoretician" was Arius (c. 256-336), who was a priest in Alexandria. He taught that God is one, un-begotten, and shares nothing in His Self. The pre-incarnate Jesus is divine, but nonetheless was created by and consequently inferior to the Father. Though Arianism was declared heretical in the Council of Nicaea, it survived for some time, even among some nobility and high-ranking clergy.

Nestorius, Archbishop of Constantinople from 428-431, criticized the use of the title "Mother of God" for the Virgin Mary. He preferred the title "Mother of Christ" because Mary gave birth only to the human person of Jesus, not the divine. He preached that Jesus existed as two persons, the man Jesus and the divine son of God, the Logos, rather than as a unified person. The Council of Ephesus in 431 condemned this view, but many bishops and churches refused to denounce Nestorius as a heretic and continued to be regarded as Nestorians. This conflict led to the separation of the Assyrian Church from the Byzantine Church. The Synod held under Mar Babai (497 or 499 AD) renewed the decree of independence from Antioch and thereafter Selucia (Iraq) became the center of Nestorianism.

Another Monophysite church was founded in the sixth century by Ya'coub el- Barad'i (Jacob Baradeus). *The Biographies of Eastern Saints* by John of Ephesus describes the way in which the king of the Ghasasinah adopted the Jacobite creed: The Ghasasinah had heard of a pious hermit, Ya'coub el- Barad'i, living in a monastery in Edessa, and when the tribe was struck by pestilence, the king appealed to the hermit for help, resulting in a mass conversion. In 543 AD, the Ghasasinah, using their political connections with King al-Hareth and some Jacobite bishops, asked Empress Theodora, wife of Emperor Justinian the First to appoint two Jacobite bishops chosen by Patriarch Theodosius of Alexandria to serve in the provinces of the Ghasasinah: Syria, Arabia and Palestine. Ya'coub el-Barad'i was appointed Bishop of Edessa, responsible for the province of Syria, while Theodorus became Bishop of Busra, responsible for Arabia, the Syrian desert and Palestine, excluding Jerusalem. Thus, in 543 AD, an Arab Jacobite bishopric called the Bishopric of Ghassan was established. Most Jacobite sources testify that the Ghasasinah loathed the Christian Melkites and even refused to share bread with them.[17] Therefore, the Melkite Church established itself in different places north of Damascus.

On the eastern side, bordering Persia, the Nestorians were well established. When the Sassanid Persian kings, who were enemies of the Byzantines, saw the persecution of the Nestorians after the Council of Chalcedon, they supported their Christian subjects and showed further sympathy:

- They guaranteed protection to the Nestorians in 462 AD.
- They executed the pro-Byzantine Catholicos Babowai, who replaced Bar Sauma, the Nestorian bishop of Nisibin in 484 AD.
- They allowed the transfer of the school of Edessa to the Persian city of Nisibin after the Byzantine Emperor had closed it for its Nestorian tendencies in 489 AD.

CHRISTIANITY AND THE QU'RAN

When Islam appeared in the seventh century, Christianity was present in most parts of the Arab Peninsula and the Fertile Crescent as well as Egypt. The different creeds of Christianity were present but the Eastern Church prevailed. This Christian presence is reflected in the dialogue with Christians in the Qur'an. Christianity and Christians are mentioned in the Qur'an in 117 verses in 13 Suras. Christians are regarded as "Ahlu-l-Kitab," the people of the Book and Jesus is exalted as a prophet, a messenger of God, son of Mary, a worker of

---

[17] Al-'Ayeb, op.cit. p. 37.

miracles. But blame falls on those Christians whose belief differs from Islam. A translation of Surat Al-Nisa (chapter 4:172)[18] records this view:

> O people of the Book! Exceed not the limits and say not of Allah anything but the truth. Verily the Messiah, Jesus son of Mary, was only a messenger of Allah, and a fulfillment of His Word which He sent down to Mary, and a mercy from Him. So believe in Allah and His Messengers, and say not "They are three." Desist, it will be better for you. Verily Allah is only One God. Holy is He, far above having a son. To Him belongs whatever is in the heavens and whatever is in the earth. And sufficient is Allah as a Guardian.

And a translation of Surat Al-Ma'idah (chapter 5:73) states:

> Indeed they are disbelievers who say "Allah, He is the Messiah, son of Mary," whereas the Messiah himself said: "O children of Israel, worship Allah who is my Lord and your Lord. Surely whoso associates partners with Allah, him has Allah forbidden Heaven, and the Fire will be his resort. And the wrongdoers shall have no helpers."

This preaching must have been addressed to a quite massive Christian community. There are even echoes of some of the controversy within the Christian church itself. Surat Al-Nahl (ch.16: 104) gives a response to allegations that there were people who "helped the Holy Prophet in composing the Qur'an."[19] In the list of these names are Christian slaves and a Nestorian monk called Sergius. The Qur'an refutes these allegations saying: "And indeed we know that they say that it is only a man who teaches him. But the tongue of him towards whom their minds incline in making this insinuation is foreign while this is Arabic tongue plain and clear."

---

[18] *The Holy Qur'an with English Translation and Commentary*, edited by Malik Ghulam Farid (London, 1981).
[19] See commentary, pp. 574 -575.

CONCLUSION

Christian Arabs were among the pioneers mentioned in the "Acts of the Apostles." Missionaries reached almost all parts of the Arab Peninsula, and by the fourth century Christian communities were established in Palestine, Syria, Iraq and Qatar and Bahrain in what is called the Persian Gulf. The climax was in the fifth and sixth centuries. The migration of many tribes from the Arab Peninsula to the Fertile Crescent resulted in strong Arab presence there. The conversion of those tribes from paganism to Christianity is remarkable. The two Christian kingdoms in Syria and Iraq (Ghasasinah and Manadhira) illustrate a hegemonic presence of Christianity amongst the Arabs at the time. Christianity also had a firm footing in Yemen. It reached Mecca and Yathrib (Medina) as well as Hadramut. Although the two kingdoms of Syria and Iraq were Christian, they allied with opposing powers: the Ghasasinah with the Romans and the Manadhirah with the Persians, and they fought against each other when politics demanded.

Due to different interpretations of major beliefs, Christianity underwent controversies and conflicts that led to separations within the Church. The Eastern Church prevailed, although the Melkite church was also present. When Islam came, the Christian Arab intellectuals played an important role in the field of science and culture and supplied the Arabic culture with the fruits of the Greek philosophy and science.

HISTORICAL FACTORS THAT HAVE AFFECTED PALESTINIAN CHRISTIANS

Naim Ateek

When we consider the last 2000 years of Palestinian Christianity, we see five major factors that affected the life of the Christian Community of the land. As we briefly outline them, it is important to keep in mind that we are dealing with the past, and some of the hard facts that are mentioned must be understood in their own historical context. They do not necessarily reflect people's thinking today. I only hope and pray that we can learn from our past mistakes.

This paper is, therefore, a general introduction and it is intended to give an overall picture of a 2000 year old movement of history. Every one of the factors mentioned had an adverse effect on the Christian Church in the Holy Land and contributed to the weakening of the Christian presence in the country. I will outline them very briefly and concisely.

In an outline spanning so many years and addressing issues of history, religion, politics, and theology it is easy, inadvertently, to use a word here or there that might offend some people. This is not my intention. I hope that this paper will stimulate discussion among many Christians and encourage them to do more study and research. There are two parts to this presentation. This one considers the past history. In the second part, I will look at the future of Palestinian Christianity in the Holy Land.

BACKGROUND

- The Church was born in Palestine by the power of the Holy Spirit on the Day of Pentecost.

"When the day of Pentecost had come, they were all together in one place. And suddenly from heaven there came a sound like the rush of a violent wind, and it filled the entire house where they were sitting. Divided tongues, as of fire, appeared among them, and a tongue rested on each of them. All of them were filled with the Holy Spirit and began to speak in other languages, as the Spirit gave them ability" (Acts 2:1-4).

- The names of the countries and peoples mentioned in the book of Acts reflect a theological statement:

"...Parthians, Medes, Elamites, and residents of Mesopotamia, Judea and Cappadocia, Pontus and Asia, Phrygia and Pamphylia, Egypt and the parts of Libya belonging to Cyrene, and visitors from Rome, both Jews and proselytes, Cretans and Arabs..."(Acts 2:9-11).

The writer Luke wanted to tell us that on the Day of Pentecost the Gospel was preached to the known world of that time and representatives of all these nations heard it and responded to it.

- The book of Acts gives us another glimpse of the inclusiveness of the Gospel as it spread to various parts of Palestine. Besides Jerusalem, it was preached in Samaria (Nablus area) for the Samaritans (chapter 8), and in Caesarea to a small Roman community (chapter 10).
- By the end of the 4th century, Palestine had become a predominantly Christian country.

Let us now look at the five major factors that adversely affected the life and presence of Palestinian Christians from those early centuries until the present.

FIRST FACTOR: THEOLOGICAL CONTROVERSIES

1. The theological factor is the most general one and has affected the life of all the Christians in the Middle East, including Palestine.
2. Up to the first part of the 4th century, although the church was taking root in various countries and among different races and cultures, it was still perceived as one. Christians everywhere recognized that they

belonged to the same "One Lord, One Faith, and One Baptism" (Ephesians 4:5).

3. Soon, however, difficulties and misunderstandings began to emerge as a result of theological, political, cultural, and geographical differences. Some Christians were living inside the Roman Empire; others were living outside it. Some spoke Greek, others spoke Aramaic and other languages. Some used Hellenistic patterns of thought; others employed Semitic thought patterns. There were cultural and political differences. Some were governed by the Roman Empire while others were governed by the Persian Empire as well as other differences.

4. There were no printed Bibles in those days accessible to people.

5. The Church was caught up in bitter controversies. The most excruciating issues related to the relationship between Jesus Christ and God. At the same time, the Church was determined to maintain the faith in the Oneness of God. Consequently, a number of Church Councils were held that brought together hundreds of bishops from East and West across the universal church to agree on the basic doctrines and principles of the Christian Faith.

6. The first four general Councils were held during the 4th and 5th centuries and determined some of the basic doctrinal challenges that confronted the whole Church especially the formulation of the Christological and Trinitarian dogmas: Nicea in AD 325, Constantinople in 381, Ephesus in 431, and Chalcedon in 451. By the end of the 5th century and as a result of the decisions of these Councils and the unresolved differences among the bishops, the first division took place within the body of the Church. This resulted in major schisms and the separation of most of the Christians of today's Middle East — The Assyrian Church of Iraq, the Coptic Church of Egypt, the Church of Ethiopia, the Syrian Orthodox Church, and the Armenian Orthodox Church.

7. It took the Christians many centuries to realize that the separation that took place in the 5th century was not actually due to basic theological differences as much as differences in linguistics, philosophical backgrounds, theological interpretations, personalities, and even political factors.

8. The Byzantine Orthodox Church and the Catholic Church, however,

continued to be united and in communion with one another. They held three subsequent councils together between the 6th and 8th centuries.

9. By the middle of the 5th century, Palestine already had some Copts, Syrians, Armenians, and Ethiopians who were living close to the Holy Places, and although they enjoyed good relations with Orthodox Christians, the fracture had already taken place within the one church.

10. This first great rift within the Church resulted in the alienation of Christians from each other as well as resentment, hostility, broken fellowship, denunciation, and rejection of the sacraments of the "other."

SECOND FACTOR: THE COMING OF ISLAM

1. The coming of Islam in the 7th century was welcomed by many Eastern Christians in order to get rid of the cruelty of the Byzantine Empire. In fact, some Eastern Christians fought alongside the Muslims against the Byzantines.

2. Generally speaking the Arab Muslim rulers were very tolerant towards Christians and Jews. Many Christians and Jews occupied prominent government positions within the Muslim state.

3. With the passage of years, the non-Arab Muslim rulers became less tolerant, and this intolerance resulted in greater hardships and persecution of Christians.

4. Such a situation caused the movement of many Christians from the Arab peninsula towards what we know today as Syria, Lebanon, Jordan, and Palestine.

5. Furthermore, to escape the payment of the special tax for non-Muslims (al-jizyeh) and also to avoid persecution, many Christians became Muslim. By and large, it was a conversion of convenience rather than conviction.

6. One indication is the names of dozens of villages and towns throughout Palestine that begin with the word "Deir," which refers to a convent, monastery or church. Most of these towns are totally Muslim now but were at one time Christian.

7. It is true that the coming of Islam lifted the yoke of the Byzantines off the shoulders of the indigenous Christians of the Middle East, but it weakened the Christian community through apostasy to Islam.

THIRD FACTOR: THE CRUSADES

1. In 1054, forty-five years before the first Crusade started (1099), the break between the Byzantine Orthodox Church in the East and the Roman Catholic Church in the West took place. This resulted in the second major division within the Christian Church.
2. When the Crusaders came to Jerusalem, they perceived not only the Muslims as their enemies but also the Jews as well as the indigenous Christians of the land, who were largely Orthodox.
3. The Orthodox Patriarch was removed and replaced by a Latin Patriarch.
4. Beginning with the Crusades, every major Orthodox Church in the East split and a segment of the church went into communion with Rome while retaining its eastern character and liturgy. In historical order this is the picture that emerged:

- In 1182, the entire Maronite Church, which had remained faithful to the principles of Chalcedon, affirmed its full unity with Rome.
- In 1672, a segment of the Assyrian Church of the East reunited with the Catholic Church and became known as the Chaldean Church.
- In 1724, the Melkites issued a declaration of Roman/Melkite union, remaining loyal to Rome when the Orthodox Church split in two. They became known as Greek Catholics and today form the largest Christian community in the state of Israel.
- In 1742, the Armenian Catholics were officially recognized by the Pope as in union with Rome, having made many efforts to restore relations with Rome from the time the Armenian Orthodox Church was established after the Council of Chalcedon.
- In 1783, the newly elected Patriarch of the Syrian Orthodox Church declared himself and the Church in unity with Rome, making permanent the two distinct branches of the Syrian Church.
- In 1895, Pope Leo III established a Patriarchate of the Coptic Catholic Church separate from the Coptic Orthodox Church, finalizing many earlier attempts at union.

5. These divisions left the Christians of the East weaker and fragmented, with much bitterness and hostility towards one another.

6. The bitter legacy of the Crusades upset the lives of all the Christians of the East vis-à-vis their Muslim neighbors and created suspicions and, at times, accusations of collaboration with the West. Even today the tension, at times, surfaces.

7. These church schisms into Orthodox and Catholic branches became the third major division within Eastern Christianity.

FOURTH FACTOR: THE PROTESTANT MISSIONARY MOVEMENT: THE RISE OF WESTERN POWERS AND COLONIALISM

1. In the 16th century the Roman Catholic Church in Europe experienced divisions within its own ranks. It started with what became known as the Protestant Reformation. Many churches in Europe separated from Rome and formed their own national and confessional churches. Further splits took place from within these churches. Eventually, many new denominations came into being.

2. By the beginning of the 19th century, the great Protestant Missionary Movement started. In some places it preceded the political colonization of that country. At times it followed it.

3. To Palestine, the missionaries came while the Ottoman Turks were still in power. Generally, colonialism followed after the end of World War I.

4. The American Presbyterians went to Lebanon, Syria, and Egypt.

5. The Anglicans and the Lutherans came to Palestine.

6. New Protestant and Evangelical churches began to form and to solicit members from the Orthodox and Catholic churches of the land. This created the fourth division within the church.

FIFTH FACTOR: ZIONISM AND THE STATE OF ISRAEL

1. The Zionist Movement did not differentiate between Palestinian Christians and Muslims. They were both Palestinians and they needed to be eliminated or ethnically cleansed for the success of the Zionist project.

2. Therefore, when the state of Israel came into being, approximately 750,000 Palestinians – Muslims and Christians – were displaced.

3. The Jewish state was established on 78% of Palestine.

4. With the establishment of the state of Israel on most of the land of Palestine, the country itself was divided and the Christian community was split between those who were driven out and those who stayed under Israeli rule.
5. Most Christians and their clergy became refugees and were not allowed by Israel to return to their homes in contravention of UN resolutions.
6. The decline in Christian numbers weakened the church further. Many Christian refugees emigrated to the West largely to escape economic hardships and to seek a decent life for themselves and their families. Furthermore, many Christians who were living in Israel emigrated to the West as well fleeing from discrimination and economic difficulties.
7. The same policies of discrimination have been used by Israel after it occupied the West Bank and Gaza. Due to political instability, many Palestinian Christians have been emigrating on a steady basis. Today more Palestinian Christians live outside Palestine than inside.

CONCLUSION

When one summarizes the last 2000 years of Palestinian Christianity, these five major factors are certainly obvious. Every one of them affected the Christians in Palestine and left them weaker and more vulnerable than before.

It is possible to summarize this outline in the following way:

1. Internal factors weakened and divided the Christians, namely, the early theological controversies, the consequences of the coming of the Crusades (and the Catholic Church) and the coming of the Protestant Missions from the West. Historically speaking, these factors divided the Church and weakened its witness and unity. Some emphasize the fragmented Body of Christ while others see a beautiful mosaic and a rich heritage of the Christian presence in the land.
2. External political and religious factors first surfaced with the coming of Islam. The Muslim conquest not only had political consequences but also produced effects and ramifications of a new religion that eventually led to the weakening of the Christian community through apostasy to Islam.
3. Another external political factor was the coming of Zionism and the

establishment of the state of Israel. The Zionists wanted the land without the people. The state of Israel created policies to reduce the number of Palestinians in the land, including the number of Christians.

In light of this brief outline that spans 2000 years, we believe that in order to be faithful to God, we must address the following areas in our ministry at Sabeel:

1. We must address the internal agenda within the Christian community; i.e. the divisions, separation, bitterness, and resentment that resulted from the divisions within the Christian community of the land. We need to create a spirit of repentance, forgiveness, and love for each other. All of us have sinned against God because we have failed to love. We must work ecumenically to increase the love and to remove the walls of separation among us. Although some Christians interpret history differently, we need to see the rich mosaic of Christianity in the Holy Land today rather than emphasize its fragmentation.

2. We must address our interfaith relations with Islam and Muslims as well as with Judaism and the Jewish people; and work for greater understanding especially in view of the rise of religious fundamentalism and extremism.

3. We must address our relationship with Israel. We must work for a peace based on justice that would lead to reconciliation among all the people of the Holy Land.

The past contains much pain and sorrow from the internal as well as external factors. We still suffer as a result of the past. Our historical memory in the Middle East is very long, vivid, and sharp. Historical events are not easily forgotten. History moves slowly in this part of the world. If we continue to live only in the past and to dwell only on the past, we can never move forward with God into the present and the future.

As we look at the past, we realize that we have survived by the Grace of God. Because we walk with God, we cannot lose hope. Our hope is firmly based in God "who in Christ, [as Paul said], always leads us in triumphal procession and through us spreads in every place the fragrance that comes from knowing him for we are the aroma of Christ..."(2Cor. 2:14-15).

THE GREEK ORTHODOX PATRIARCHATE OF JERUSALEM

Archbishop of Constantina Aristarchos

The Greek Orthodox Patriarchate of Jerusalem is accepted historically as the Mother of Churches. Its Jewish origins are in its Founder Himself with the circle of the twelve apostles taught by Him and enlightened by the Holy Spirit on the day of Pentecost to speak in the tongues of all nations the mighty works of God (Acts 2): "In that same day there were added unto them by baptism about three thousand souls" (Acts 2:41) and that event constituted the church in its first dynamic appearance in the world. Its Greek background is in the Greeks who asked the apostle Philip to see Jesus (John 12:20-22). It is also in the many pagan Greeks who, when the Church opened itself to the nations with the family of Cornelius the centurion (Acts 10), died as Greeks like the "corn of wheat in the ground" (John 12:25) and "were cut out of the wild olive tree and were grafted to the good olive tree" (Rom 11:24). With this incorporation, uncircumcised and circumcised alike fulfilled their call from Christ "to be reconciled both unto God in one body by the cross" (Eph. 2:16).

This body of Christ with Jerusalem as its See preached His truth in the land of the Revelation, the Holy Land and beyond it "unto the uttermost part of the earth" (Acts 1:8). Its first bishop was James, the brother of the Lord according to the flesh (Gal. 1:19). It survived the three centuries of persecutions, offering many martyrs to the church among whom was the first martyr, Stefan the deacon (Acts 6). It had the good fortune of enjoying as its centers of worship throughout the centuries the first two magnificent churches of Christianity built by the Emperor St. Constantine and his mother St. Helen: the Church of the Anastasis (Resurrection) in Jerusalem and of the Nativity in Bethlehem. In one of these churches, the Chapel of Calvary, St. Cyrillos, Bishop of Jerusalem, delivered his Catechises (348 AD) as a trans-temporal theological monument of Christian initiation. To provide continuous worship in these churches, one of the most ancient monastic orders, the Order of the Spoudai (industrious) monks or the Brotherhood of the Holy Sepulcher, established itself.

Although the center of gravity of this church was always Jerusalem, other cities of its jurisdiction were developed as foci of Christian spirituality under the influence of certain illustrious personalities: Caesarea, with the ecclesiastical authors Origen and Eusebius in its high theological school; Bethlehem with St. Jerome, the biblical scholar from Rome; the previously Hellenistic and idolatrous Gaza as a center of Christianity by efforts of St. Porphyrios the Thessalonian and as the first center of Palestinian monasticism by the indigenous St. Hilarion, disciple of St. Antony the Great; the desert as a city with St. Euthymius from Armenia and St. Sabas and St. Theodosios the Cappadocian as leaders of Palestinian monasticism and defenders of the Christological doctrine of Chalcedon (451 AD). This Ecumenical Synod, via the efforts of St. Juvenal, promoted the Church of Jerusalem to the status of Patriarchate and confirmed its jurisdiction in the three Palaestinas, which in today's terms comprise Israel, Jordan, the Palestinian autonomy and the peninsula of Sinai. In this golden era of the Church of Jerusalem, numerous churches and monasteries were built all over the Holy Land by the help of Roman Byzantine Emperors and provided a rich pastoral, social and cultural activity. This way the holy places were maintained as loci of worship, education and transformation.

In 614 AD the Jerusalem Church experienced the consequences of the Persian invasion. In 629 it recovered somewhat as the Emperor Heraclius brought back to Jerusalem the pillaged Holy Cross and the abducted Patriarch Zacharias. A decade later, in 638, the church of Jerusalem stood in need of the diplomacy of the great theologian and church father Patriarch St. Sofronios for the transmission from a Christian Byzantine political sovereignty to a Muslim one. The then-signed agreement with Caliph Omar Ibn El-Khattab became the road map of the relations between the Church of Jerusalem and the Muslim world for the centuries to come. According to this agreement, the church from that time on became a minority, the *rūm millet*, with certain rights and with the Patriarch as ethnarch. St. John of Damascus and the great theologian of St. Saba's convent contributed to this new framework of relations. With this identity the Church of Jerusalem overcame the adversities of the Crusader and the Mamelukian periods and defended its natural and legitimate rights in the Holy Land during the Turkish period vis-à-vis the concerns of the other Christian denominations.

The same church, with this uninterrupted history and patriarchal succession, continues its life and mission today in its designated ecclesiastical territory of the Holy Land. It sees its mission in safeguarding the Holy Shrines as places of the Revelation, i.e., the birth, crucifixion and resurrection of the Incarnate Word of God, and in guiding its Orthodox congregation according to that Revelation. It is ruled by an 18 member Synod presided over by the Patriarch. The Patriarch is, in addition, the Superior of the Brotherhood of the Holy Sepulcher, which has been an integral body of the Patriarchate since the 4th century and which has 113 members today.

The congregation of the Patriarchate in Israel, Jordan and the Palestinian Autonomy is estimated at about 300,000 members. It is served pastorally in towns and villages according to parishes, 25 in Israel, 30 in Jordan and 15 in the Palestinian Autonomy. The convents of the Patriarchate throughout its jurisdiction number 51. The married parish priests of the Patriarchate are about 100. The Greek-speaking congregation has been a minority for the last decades. The overwhelming majority of the congregation, known as "Rūm Orthodox," is Arabic-speaking, with Israeli, Jordanian or Palestinian national identity. For this congregation the Patriarchate demonstrates a policy respectful of its cultural heritage. The Patriarchate translated the Scriptures, as well as the liturgical and other church religious books, into Arabic from the time the Greek language was no longer in use. The concern of the Patriarchate was to safeguard their religious identity as Rūm Orthodox Christians and not by any means to alienate them from their national identity. The collection of 200 Arabic manuscripts in the Patriarchate Library is proof of this attitude. The Patriarchate faces with the same pastoral responsibility and sensibility the Russian speaking congregation by the appointment of Russian speaking priests and translation of books into Russian.

The Patriarchate puts a special emphasis on education. It maintains a Seminary on Mt. Zion for the education of those who prepare themselves for the priesthood. It maintains elementary and secondary schools in Jordan, Israel and the Palestine Autonomy. These 18 schools employ 680 faculty and staff and educate 8,500 pupils. The Patriarchate is ambitious to upgrade its system of education for the greatest benefit of the pupils independent of denomination or religion.

The Patriarchate operates a printing press, established in 1853, that produces many editions in Greek and Arabic. Furthermore, the press has issued a scientific magazine, *Nea Sion*, since 1904. The Patriarchate maintains a library with 15,000 printed books and 2,000 manuscripts in Greek, Arabic, Aramaic, Slavonic, Georgian and Ethiopian languages. The Patriarchate issues and distributes *gratis* for all its parishes the pamphlet of "Nur-Il-Masih – Light of Christ" containing the Epistle and Gospel reading of every Sunday with patristic exegesis. The Patriarchate has built recently two new churches in Jordan and has started to build one in Qatar. The Patriarchate maintains in its bosom the Polyclinic of St. Benedictos, a well-organized outpatients' system covering the health needs of everybody for a minimal payment. The Patriarchate cooperates with the other Christian communities regarding issues of common Christian concern, participates in the inter-Christian and inter-religious dialogue and is a member of the WCC.

These are the highlights of Patriarchate life and activity in the past and today, presented as modest objective information. Through them the open-minded seeker will be convinced that the Patriarchate has struggled throughout the centuries to witness to the Christian Revelation in its geographical context and to guarantee in it the Christian identity of its faithful, independent of nationality. The Patriarchate sees the reason of its existence as the continuation of this mission under today's difficult circumstances. Under these circumstances of regional violence and political uncertainty and instability, the Patriarchate exercises its role of reconciliation. It experiences as a church the inner peace of its Founder and transmits it to its political, religious and social environment.

The Patriarchate exercises its mission in its ecclesiastical territory divided, perhaps for the first time in its history, into three political sovereignties with opposing interests. Only by the guidance of the Holy Spirit can the Patriarchate avoid a fall from such an acrobatic process. The tense political atmosphere influences the life of its members economically, educationally and in many other ways. The Patriarchate tries, in its capacity, to support its faithful morally and materially to restrain them from emigration and to keep them in the homeland of Christianity. At this point, all Christians of the Holy Land need the solidarity of their fellow Christians who live in more advantageous societies.

The Patriarchate is aware of the significance of the earthly Jerusalem to itself and to the followers of the three monotheistic religions, without losing the vision of the heavenly Jerusalem. The Patriarchate has had the spiritual power to overcome its recent crisis of changing leadership and under the wise guidance of its new Patriarch Theophilos III tries fervently to keep its religious identity as a beneficial factor for its members and for the citizens of the states in which it exists.

THE ARMENIAN CHURCHES
IN THE HOLY LAND

Archbishop Aris Shirvanian

The history of The Armenian Church in the Holy Land can be traced back to the beginning of the fourth century, after Christianity was adopted as the state religion in Armenia in 301 AD by King Tiridates III through St. Gregory the Illuminator, who became the first Catholicos. Thus Armenia became the first nation officially to adopt Christianity.

According to Armenian tradition, both King Tiridates and St. Gregory came and spent some years in Jerusalem during the excavation of the site of the Church of The Holy Sepulchre by the Queen Mother St. Helena, mother of the Emperor Constantine the Great of the Roman Empire. Armenia was an ally of Rome then. Adoption of the new Christian religion motivated Armenians to come to Jerusalem and to take great interest in the Holy Places connected with the life and work of salvation of Our Lord Jesus Christ. Armenia is a far away country in the Caucuses in Asia Minor. It is the biblical land of Mount Ararat, where, according to the story of Genesis, Noah's Ark landed.

King Tiridates participated in the construction of the Church of the Holy Sepulchre, which was completed in 335 AD. He also took part in the building of the Church of Nativity. The Emperor donated the convent of St. James as well as the site of Calvary to King Tiridates for the use of pilgrims. Since at the time there was one common Christian faith, there was no discrimination among the faithful, but they were distinguished only by language and rituals; therefore each would have an altar and a place of worship. However, they all were subject to the authority of the Patriarch of Jerusalem. This was the situation in Palestine until the fifth century. Three Ecumenical Councils were convened by reigning emperors: Nicea in 325 AD, Constantinople in 381 AD and Ephesus in 431 AD. Throughout this time, the Church in

Jerusalem had remained united in one faith in Our Lord and Savior Jesus Christ. It is important to mention here that asceticism in the 4th century gave way to monasticism in Egypt and in Palestine. Although until that time the Egyptian and the Judean Deserts were inhabited by hundreds of ascetics, each dwelling in a cell or a shack, living alone came to be considered as less beneficial than a communal fraternal life which would serve the common good. Therefore, individual ascetics began gathering around a leader along the River Nile and started building monasteries with churches, thus initiating a communal life in each monastery. A similar development took place in Palestine. Ascetics in the Judean Desert started coming together to build monasteries, and in Jerusalem monasteries began to be built in and around holy sites. An Armenian priest, Anastas, who had come on a pilgrimage to Jerusalem in the seventh century, drew up a list of seventy Armenian monasteries in Jerusalem, some of them built by princely dynasties of Armenia. Father Anastas acted at the request of an Armenian prince, Hamazasb Kamsarakan, to whom he presented his report after his return from the pilgrimage. However, some of those monasteries were abandoned by the Armenian monks due to persecutions against them by the Pro-Chalcedonian Emperor Justinian (527 AD) and Greek clergy. Later, during the Arab conquest of Palestine in the seventh century, some of the monasteries were ruined or confiscated due to heavy taxes levied against them. After those calamitous centuries had passed, many Armenian churches were built on the Mounts of Sinai and Tabor in the region of Tiberias and in other parts of Palestine, including Nablus, Gaza, Jericho, the River Jordan, Nazareth and Caesarea. Unfortunately these churches do not exist anymore as they were either ruined or were converted into mosques.

The Chalcedonian controversy (451 AD) had adverse consequences in Jerusalem, where eventually the Church split into two camps: the Greek Orthodox supporting the Chalcedonian doctrine of two separate natures of Our Lord Jesus Christ, the divine and the human, and the Armenians, Copts, Ethiopians and Syrians upholding the doctrine of one united nature of Our Lord according to the teaching of St. Cyril of Alexandria in the Ecumenical Council of Ephesus of 431 AD.

With the rise of Islam, early in the seventh century, Christianity came under attack. However, during the Arab invasion of Palestine, the Armenian Patriarch Abraham I made a trip with a large delegation of Armenian clergy to Mecca to meet the Prophet of Islam Muhammad and to ask him for protection for themselves and for the properties of Armenians in and around Jerusalem.

He received Prophet Muhammad's pledge in writing, whereby possession of the following sites was given to Patriarch Abraham I and his clergy and to their followers, the Ethiopians, Copts and Syrians: St. James Cathedral, the Convent of the Olive Tree (i.e., of the Holy Archangels), The Convent of the Prison of Christ (Caiaphas' House), St. John's Chapel and the Chapel in Nablus, and the Church of the Holy Sepulchre, including the chapels in the rear and the Holy Tomb of Christ, as well as Calvary. He also guaranteed their possession of all their monasteries, churches and other properties. When Caliph Omar Ibn El-Khattab besieged Jerusalem, the Greek Patriarch Sophronios and the Armenian Patriarch Abraham I urged him not to attack the Holy City of Jerusalem, and they voluntarily surrendered it to him. Thereupon Omar gave his *firmans* to them in 638 AD confirming them as Patriarchs and granting them the right of the possession of their churches and properties.

In 1099 AD, when the Crusaders liberated Jerusalem and the Holy Tomb from the Muslims, one of their leaders, Godfrey of Bouillon, a French nobleman, was chosen and consecrated King in the Holy Sepulchre. However, because of his humility, he declined to use the title of King, preferring the title of "Protector of the Holy Sepulchre." At that time Greeks, Armenians and their followers were its guardians. The new king appointed twenty Latin clergy to serve in the Holy Sepulchre. The Armenian Catholicos, Gregory II, who was on a pilgrimage together with the Armenian Patriarch, visited King Godfrey and congratulated him on his accession to the throne. In this period (1222 AD), a great number of Armenians lived in Jerusalem in the Armenian Quarter

In 1187 AD, Sultan Saladin conquered Jerusalem. He expelled the Latins and converted their churches into mosques. However, he allowed the Greeks, Armenians and their followers to continue worshiping in the Holy Sepulchre Church. The Armenian Patriarch Abraham III met Saladin and expressed loyalty to him. He also showed Saladin the *firmans* given by the Prophet Muhammed, Omar Ibn El-Khattab and Ali to the Armenian patriarchs, and requested him to re-affirm them by his own *firman*, thereby confirming the possessions and the privileges of the Armenian Patriarch. Saladin granted Patriarch Abraham III his *firman* that same year.

The Armenian kings of Cilicia paid special attention to the Armenian Patriarchate by donating properties and other gifts. St. James Monastery on Mount Zion was the center. Members of St. James Brotherhood not only maintained their acquired properties faithfully, but also upheld the orthodoxy of the Armenian Church, even against the pro-Latin policy of the Armenian kingdom of Cilicia, a policy which was motivated by political gains. For that reason Patriarch Sarkis I refused to submit to the directives and Latinizing attempts of the Armenian kingdom and severed his administrative ties with the Catholicos of Cilicia in 1311 AD. He received a *firman* from the ruling Sultan Nasser Muhammed of Egypt confirming him as Patriarch of Armenians and of their followers, the Copts, Ethiopians and Syrians. Thus he only maintained his spiritual ties with the Catholicos of Cilicia in the form of having him consecrate bishops for Jerusalem and bless the holy oil.

In 1517 AD, the Turkish Sultan Selim I occupied Jerusalem. He visited the holy places, especially the Holy Sepulchre Church, and gave assurances to the Christian denominations owning it. He also gave a *firman* to the Armenian Patriarch Sarkis II, recognizing his authority and the right to his possessions and properties. His successor, Sultan Suleiman I, imprisoned all the members of the Franciscan Order. The Armenian Patriarchate maintained the Franciscan holy places for them. The Muslims took the Cenacle from them. The Armenian Patriarchate hosted the Franciscans for seven years in the Convent of the Holy Archangels until they purchased St. Savior's Monastery in the Old City from the Georgians and moved there.

During the Ottoman rule of Palestine, the Armenian Patriarchate generally enjoyed the support of the Turkish sultans who granted them privileges by their *firmans* until the end of 1918 AD. Two outstanding Patriarchs were Gregory V Baronder (1613-1645) and Gregory VI the Chainbearer (1715-1749), who paid off the heavy debts of the Patriarchate, renovated the holy places and churches, and purchased new lands and houses in the Armenian Quarter.

Disputes arising in the holy places because of the rivalry among the Greek Orthodox, Armenian Orthodox and Franciscans and because of the prevalent corruption of government officials finally were brought to an end by a *firman* in 1852 by Sultan Abdul Mejid. This document constitutes the official Declaration of the Status Quo in the Holy Places. He confirmed it again in 1853 by another *firman*. In 1878, the Treaty of Vienna specified that no alteration was to be made in the Status Quo without the general consent of the Signatory Powers. This has been the law governing the Holy Places ever since and it has brought stability and generally peaceful co-existence among these communities guarding them. If a dispute is not resolved among the three major communities owning the Holy Places, or the minor communities of the Copts, Syrians and Ethiopians, then the matter is referred to the ruling Government for a resolution.

Presently the Armenian Patriarchate has jurisdiction over the Armenian communities living in Israel, the Palestinian Territories and Jordan with an estimated 25,000 members. There are 2,000 Armenians in Jerusalem, 18,000 in the Jaffa-Tel Aviv area, Haifa and Nazareth, and 5,000 in Palestine and Jordan. The Armenian Quarter covers one-sixth of the Old City.

The Patriarchate is headed by a Patriarch elected for life by the members of St. James Brotherhood. The incumbent Patriarch is His Beatitude Archbishop Torkom Manoogian, who manages the day-to-day affairs along with the Holy Synod.

St. James Cathedral with the Monastery is the seat of the Patriarchate situated on Mount Zion in the Old City of Jerusalem. Its history can be traced back to the fourth century. It is the historical site of the house of the first Bishop of Jerusalem, St. James the Apostle, the Brother of the Lord, who was martyred; his relics are buried under the Main Altar. In addition, the head of St. James the Apostle, son of Zebedee, beheaded by King Herod Agrippa, is also buried in a Chapel.

The Patriarchate includes the following institutions: the Administration building, comprised of the Patriarch's office, residence and reception hall, the departments of Ecumenical and Foreign Relations, Real Estate, Finance and the Archive and the Chief Dragoman's office; the Grand Sacristan's Office and residence; the Alex and Marie Manoogian Theological Seminary with 40 students receiving training for priesthood; the Holy Translator's High School with 120 students; the Calouste Gulbenkian Library with over 100,000 books in different languages; the Library of Manuscripts at St. Theodoros Church with 4,000 valuable manuscripts; the Edward and Helen Mardigian Museum; the Bookstore and the Printing Press, which publishes the magazine *Sion* and religious books.

The Patriarchate has two other Convents in Jerusalem, that of the Holy Archangels on the site of the House of the high priest Annas, and that of St. Savior on the site of the House of the high priest Caiaphas near Zion Gate. It also has a Convent attached to the Church of the Nativity in Bethlehem, St. Nicholas Convent in Jaffa, St. George's Convent in Ramle, a church in Haifa and a church in Amman, Jordan.

Three cultural and sports' clubs in the Armenian Community maintain cultural, social and sports activities. A very important event is the annual commemoration of the Armenian Genocide of 1915 by Ottoman Turks when one and a half million Armenians were exterminated. Thus far, Turkey refuses to accept its responsibility as a perpetrator of this Genocide.

Daily worship services are conducted at St. James Cathedral, The Holy

Sepulchre Church, St.Mary's Church in Gethsemane and in the Church of Nativity.

What challenges do we face at present? With our shortage of manpower and because of our financial limitations, the Armenian Patriarchate faces a number of challenges. Here are some of them:

- To keep our Orthodox Christian faith and its spiritual and moral values at a high standard and not let them be devalued by the generally non-Christian environment in which we live. We keep our heads high as Christians and endure some anti-Christian offensive remarks and spitting by extremist orthodox Jews.
- To preserve our Armenian identity by teaching our native tongue and history and by promoting our cultural heritage.
- To maintain and safeguard our international Christian Holy Places as their guardians together with the Greek Orthodox and the Franciscan communities, and our centuries-long rights and privileges, based on the prevailing Status Quo.
- To maintain our private convents, churches, buildings and other properties in good condition at a very heavy financial cost.
- To provide housing, medical and financial aid and food to the needy.
- To maintain fraternal and harmonious relations with our sister churches with different traditional and theological backgrounds.
- To establish dialogue in an ecumenical spirit with religious leaders of the other two monotheistic religions, Judaism and Islam, in order to find a common ground in the faith of one and the same God, and with the goal of promoting love and peace among their followers.
- Last but not least, to promote the message of a permanent peace and justice for all the people inhabiting this Holy Land by urging Israeli and Palestinian leaders to refrain from destructive violence against each other and to look for constructive ways and means to share this holy city of Jerusalem and this Holy Land for all.

The message of the coming of the Son of God as Our Savior was and remains "peace in this world and goodwill amongst men." We should commit ourselves tirelessly to work until that peace and goodwill become reality.

THE COPTIC CHURCH

Archbishop Anba Abraham

The word Coptic derives from the Greek word *Agapitos*, which was in turn derived from *Hikaptah*, one of the names of Memphis, the first capital of ancient Egypt. The modern use of the term "Coptic" describes Egyptian Christians as well as the last stage of the ancient Egyptian language script.

The relation of the Coptic Church to the Holy Land dates back to the first century, when the land of Egypt was blessed by the visit of the Holy Family to fulfill the prophecy of Isaiah, "Blessed be Egypt my people" (19:25). Saint Mark the evangelist established the Coptic Church of Alexandria in the middle of the first century when he was martyred on Easter of 68 AD. Saint Mark himself is considered to be the first Bishop. The present Patriarch is His Holiness, Pope Shinouda III and he is the 117th of St. Mark's successors.

Our church is known as a church of martyrs. The worst time was during the rule of the Roman Emperor Diocletian, when hundreds of thousands of Christians were martyred. We adopted a special calendar marking the beginning of his rule on the 11th of September, 284 AD, which is called the year of the martyrs. Our church has offered many martyrs through its different periods.

The Coptic Church produced the School of Alexandria, which taught many of the spiritual leaders and the early fathers of the universal church. In 1893 the Coptic Church reestablished the theological college, which now has campuses in Cairo, Alexandria, New Jersey and Sidney, where priests and others study and qualify for ministry.

Christian Monastic life was initiated in Egypt by Saint Antony, Saint Pachom and Saint Makarious and has spread to the Holy Land, Syria, Iraq, Asia Minor and the West.

Today, in Egypt, there are over 14 million Copts out of a population of some 75 million Egyptians. They pray and share communion in daily masses in thousands of Coptic Churches in Egypt. Additionally, there are another one and half million emigrant Copts. Inside Egypt, Copts live in every province. Our cultural, historical and spiritual treasures are spread all over Egypt.

The Coptic Church in the Holy Land is considered to be an historic extension of the neighborly relations between Egypt and the Holy Land which started with the visit of the Holy Family to Egypt. The Coptic Church in the Holy Land grew after the visit of Queen Helen, the mother of the Emperor Constantine, when she found the Holy Cross and built the Church of the Holy Sepulchre. The Copts started to visit the Holy Land and to set up churches to take care of their own affairs. The historical documents testify to our Coptic existence. One of them, the letter from Paula to her friend Marcella in Rome in 386 AD, mentions the Copts as a community in the Holy Land.

Political circumstances play a role in decreasing or increasing the number of our Coptic population, as is true for other communities in the Holy Land. We suffer from emigration which results from the current social, economic and political circumstances. There are about 10,000 Christians who live in and around Jerusalem today, but they are not gaining in numbers; they are diminishing. In 1948 there were 30,000 Christians in Jerusalem and normal demographic growth should have increased their numbers today to 120,000. However, the number of Christians has fallen sharply all over the Holy Land. A century ago, they were 10 percent of the population between the Jordan River and the Mediterranean Sea. Today they are less than 2 percent, about 130,000 in Israel and about 50,000 in Palestine.

The Coptic Church achieves its role in the Holy Land through monasteries and educational and social institutions which support the faith of the people and help to support the Christian spiritual identify of the Coptic Church with its sister churches and communities.

The churches in the Holy Land face many challenges, the most compelling of which is maintaining its strong existence despite the political and economic difficulties which push believers to emigrate to the West. This matter should be studied and co-operation developed throughout all the churches and among our beloved throughout the world to find means of encouragement for our people to stay and to offer them welfare and a meaningful life.

The challenge of faith, within a world of troubles and ideas which resist religion and among the temptations of materialism and the flood of information through the mass media, is how we can unite our people, especially the youth, with our Savior Jesus Christ. Our message to you, beloved brothers and sisters, is a call to pray together for peace between God and us, peace in ourselves by repentance and holy life, and peace in our Holy Land and all over the world. We want you to share with our people in the Holy Land their joy and troubles. We are asking you to pray that the Holy Spirit fill us all so that we can be witnesses to our Lord "in Jerusalem, Judea, Samaria and unto the uttermost part of the earth" (Acts 1:8).

SYRIAN ORTHODOX PATRIARCHATE OF ANTIOCH IN JERUSALEM, JORDAN AND THE HOLY LAND

Archbishop Mar Sewerios Malki Murad

Our nation of Antioch was the home of the first believers in our Lord Jesus Christ and the first nationality to adopt Christianity, for the Aramaic people were the first followers of the Apostles. In the time of Our Lord, the Arameans were the majority in the Middle East, especially in Greater Syria and the Land of the Euphrates. That is why Jesus Christ spoke the Aramaic language, which was at the time the language of the ordinary people while Greek was the official language as well as language of the sophisticated class.

We are proud to say that the first believers who were called Christians were from Antioch and the first Patriarchal Throne was placed in Antioch in 37 AD by St. Peter, the Great Apostle. This was four years after the Ascension of our Lord.

The Patriarch of Antioch, who was Syrian, governed a jurisdiction that extended all over the continent of Asia, even including India, as was verified by the Holy Synod of Nicea in 325 AD. This rule continued until the differences and struggles started between the Christians during the Holy Synod of Chalcedon in 451 AD, which focused on disagreement concerning the Nature of Christ.

We are also proud that our forefathers spoke the Aramaic language, the language spoken by Jesus Christ, His Mother, the Apostles and all their followers. They have blessed this language, which we are still using today in our services and prayers. A great many of our people and communities around the world use Aramaic as a means of communication in their daily lives in addition to the language of the country in which they live.

Our forefathers translated all sciences from Greek to the Syriac Aramaic language and added to them, especially in Math and Science. Our history is full of such scientists and scholars. Then they also translated the books to Arabic. Later in history, the Muslim Arabs transferred this knowledge and science to the West through Spain.

Until 1286, our Church played a major role in the East, but due to the wars and the rule of the Ottomans, our role was reduced and many of our rights were lessened because of lack of justice and peace in the world. After World War II our Church regained its freedom little by little and many of our people emigrated to the USA, Latin America and Europe, thus becoming dispersed around the world. Now the number of the Syrian Aramaic people reaches five million: one million in the Middle East, one million in Europe and America and three million in West India. The head of our Church, Our Patriarch, His Holiness, Patriarch Zakka Iwas I, resides in Damascus, Syria.

The Syrian Orthodox Church provides many services. The most important service rendered to the people is strengthening and preserving the believers and their Christian identity. As Christian and Syrian Aramaic believers, we stress our belief in our Lord and spread His Love and Principles to the people. Other vital services include:

- Welcoming pilgrims from all the nations of the world to the Holy Land.
- Spreading the Aramaic language, the language of Our Lord, and preserving this great heritage.
- Spreading peace and justice and the teachings of Our Lord through prayers and mutual gatherings.
- Publishing religious books and periodicals and magazines for Christian awareness for all our Syrian communities in the world and for all other communities and nations as well.
- Supporting the School of St. Aphrem the Syrian in the district of Bethlehem, to serve all Christian communities in general, and our Syrian Orthodox community in particular, and to help preserve both the Christian identity and the Aramaic language, which is presently being taught to the children of the school.
- Providing support and financial and spiritual aid to all needy families in the Holy Land to preserve the Christian presence and stop or eliminate emigration.

We also face many great problems. The most difficult challenges faced by our church leaders and congregations are war, lack of security and the difficulties of transportation and movement due to current economical and political burdens. Other challenges include:

- The educational burden of providing for students in schools and universities
- Provision for the needy and the poor
- Housing projects for young couples and the newly married
- Provision of employment through small income-generating projects
- Issuing permits for our community to participate in church celebrations and festivities
- Medical services and insurance provision

We ask all decision makers in the world to work hard to stop war and try to bring peace and justice and security to this troubled world and its people. Once these challenges are lessened, we shall live in dignity and security like all other nations.

THE CATHOLIC CONTRIBUTION
TO THE CHRISTIAN PRESENCE
AND WITNESS IN THE HOLY LAND

Father Frans Bouwen

From the beginning, it is important to note that in the Middle East and in the Holy Land most specifically, history never belongs to the past, but is part and parcel of the present. Therefore to address the subject of "The Catholic Contribution to the Christian Presence and Witness in the Holy Land," it will be necessary to take a quick look at history so as to reflect on the Catholic contribution today. Hence this paper will contain three parts: 1) a quick look at history; 2) present contribution and witness; and 3) questions and challenges for the future.

A QUICK LOOK AT HISTORY

If we want to reflect on the specific Catholic contribution and witness in this country today, it is not necessary to go very far back in history. During the whole first millennium, there was full communion between the Church of Jerusalem and the church in the West, particularly the Church of Rome. As a consequence, the Western presence in the Holy Land integrated harmoniously with the Church of Jerusalem, under the guidance of its local bishop or patriarch. During that period, there was a varied, almost continuous, although rather limited Western presence in the Holy Land, be it through pilgrims, monastic communities of men and women, or biblical scholars like Saint Jerome, but they were fully part of the local Christian presence and witness, with its unity in diversity.

The first distinctive – and separate – Catholic or Western presence and activity goes back to the time of the Crusaders. It is not the place here to analyse or evaluate that historical episode in all its complexity, but we have to be aware that their passage left a deep imprint on the Christian communities in the Holy Land and the Middle East, and perhaps even more on the Arab and Muslim world. Recent history has shown more than once that every authoritarian or aggressive intervention by the West tends to be interpreted as some new kind of crusade. This is a lesson that we should never forget: every external, especially Western, intervention in the Middle East is a complex reality and has to be evaluated very carefully. In particular, any attempt to impose an external solution often attains the opposite effect.

With regards to the Catholic presence in the Holy Land, the next important fact is the arrival of the Franciscan Friars, in the 14th century. They came in the first place to take care of the Holy Places in the name of the Catholic Church. As such, they played their role in the dynamics of the intricate relations around the Holy Places. This is not our first concern here, but we cannot exclude it entirely, because the care for the Holy and Biblical Places is also part of the ministry of the church in the Holy Land. Because of the fact that Catholics and Orthodox were at that time no longer in communion, these relations were more than once marked by tension and conflict. At the same time, however, the Franciscan Friars also developed a network of pastoral, educational and social activities around the Holy Places where they were present, creating small Catholic Latin communities and schools, and starting different initiatives in the field of health care and assistance to the needy.

The real development of the Western Catholic presence happened at the time of the reestablishment of the Latin Patriarchate in Jerusalem in 1847. This initiative has to be seen in the larger context of the new possibilities for the arrival of great numbers of Western missionaries of various other denominations in the Holy Land during that period as a consequence of the decline of the Ottoman Empire. Many of these missionaries came to help the local Christian community that had been living, for several centuries, under very difficult circumstances. Unfortunately, they came with the theology and the ecclesiology of that time. For Catholics in the 19th century, working for the renewal and unity of Christians meant to work for their return to Rome. Hence, they embarked on an active "missionary" approach towards the existing local Christian communities. We should be careful not to judge these missionaries with our present day ecumenical theology and experience. Their arrival brought some real renewal for the local community, in the spiritual, cultural and social fields. However, we must also recognize that this missionary activity – by Catholic, Anglican and Evangelical Churches – has caused a fragmentation of the existing local Christian community, not only from the religious point of view by creating new churches and communities, but also in the cultural field, by constituting different culturally and nationally isolated islands, according to the language and the history that was taught in the schools and the links that were created with the countries the missionaries came from. This has weakened the cohesion of the local community and it is only little by little that these handicaps are being overcome today.

Finally, it should be noted that the Catholic presence in the Holy Land is not restricted to the Western or Latin Church. There is also a considerable Oriental Catholic presence, especially the Greek (Melkite) Catholic Church and the Maronite Church. These communities were established even a short time before, in this country. They were more locally rooted, had less foreign personnel and fewer means, but they developed similar pastoral and social activities. Their contribution to the Catholic presence and service in this country should not be underestimated, particularly in Galilee.

PRESENT CONTRIBUTION AND WITNESS

If one wants to have an idea of the variety and importance of the Catholic presence in the Holy Land today, it would be sufficient to refer to the *Directory of the Catholic Church in the Holy Land*. There one can find all necessary details concerning all six different Catholic Churches: 1) the Latin Patriarchate, 2) the Greek Catholic Archdiocese of Galilee and Patriarchal Exarchate in Jerusalem, 3) the Maronite Archdiocese of Haifa and Patriarchal Exarchate of Jerusalem, 4) the Armenian Catholic Patriarchal Exarchate, 5) the Syrian Catholic Patriarchal Exarchate, and 6) the Chaldean Catholic Patriarchal Exarchate. There is also a full list of about thirty religious congregations of men and about seventy religious congregations of women, with their communities and institutions. Additionally, there are the many educational institutions: Bethlehem University, Catholic Theological Faculties, Biblical institutes, seminaries, kindergartens, primary and secondary schools. It would also be impossible to mention all of the many medical, social and charitable institutions which try to be of service to the Christian community, as well as to the wider human community in the Holy Land.

Instead of presenting a whole list of names and numbers, I prefer to concentrate on an ecclesial event that has been central to all the Catholic Churches in the Holy Land in the past 10 years: the *Diocesan Synod of the Catholic Churches in the Holy Land*. In the Catholic Church a diocesan synod is a long reflection process of deepening and renewal under the guidance of the local bishop and with the collaboration of all the members of the church community: clergy, religious men and women and lay people. In our case, it involved all the Catholic Churches, Western and Oriental, in Israel, Palestine and Jordan, and was placed under the auspices of the Assembly of Catholic Ordinaries (or Heads of Churches) of the Holy Land.

Among the main objectives of this Synod were: (1) Bringing the churches home to this country and this region; because the Catholic communities in the Holy Land are to a large extent the fruit of missionary activity coming from abroad, the Western influence often remains very strong in organisation and outlook; (2) promoting a more active involvement of the faithful: most of the time they have been on the receiving end so it is time for them to take the initiative in order to make the churches their own; (3) facilitating a closer collaboration between the different Catholic Churches, Western and Oriental, and between the many religious congregations or institutions; and (4) elaborating together a common vision for the future in the midst of the continuously changing political and social situation and facing the uncertainty of the future together.

After an initial preparation that lasted three years, the synodal process went on for five years, from 1995 till 2000. At the concluding general assembly, in February 2000, a *General Pastoral Plan* was elaborated and later approved by the Heads of the Catholic Churches as the basis for future pastoral work. It has been published in the form of a booklet of almost 200 pages in Arabic, English, French and Italian. As was already the case in the synodal process itself, the main themes are grouped under three headings: "Believing in Christ," "Participating in the Church," and "Witnessing in Society." These headings already constitute a whole program!

The third dimension, "Witnessing in Society," is perhaps more directly in the line of the general theme of the present Sabeel Conference. However, it is clear that no effective or authentic Christian witness in society is possible without a deep personal faith and without an active participation in the life of the church.

After the conclusion of the synodal process and the publication of the *General Pastoral Plan*, a whole mechanism was established to implement the main themes. In the first place, a General Pastoral Committee, with local branches in each of the three main regions, Israel, Palestine and Jordan, was established. It is obvious that a great amount of work remains to be done. It is not sufficient to repeat general principles and to outline concrete proposals. However, it may be said that this *General Pastoral Plan* constitutes a true program and contains the main elements for an active contribution for the present and future of the Christian community in the Holy Land, as well as for a true witness and service in the wider human national community. This initiative illustrates the vision and efforts of the Catholic Church much more clearly than a simple list of activities.

To illustrate more explicitly a few specific points, it is best to quote some passages of the *Pastoral Plan* on certain topics that are essential to the Christian presence and witness in this country: schools, inter-religious dialogue, involvement in political life, ecumenism:

- *Education, schools*: From the very beginning, education has been one of the main efforts of the Catholic presence, similar to that of the Anglicans and Lutherans, and even today it mobilizes tremendous energies and requires considerable financial means. This service has always been considered of essential importance, not only in the building up of the Christian community but also as a service to the larger human society. The first aim of this educational effort is, of course, the Christian formation of children and youth. However, about half of the pupils and students of these schools are Muslims. Nevertheless, in spite of the many energies and expenses involved, the Catholic Church would very much like to continue this effort, because this common education of Christians and Muslims is seen as an extremely important factor in the coexistence of the believers of these two religions. Such an education for coexistence or pluralism has, of course, very concrete demands. *The General Pastoral Plan* says:

    The school does not live in isolation from society. Rather the school is an institution within the society and for the sake of society.... As the society in which we live is characterised by religious pluralism, it is necessary that this dimension of our schools' reality be integrated in our educational and pastoral planning. In this way, the school can be an exercise in interaction with the religiously different other, developing a positive model of fraternity and co-existence. (p. 122)

A little more than 30 years ago the Catholic Church opened the Catholic University of Bethlehem. In the first place, the University offers the young generation the possibility to start university studies in this country rather than having to go abroad, with the danger of never coming back. Therefore the University fulfils a real need and also concretely offers training for job possibilities like hotel management, tourism, business management, and teacher training. Bethlehem University also provides a major contribution to Muslim-Christian coexistence, with two-thirds of the students and one-third of the teaching staff being Muslims.

- *Social work and health care*: In the field of health care and social service, the Catholic Church has always engaged in an intense and varied activity: hospitals, clinics, homes for elderly people and dependent children, centers for disabled persons, as well as charitable and humanitarian organisations. This was and still is of special importance at times and in places where a governmental policy in those fields is almost non-existent or impossible, given the political and social context. In this field, too, the outreach to the wider human community, beyond the borders of the Christian community, is a constant dimension of the Christian presence and witness: it is part and parcel of Christian service without exclusion or discrimination; it is also a concrete expression of the fact that the life and future of the Palestinian Christian community is inseparably linked to the life and future of the Palestinian Muslim community.

- *The Christian presence in public life*: Active involvement in public and national life, whether in the political, economical or cultural sphere, is of primordial importance for the future Christian presence in this part of the world. If our Christians want to have a place in this country in the future, they have to collaborate from now on in the building of the nation and in shaping its political forms. Many recent interventions of church leaders underline this need, and several Catholic organisations have organised study sessions and public panels on this question. "The General Pastoral Plan" says in this context:

> Participation in the life of society is both the right and the duty of the faithful. The basic role of the church is one of spreading awareness among the faithful of the importance of the political domain, involvement in it, the faith vision that is incorporated in this involvement and the values that support it.... It is important that our churches develop a serious reflection on political issues with their faith as the point of departure and deriving from the conditions of society and its needs, so that this reflection might be both a support and a motivating factor for the faithful in their participation in political life at all levels and in all forms, including the preparation of leaders needed in this area. (p. 164)

- *Ecumenism*: For the small Christian community in the Holy Land, divided into so many different churches and denominations, working for Christian unity and collaboration is not a matter of choice; it is an issue of vital importance for the future. Many times, lay people take the lead in this field, pushing their leaders to meet, to consult and to arrive at a common stand on major contemporary issues, for instance, those concerning justice and peace. Lay persons of our different churches work spontaneously together in daily life. They are happy to see that their leaders meet more and more often, address common messages to them at the occasion of Christmas and Easter or when some urgent issue emerges. On this point, "The General Pastoral Plan" quotes a pastoral letter of the Council of Catholic Patriarchs of the East, saying:

> Before us, there is a vast, open area for collaboration in various services, like building churches and using them, building schools and hospitals where needed, development and social programs, helping the needy, housing plans, the media and the press, etc. It is necessary that we address the problem of emigration with all available means. Together we must work in the path of justice and peace, through active and rightful participation of Christians in public life. Together we must treat

the problem of the churches in our relations with the official authorities. Together we must develop our relations with our Muslim and Jewish brothers and sisters. (p.138)

- *Interreligious dialogue*: Interreligious relations and dialogue constitute a permanent dimension of every aspect of the life of our churches in the Holy Land. What is needed is not so much a theological or directly religious dialogue, but a dialogue of life promoting mutual coexistence and common commitment for the building of a more just and fraternal society. "The General Pastoral Plan" states, concerning the dialogue with Muslims:

> Our Catholic Churches in the Holy Land, ... seeking to serve the faithful as they embark on the third millennium and preserving the unity of our people, understand that it is essential to accentuate the framework of Christian-Muslim dialogue, which guarantees fidelity to God and to our people. Our churches look to the positive and the negative of the past in order to strengthen the positive and to avoid the negative...for the sake of peace, harmony and cooperation. (p. 152)

As to the dialogue with Jews, the Plan notes:

> The building up and development of a positive relationship with members of the Jewish religion in our countries is not easy because of certain adjacent negative conditions. However it is essential that work begin now in establishing positive and fruitful relations. This is required both by the reality that we experience and by the Christian evangelical values in which we believe. (p. 155)

The text also insists on the fact that the two dialogues should not be separated: Relationship cannot be divided up, relationships in our countries being tripartite, among Muslims, Jews and Christians. The future of our countries is also founded on these relationships. They must develop simultaneously rather than any relationship being at the expense of another (p. 157).

CHALLENGES FOR THE FUTURE

Is it still necessary to offer some questions and challenges for the future? It is clear that almost all the issues mentioned until now remain an open task for the future. However, these main points briefly serve as a conclusion:

- *Christian presence*: The future of the Christian presence is undoubtedly the most frequently cited challenge. It is at the same time the one that recapitulates in some way most of the other ones. It entails in the first place the whole question of the emigration of Christians from the Middle East and especially from the Holy Land. Emigration in turn is closely linked to the prevailing political and economical situation. As long as there is no greater stability in the region, violence will not disappear and extremism will continue to flourish. Therefore working for a just and durable peace is also working for the future Christian presence in the Holy Land, besides its being a permanent calling for every Christian person and community. The future of the Christian presence is, of course, also inseparably linked with inter-religious dialogue and coexistence, as we have already seen.

- *Bringing our churches home to this country*: Another important challenge for this Christian presence is the effort to bring our Churches truly home to this country and to the present time. This is especially true for the communities that were created as a result of a Western missionary activity, but it is also in some way true for the traditional Oriental churches. Almost all the Churches need some new form of enculturation, with regards to the social and political context of the Holy Land as well as to the changing circumstances of today. Our churches should neither live in the West nor in the past but should be present and should witness and serve in this country, today. When the local Christians discover that they are the church and that they have an irreplaceable role to play, the future of the Christian presence in this region can be viewed with confidence. The church must help the faithful to discover that being a Christian in the Holy Land is a special vocation: a vocation to bear witness to the events of the Gospel on the spot where it all took place, as well as a vocation to bear witness in the midst of

Muslim and Jewish believers. None can replace them in this vocation.

- *Communion with the worldwide Christian community:* On the one hand, we are used to saying that the Christians in the Holy Land are in need of the solidarity of their Christian brothers and sisters around the world. And this is profoundly true! However, on the other hand, to the extent that the Christians in the Holy Land really discover and live their own specific vocation, they can contribute something unique to the worldwide church: a generous welcome in the Land of the Bible and of Jesus, with a faithful and uninterrupted witness to Christ throughout the centuries in spite of extremely difficult historical circumstances. Their witness means that the many Christian pilgrims who visit this country can go back home enriched not only because of the ancient stones or places they see but still more thanks to the living Christian community they meet, a community that sees itself in continuity with the first community of the Book of the Acts of the Apostles, devoted to the teachings of the apostles and to the communal life, to the breaking of the bread and to the prayers, and having all things in common (cf. Acts 2: 43-44).

THE HISTORY OF PROTESTANTS
AND EVANGELICALS IN PALESTINE

Y. Lynn Holmes

Unlike the Catholics, the Orthodox, the Copts, the Armenians, and other Eastern branches of the Christian faith who had been in the Holy Land for centuries, the Protestants and Evangelicals were latecomers on the scene of Palestinian Christianity. This paper offers a brief summary of the beginning, the growth, and the problems of the Protestant churches in Palestine.

Until the first decades of the nineteenth century, contacts of the Protestants and Evangelicals with the area of Palestine had been rather insignificant and irregular. Protestant involvement in Palestine began with the visits of itinerant missionaries in the early 1800's, but thereafter became stronger and more continuous on the part of a few groups.[1]

Historically, the advent of Protestantism in the Arab world was a by-product of the movement of the Protestant religious awakening of the eighteenth and early nineteenth centuries, which emerged in the United States and Britain. Protestant missionaries from these countries went out to fulfill the command of Christ to take the Gospel "unto the uttermost parts of the earth."[2]

The first Protestant mission work in the Middle East was begun by the American Board of Foreign Missions and by the Church of England through

---

[1] Jaeger, d.-M.A. (ed.), Papers Read at the 1979 Tantur Conference on Christianity in the Holy Land (Studia Oecumenica Hierosolymitana, Vol. I), Jerusalem: Ecumenical Institute for Theological Research, 1981, p. 287.

[2] Talal, El Hassan, *Christianity in the Arab World*, London: Arabesque Int., 1995, p. 85 and Ateek, Na'em S. *Toward a Strategy for the Episcopal Church in Israel with Special Focus on the Political Situation-Analysis and Prospect* – Dissertation/Project, San Francisco Theological Seminary, 1982, p. 8.

its London Society for Promoting Christianity among the Jews (LJS).[3] The Protestants and Evangelicals were badly handicapped in the beginning because, unlike the traditional churches of the Middle East, they had no legal status in the Ottoman Empire. Any building activity on their part was plagued with obstruction, the new faith of their converts was unrecognized, and, importantly, they had no official backing from major governments.[4]

Protestant activities in Palestine began with the Anglican and Lutheran Churches and the Church of Scotland in the early nineteenth century, and they were joined by other Protestant and Evangelical groups in the twentieth century.

ANGLICAN/LUTHERAN UNION

After exploratory visits to Jerusalem in 1820 and 1824, LJS dispatched Dr. Dalton, its first medical missionary, to launch its work. This first venture encountered obstacles, and only in 1833 did Rev. John Nicolayson, a Dane, begin work of a permanent nature.[5]

King Frederick William IV of Prussia proposed setting up an Anglican bishopric to which a Lutheran mission might be appended, envisioning a worldwide Protestant union with Jerusalem as its center. Frederick's proposal was presented to Queen Victoria and to the Archbishop of Canterbury, and an agreement was reached establishing the Anglican/Lutheran bishopric in Jerusalem in 1841.[6] The nominee for the new bishopric, if not already an Anglican, was to become one. Nominations for this position would be alternately filled by the British or Prussian kings.[7]

The first person sent to Palestine under this arrangement was Dr. Michael Salomon Alexander (1841-1845), a convert from Judaism. His main task was the conversion of local Jewry, but his work was brief and relatively ineffective.

---

[3] Colbi, Saul P., *Christianity in the Holy Land: Past and Present*, Tel Aviv: AM Hassefer, 1969, p. 86.
[4] Ibid., p. 87.
[5] Ibid., p. 86.
[6] Prior, Michael and Taylor, William (eds.), *Christians in the Holy Land*, London: World of Islam Festival Trust, 1944, p. 131.
[7] Op. cit., Colbi, p. 86.

A Prussian nominee, Samuel Gobat (1846-1879), a Swiss Protestant, succeeded Alexander and began proselytizing among the non-Protestant population. Direct work among the Muslims was difficult and likely to endanger the status of the mission, but work among Christians was looked upon with indifference by the Ottoman government. Thus, Gobat turned to the Eastern Christians. Mindful of the agreement made when the bishopric was established not to interfere in the affairs of the Eastern Churches, he thought that opening schools and distributing Bibles among the Eastern Christians would not be an infringement of this agreement. Although he may have been pursuing these educational activities in good faith, the ultimate result was that many youth educated in Anglican schools abandoned the Eastern communities to join the Anglican Church. As a result, congregations sprang up in all the main Christian towns, most with Arab clergy and an Arabic translation of the Book of Common Prayer.[8]

The building of Christ Church just inside the Jaffa Gate in Jerusalem was completed under Bishop Gobat and consecrated in 1849. It was then the only Protestant church in the Middle East.[9] In 1853, Gobat opened a school on Mount Zion in Jerusalem, which was later enlarged and named after him. In the 1860's he opened schools in Bethlehem, Beit Jala, Ramle, Jaffa, Nablus, Rafidiah, Nisf al-Jabal, Zebabdeh, Burqin and Shfaram. The Church Missionary Society of the Anglican Church (CMS) also opened several schools in and around Nazareth, so that by the end of the nineteenth century, the church was maintaining thirty-one schools, with almost 1800 students, in the whole of Palestine.[10]

Thanks to the extensive educational activity of the episcopate of Samuel Gobat, the Arab-Anglican congregation grew to more than a thousand faithful. Special churches had to be built for them: Christ's in Nazareth (1871), St. Paul's outside the new Gate in Jerusalem (1874), St. Philip's in Nablus (1882) and St. Andrew's in Ramallah (1888).[11] The thirty-three-year episcopate of Bishop Gobat was to be the most decisive in the development of the Anglican Church in Palestine. Indeed, Bishop Gobat was the founder of the Arab-Anglican Church in Palestine.[12]

---

[8] Ibid., p. 87.
[9] Ibid., p. 88.
[10] Ibid.
[11] Op. cit., Prior, p. 241 and Op. cit., Ateek, p. 36.
[12] Op. cit., Colbi, p. 89.

In 1886, the union between the Lutheran Church and the Church of England in affairs of the Anglican bishopric of Jerusalem ended and each denomination thereafter conducted independent activities. This Anglican-Lutheran joint venture had lasted thirty-five years, most of it during the time of Bishop Gobat.[13]

THE ANGLICAN CHURCH

George Francis Popham Blyth, the first Bishop of the purely Anglican work, served from 1887 to 1914. A major controversy concerning proselytism amongst the Eastern Churches led to his seeking independence from the CMS' financial support.[14]

In 1905 a great step toward the indigenization of the church was taken with the formation of the Palestine Native Church Council in which local clergy and laity united to establish a self-governing, self-supporting church. A most important development was CMS' handover in 1906 of several institutions and responsibilities to Anglican-Arab Christians governed by the Council.[15]

While Blyth was Bishop, St. Luke's Church in Haifa was consecrated in1899, along with its school and hospital. On October 18, 1898, the collegiate church of St. George the Martyr was consecrated in Jerusalem. The compound included the bishop's residence, the house of the clergy, the choir school and St. Mary's Girls' Home or Orphanage. In 1910 Edward's Tower was added to the main church.[16]

The period immediately following the ravages of World War I was a difficult one for the Anglican Church. Bishop Blyth died in 1914, shortly after the outbreak of the First World War. His successor, Bishop Rennie MacInnes (1914-1931) was unable to assume his responsibilities or to enter the cathedral until hostilities ended. Arriving in 1918, he found work at a standstill, with the native Arabic clergy carrying on as best they could without outside help.[17]

---

[13] Ibid.
[14] Ibid., p. 90 and Op. cit., Prior, p. 132.
[15] Ibid.
[16] Ibid., pp. 90, 112.
[17] Ibid., p. 112 and Op. cit., Jaeger, p. 244.

During the thirty years of the British Mandate of Palestine, the Anglican Church recruited members mainly among the civil servants, such as the British garrison and the constabulary of the Mandate government. The work grew and developed. New churches and charitable and cultural institutions were founded, and Arab membership was enlarged by proselytes from the other churches in Palestine.[18] Although the Anglican Church remained the largest Protestant denomination in Palestine after the end of the Mandate, its influence was diminished.[19]

The Jewish-Arab War of 1948 left its mark on the life and works of all of the Palestinian Christians. Most of them fled the terror of the war or were expelled from their homes. For nineteen years all Christian churches of Palestine were split, including the Anglican Church. Only a small remnant of Anglicans remained in Israel, while most church members lived on the West Bank of the Jordan, or were scattered throughout Lebanon or other Arab countries.[20]

After the fighting of 1948 split the country, the dwindling Anglican Church in the Jordan-administered territory had to be reorganized. The CMS handed over to the Arab Episcopal Church its hospital and schools in Nablus and Zebabdeh, and all other property in the West Bank.[21]

Before the events of June 1967, there were large Anglican congregations in East Jerusalem and in Ramallah, and smaller ones in Bethlehem, Bir Zeit, Nablus, Rafidiah, Zebabdeh and Aboud. Schools were maintained in Jerusalem and in Ramallah, Nablus and Rafidiah, a hospital in Nablus and an orphanage in Hebron.

The Arab Episcopal Church, with some nine hundred followers in Israel, was remarkably autonomous in administration and finance, and recognized the Archbishop's authority only in spiritual matters. Its congregations were in Nazareth, Shfaram, Rene, Kafr Yussif, Acre, Haifa, Jaffa, Ramle and Jerusalem, with elementary schools in Haifa and in Nazareth and a girls' orphanage in Nazareth. The European branch of the Anglican Church was concentrated in Jerusalem, Jaffa, Haifa and Lod.[22]

The Gaza Strip has very few Protestants. The Arab al-Ahli Hospital, established in 1908 by the CMS, is the only non-governmental hospital and

[18] Ibid., p. 139.
[19] Op. cit., Ateek, p. 70.
[20] Op. cit.,, Colbi, pp. 150-151.
[21] Ibid., p. 151.
[22] Op. cit., Prior, p. 63.

the major Protestant activity in Gaza. When the CMS terminated its services in Palestine, the Arab-Anglican diocese assumed and still maintains control of the hospital.[23]

When Israel captured and occupied the West Bank and the Gaza Strip in 1967, the Anglican Church had about 2300 members in Israel and in the Occupied Territories in twenty-eight congregations, of which six were primarily English speaking.[24.]

The Anglican Archbishop in Jerusalem, Dr. Angus Campbell MacInnes, was succeeded in 1968 by Dr. George Appleton, Metropolitan of West Australia. He was charged with finding the right ecclesiastical formula to enable the Anglican Church to meet the political and military problems of the Middle East.[25]

Some very important changes had begun to take place in the Anglican Church in the Middle East as early as 1958. At that time the Reverend Najib Cubain was appointed as the first Arab Bishop in the Middle East, and he served as the Bishop of the Diocese of Jordan, Lebanon and Syria until 1976. In 1976 the Anglican dioceses were re-organized, and in the new Diocese of Jerusalem, the Reverend Faik Hadad was elected Bishop, serving until 1984. After Bishop Hadad, the Reverend Samir Kafity (1984-1998) and the Reverend Riah Abu-El Assal (1998-2007) were elected Bishops. In 2007 the Reverend Suheil Dawani was elected Bishop of the Diocese.

THE LUTHERAN CHURCH

Even before the end of the Anglican-Lutheran joint venture, the Lutherans had initiated a number of projects. After 1851 the Talitha Kumi Girls' School began and Deaconesses of Kaiserwerth founded a hospital in Jerusalem and built welfare institutions in Bethlehem and Haifa. In 1858 a hospice sponsored by the Evangelical branch of the Knights of St. John was established in the Via Dolorosa. In 1860 the family of the German missionary, Johann Ludwig Schneller, began its work of orphan care and rehabilitation and soon founded the great "Syrian" orphanage in Jerusalem, with branches in Nazareth and Bir

---

[23] Ibid., p. 134 and Op. cit., Colbi, p. 167.
[24] Op. cit., Colbi, p. 167.
[25] Ibid., p. 90.

Salem. A landmark in the development of Lutheran missionary work in Palestine was the acquisition of the Muristan area in the vicinity of the Church of the Holy Sepulchre. There, in 1871, the Lutheran Church built the Muristan Chapel, which was used as a place of worship for the German congregation until 1898, when the Church of the Redeemer was completed.[26]

The German institutions quickly revived works interrupted by World War I. Schneller's orphanage reopened in 1921 and cared for a great number of war orphans. In 1923 the Jerusalem Hospital of the Kaiserswerth Diakonissen was returned to its owners by the British. The Talitha Kumi Girls' School and the German Evangelical School were reopened soon afterward. The Augusta Viktoria Complex reverted to its German owners in 1928.[27]

Meanwhile, many former pupils of the German Lutheran institutions favored the formation of an Arab congregation, requiring a setting other than the one for Germans. Consequently in 1929, the first Arab Lutheran congregation was organized and others followed.[28] In the 1930's, the activity of the German Lutherans grew steadily outside Jerusalem as well as in Jaffa, Haifa, and al-Bassa, a village near the Lebanese border.[29]

When the Second World War broke out, most of the members of the German community were arrested, placed in special camps, and eventually deported to Australia, disrupting the countrywide work of the community. German property was vested in a Custodian of Enemy Property. Ecclesiastical buildings were taken over by the Anglican Church. The German hospital became a government one, the Augusta Viktoria complex served as a British military hospital, and the Syrian Orphanage housed British families evacuated from Egypt.[30]

At the end of hostilities, the general atmosphere in Palestine did not favor renewal of German activity. The initiative for matters pertaining to the German Lutheran Church in Palestine was entrusted to the Lutherans of the United States, and, at the end of 1946, the National Lutheran Council opened negotiations with the British Mandatory Administration to regain some of the confiscated property. The outbreak of Jewish-Arab hostilities and the subsequent

---

[26] Ibid., p. 114.
[27] Ibid., and Bailey, Betty Jane and Bailey, J. Martin, *Who Are the Christians in the Middle East*, Grand Rapids: William b. Eerdmans Publishing Co., 2003, p. 107.
[28] Ibid., p. 114.
[29] Ibid.
[30] Ibid., pp. 115, 140-141.

partition of Palestine opened up possibilities for a fairly rapid revival of German Lutheran work in the part of Palestine within the Kingdom of Jordan.[31]

After the partition of the Holy Land in 1948, Lutheran Church property in East Jerusalem was composed mainly of the Muristan compound (with the Church of the Redeemer, a school and a hospice) and of the Augusta Viktoria complex on the Mount of Olives. Outside Jerusalem, there were church buildings and educational institutions in Beit Jala, Bethlehem and Beit Sahour.[32] In Jordan the Lutheran Church took up its work again with support of the Lutheran World Federation and others. The Augusta Viktoria complex was transformed into a huge hospital, first administered by the Red Cross and afterwards by the Lutheran World Federation, together with the UN. Other Lutheran facilities like the Talitha Kumi School for Girls, the Leper Hospital and the German Evangelical Institute for Archaeology were also reopened.[33]

The years following the partition of Palestine saw the gradual rise of an Arab Evangelical community in the Jordanian-occupied part of the Holy Land with Arab congregations in Jerusalem, Bethlehem and Beit Sahour. In 1957 a fourth congregation was established in Ramallah, which in 1963 built the Church of Hope, including a pastor's residence and a community center. The primary schools in Jerusalem, Bethlehem and Beit Sahour were enlarged and modernized, and a secondary school was opened in Bethlehem[34].

Following the Six-Day War in 1967, five of the six Arab-speaking congregations were in the occupied West Bank. Since 1995, the congregations in Beit Jala, Bethlehem, Beit Sahour, and Ramallah have been within the area administered by the Palestinian National Authority. Today the church is largely made up of refugees, many of whom fled Lydda, Ramle, and Jaffa in 1948. The first Palestinian bishop, the Right Reverend Daoud Haddad, was consecrated in 1979[35] and subsequent bishops have come from the local Palestinian church.

The focus of ministry of the Lutheran Church in Palestine has been in the field of education, although a number of the churches pursue a variety of social services, including an international hostel. Five schools and two boarding homes have an enrollment of more than three thousand pupils. Close

---

[31] Ibid., p. 151.
[32] Ibid., p. 152.
[33] Ibid., pp. 152-153.
[34] Op. cit., Bailey, p. 128 and Op. cit., Prior, 128.
[35] Ibid., p. 107.

relationships exist with other Lutheran endeavors in the area including the Lutheran World Federation, and Danish, Finnish, Swedish and Norwegian Lutheran bodies.[36]

THE CHURCH OF SCOTLAND

The Church of Scotland first became interested in missionary work in Palestine in 1839 following a visit by a commission of inquiry. As the Church of England had started its proselytizing activities in Judea, the members of the Scottish commission suggested that the work of their Church be confined to the Galilee area. Consequently, missionary work among the Jews was initiated in Safed in 1852, but was given up shortly afterwards. In 1863, a Scotswoman established the Tabitha Mission for Girls in Jaffa, and in 1875, a boarding school and later a day school were added.[37] In 1885 Scottish medical work began in Tiberias, and in 1894 a hospital was built on the shore of the Sea of Galilee with a maternity ward added in 1912.

The Church of Scotland also launched educational activities in Tiberias by opening a school for girls in 1888, followed by a school for boys and other schools in Safad. About the same time, the Edinburgh Medical Missionary Society inaugurated a hospital in Nazareth and by the turn of the nineteenth century, a hospital was built in Hebron.[38]

The outbreak of the First World War disrupted the educational and medical work in Galilee but work resumed under the more favorable conditions of the British Mandate. Schools in Jaffa and Safed were reopened, though not those in Tiberias.[39]

A special pride of the Church of Scotland is St. Andrew's Church in Jerusalem, built in memory of men from the Scots regiments who died to free the Holy Land. The foundation stone was laid in 1927, and the church opened in 1930.[40]

---

[36] Op. cit., Colbi, p. 92.

[37] Ibid., p. 93.

[38] Ibid. This was later transferred to the Church of Scotland, which in 1922 transferred it to the Church Missionary Society, a body connected with the Anglican Church.

[39] Ibid., pp. 93 and 113.

[40] Wikipedia, "St. Andrew's Church, Jerusalem," p. 1 and Op. cit., Prior, p. 113.

The Church of Scotland became less influential with the end of the British Mandate in Palestine. Its congregations diminished, but its cultural activity and good works flourished. It had a church and hostel in Jerusalem, a church, school, cultural center and clinic in Jaffa, a church and hospice in Tiberias, and a hospital in Nazareth with a nearby school to train Arab nurses. It has recently refurbished the Church of Scotland Center and the Scots Hotel in Tiberias.[41]

OTHER PROTESTANT AND EVANGELICAL GROUPS

Besides the long-established Anglican, Lutheran and Church of Scotland Churches, a number of smaller denominations, primarily Evangelical and Fundamentalist and headquartered in the United States, pursued missionary activities in Palestine. After the Six-Day War, missionaries throughout Palestine who had begun their work only after the partition of 1948 but who were connected with the same organizations abroad, finally had opportunity to meet. The total community of Arab evangelicals is estimated at 5,000.[42]

THE SOUTHERN BAPTIST CONVENTION

The largest of these groups are the Baptists. Shukri Musa, who was baptized at the First Baptist Church in Dallas, Texas, is the first known modern Baptist to enter Palestine. He arrived in 1911 and founded a church in Nazareth. The Southern Baptist Convention sent missionaries for the first time in 1923, establishing a congregation in Jerusalem in 1925 and another in Haifa in 1936.[43]

The Second World War, the conflict in 1947, and the 1948 War set back Baptist work, especially in Jerusalem and Haifa. Missionaries left and many church members fled to other countries in the Middle East. The Nazareth Baptist Church was less affected because the local church members took over the leadership role. In 1949-1950, missionaries started to return and worked

---

[41] Ibid., and Op. cit., Prior, p. 140.
[42] Op. cit., Colbi, p. 169.
[43] Haddad, Fuad, "Baptist in Israel Today," *The Baptist Studies Bulletin*, December, 2004, Vol. 3, No. 12, p. 4.

with local believers to reorganize the Baptist work in Israel. In Nazareth the first indigenous pastor was ordained in 1960.[44]

After the beginning of the State of Israel, the Southern Baptist Convention generously subsidized the Baptist mission work. For many years they were probably the busiest Protestant group in Israel, principally in Nazareth, with a church and a school of 570 pupils. From Nazareth, activity among the Arabs was widespread, and churches were built in Cana, Rama, Turan and Acre. The George Truett Orphanage, formerly in Nazareth, was moved to Petach Tikva, where the campus served as a cultural center and a farm.[45]

Later the Southern Baptist churches were turned over to the Association of Baptist Churches in Israel, which is an association of locally-controlled Baptist churches. The Southern Baptist Convention withdrew in 1994, but the Baptist Village near Petah Tikva is still managed by the International Mission Board of the Southern Baptist Convention.

Currently there are twenty Baptist churches in Israel, of which fifteen are Arabic Churches. The others are Hebrew, Spanish and Russian. They are all organized under the Association of Baptist Churches in Israel (ABC) with no relationship to the Southern Baptist Convention. With around 800 baptized members in Israel and a community of around 3000 people, the Association of Baptist Churches in Israel is the largest individual evangelical body in Israel.[46]

THE QUAKERS

There has been an active and vibrant Palestinian Quaker community in Ramallah since the late 1800's. The Palestinian Quaker community grew up around the Friends Girls Schools established in Ramallah in 1869 and the Friends Boys School established in El-Bireh in 1901. In 1910 this community built the Ramallah Friends Meetinghouse and later added another building that was used for community outreach. Friends played a vital role in the community in 1948 when the buildings and grounds of the Meetinghouse became the home to many Palestinian refugees. Throughout the years, the members of the Ramallah Friends Meeting organized numerous community

---

[44] Ibid.
[45] Op. cit., Colbi, p. 141.
[46] Wikipedia, "Association of Baptist Churches in Israel," p. 1.

programs such as the Children's Play Center, the First Day School, and women's activities.

By the early 1990's the Meetinghouse and Annex, which housed meeting rooms and bathroom facilities, fell into disrepair as a result of damage inflicted by time and impact of conflict. So serious was the deterioration of the Meetinghouse that by the middle 1990's it was impossible to use the building at all. The Meetinghouse, which had served as a place of worship for the Friends in Ramallah, could no longer be used as such and the Annex could no longer be used for community outreach. Through the generous gifts of Friends in the US and elsewhere, money was raised to renovate the buildings and grounds and by November, 2004, the renovations were completed. On March 6, 2005, the Meetinghouse and grounds were rededicated to serve Ramallah Friends and the Palestinian community at large.[47]

The number of Palestinian Quakers currently living in Ramallah is small but the Quaker presence is felt and appreciated by the community. As is the case in the wider Palestinian community, the level of emigration brought on by the economic situation and the hardships arising from the continuing Israeli military occupation have also affected the Quaker community in Palestine.

Additional Protestant and Evangelical Groups

Other Protestant and Evangelical groups are relatively small in their numbers and their activities but they play a very important role for Protestant Christianity in Israel/Palestine.

The Christian Missionary Alliance came to Palestine in 1889.[48] It organized churches in Jerusalem (the American Gospel Church), Haifa and Beersheba, as well as outstanding activities in many villages and towns, such as Hebron, Ein Kerem, and Dhahriyeh. During the hostilities, its regular congregation was to a large extent dispersed, its educational work suspended and its well-known theological school closed.[49]

---

[47] Wardi, Ch., *Christians in Israel: A Survey*, Jerusalem: Ministry of Religious Affairs, 1950, p. 20.
[48] Op. cit., Colbi, pp. 93, 154.
[49] Ibid., p. 142.

The work of the Church of God in Palestine dates from the visit of Rev. J. H. Ingram to the Middle East. At the Church's assembly in 1946, Rev. D. B. Hatfield was assigned to Palestine. Landing in Haifa at the end of the British Mandate, he established his headquarters in Cyprus, directing the Church's work in Palestine, Jordan and Egypt.

The Church of the Nazarene has a mission in Jerusalem; it recently built a church in Nazareth and established a center, with a chapel, in Haifa. In the Jordanian controlled areas before 1967 there were two small congregations in East Jerusalem, one Arab and the other Armenian.[50]

The Pentecostal Movement is represented by several American, British and Scandinavian missionary organizations; local congregations are very small. One of these organizations, the Church of God of Prophecy put up a memorial on the Horns of Hittin, a hill midway between Nazareth and Tiberias, site of the legendary tomb of Jethro, a place of pilgrimage for the Druze of Israel. A world Pentecostal Conference in Israel organized by the Movement in 1962 drew three-thousand delegates.[49]

The Seventh-Day Adventists have a mission in Jerusalem and a center in East Jerusalem. Several Adventist families work as farmers in villages throughout the country, attracted by the facilities afforded them to keep the Sabbath.[50]

The Church of Christ maintains a center in West Jerusalem and a recently-opened secondary school in the village of Ailaboun in Galilee.[51]

The Mennonite Central Committee, with headquarters in the U.S. has distinguished itself in educational projects: a self-help needle-work center in Jerusalem, a boys' school in Beit Jala, a sewing-center in the village of Surif near Hebron, and a free kitchen in Jericho. They have a comprehensive aid program both in Jerusalem and the rural regions and have provided agricultural assistance and advice to Palestinian farmers.[52]

Other groups include the Independent Presbyterian Mission, the Open Brethren Churches, the Plymouth Brethren, the Assemblies of God and many other small Evangelical churches.[53]

---

[50] Ibid., p. 142.
[51] Ibid., p. 154.
[52] Ibid., pp. 142, 154.
[53] Ibid., p. 154 and *Ecumenical Life in Jerusalem*. Geneva: World Council of Churches, 1991, p. 41.

PROTESTANT RELATED ORGANIZATIONS

The United Christian Council in Israel is a voluntary, independent organization established in 1956 by Christian groups for mutual advice, cooperation and fellowship. There are more than twenty member bodies including groups from Norway, Finland, Great Britain and the United States. The object of this council is to work together with all Christian churches and agencies for the extension of the Kingdom of God, for the deepening of Christian witness, and to strive together for the greater strength and unity of the indigenous church.[54]

Some other Protestant related-organizations in Palestine are the Young Men's Christian Association (YMCA), with two facilities in Jerusalem, one in Nazareth, Beit Sahour and Jericho, and a hostel on the Tiberias lakeshore; the YWCA in Jerusalem; the American Institution of Holy Land Studies located on Mt. Zion in Jerusalem; and the Garden Tomb in Jerusalem.[55]

The Protestants have been impacted greatly by the political changes and military struggles of the Middle East. At times they have suffered extensively from these events. They have also been hurt by internal struggles and divisions that have too frequently split and weakened many of the churches. Many times the political, military, economic or religious situation has caused many Protestants to leave Palestine, thereby decreasing the numbers of these groups.

Though the Protestants are latecomers on the religious scene of Palestine, they have played an important role as a part of the Forgotten Faithful. Hopefully, their numbers will stabilize and begin to grow and join with the historic churches to make the Forgotten Faithful known by all Christians around the world.

---

[54] Op. cit., Jaeger, pp. 246-247.
[55] Ibid., p. 154.

THE ROLE OF THE CHURCH IN PEACEMAKING: RAISING A PROPHETIC VOICE

Bishop Munib Younan

As I was walking one day in Jerusalem, I came upon a woman visiting the Holy Land with her church group from the United States. I asked her where she had visited, and she gave me the usual list of places. Then I asked her if she had spoken with any Palestinian Christians, and she was quick to reply: "No, no, this is a church group. We're not getting political."

Think about that. To some Christians, my very existence – a brother in Christ – is seen as political. Nowhere in the world is the mix of politics and religion as potentially lethal as in the Middle East, as recent events have painfully shown. There are those who distort the holy writings and teachings to justify violence, occupation and hate, and those who try to transform political issues into religious wars. But perhaps the problem is not that we are mixing politics and religion. Perhaps it is the kind of chefs we are allowing to take over the kitchen. And their mix of extremism in both politics and religion can be deadly.

We believe that it is time for Christian churches to raise their prophetic voices and unite in their stand for common values of justice, human dignity and mutual respect for all people regardless of gender, race or creed.

If Jesus were on earth today, someone would be telling him to stay out of politics and stick to religion. But Jesus wouldn't really understand the issue. He didn't care for labels; he just believed in loving and serving the humanity of each person. His compassion and revolutionary mission led him out into the streets with the people, as he asserted by quoting the prophet Isaiah in the synagogue:

The Spirit of the Lord is upon me, because he has anointed me to bring good news to the poor. He has sent me to proclaim release to the captives and recovery of sight to the blind, to let the oppressed go free, to proclaim the year of the Lord's favor. Today this scripture has been fulfilled in your hearing (Luke 4:18).

Jesus came to embody the reign of God by turning the world upside down, by blessing the poor and the peacemakers, breaking the yokes of oppression and inviting all to the table of God's blessings, just as the prophets before him had done. There are no themes more fundamental to Hebrew scripture than justice and righteousness – right relations with people. When Isaiah called the people of Israel to repent and turn back to their covenant relationship with God, he reminded them it would mean seeking justice and correcting oppression (1:17), letting the oppressed go free, breaking every yoke (58:6). The prophet Micah spells out clearly: "What does the Lord require of you but to do justice, love kindness and walk humbly with your God?" (6:8)

Yet, some criticize Palestinian churches as being too political. **Justice is not political; it is Biblical.** It is a spiritual struggle but it arises from a real world struggle to liberate human beings from the sin of oppression and occupation. It is the very essence of the ministry of reconciliation Jesus came to bring us. Justice is by nature not balanced; it is on the side of the suffering and the oppressed, the weak and the poor.

As the Evangelical Lutheran Church in America (ELCA) put it in their *Social Statement for Peace in God's World*:

> In recalling an identity in baptism, in gathering in peace around the Lord's Table, in telling the biblical narrative, in teaching faith, hope and love, the Church promotes the basis of peacemaking for all of life…The Church is a disturbing presence when it refuses to be silent and instead speaks the truth in times when people shout out, "'Peace, peace' when there is no peace" (Jer 6:14). The Church is this presence when it names and resists idols that lead to false security, injustice and war and calls for repentance.

We therefore denounce beliefs and actions that:

- Elevate one nation or people to the role of God;
- Find ultimate security in weapons and warfare;
- Ordain the inherent right of one people, race or civilization to rule over others;
- Promise a perfect, wonderful society through the efforts of a self-sufficient humanity;
- Despair of any possibility for peace. (ELCA: *A Social Statement for Peace in God's World*, 4-5)

Palestinian Christians are called to be instruments of peace, brokers of justice, initiators of dialogue, defenders of human rights and dignity and ministers of reconciliation in our context:

> God is first and foremost the God of victims: God is one who bends down to release an oppressed people; the God who is proclaimed as good news for the poor; the God who identifies with the downcast and despised right unto death; the God who in Christ became victim of violent assault and suffered a death of torture on the cross. Just how radical the Christian message is on the point can once more be best illustrated with a reference to Christ's words in Matthew 25:35. "For I was hungry…I was thirsty…I was a stranger." In our suffering neighbor it is none other than God whom we meet. ("Vulnerability and Security: A Study from the Commission on International Affairs in Norway," 2002)

His Holiness Pope Benedict XVI once pointed out that the church "cannot remain on the sidelines in the struggle for justice." We have learned from liberation theologians like Romero, Boff and others that faith cannot be neutral when the life and death of human beings is at stake. Boff emphasizes that "the Biblical tradition is verified, made true, when it is informed by love, solidarity, hunger and thirst for justice. St. James teaches that 'faith without good deeds is useless.'" (Leonardo Boff, *Introducing Liberation Theology*).

When we look for true justice in today's world, we see the great divide between the West and the East, the haves and the have-nots, the occupied and the occupier. Nowhere is this division more apparent than the Middle East, with all of its turmoil. Today's injustice is deeply rooted in self-interest, power and economics and double standards. This contradicts the message of the cross: God has redeemed all humanity equally regardless of gender, ethnicity or race, whether powerful or weak, rich or poor, from the north or south, east or west.

Hypocritical standards for justice and ethics are at the heart of the unrest in the Middle East. We continue to believe that the road to peace in this region is through Jerusalem, because the Arab and Muslim world sees this conflict as the test of the Western world's relationship with it. The Arab world views the superpowers as upholding freedom and justice for some but not for them. They still want the US to be an honest broker in this conflict, but witness the US unequivocally supporting one side. Peace to the region will depend not on how powerful the West is or how mighty its military but on whether the international community and the worldwide church can implement a single standard for justice.

A new peace initiative through the International Crisis Group entails holding a peace conference to jumpstart these next steps:

- Support for a Palestinian national unity government, with an end to the political and financial boycott of the Palestinian Authority;
- Talks between Israel and the Palestinian leadership, mediated by the Quartet and reinforced by participation of the Arab League and key regional countries, to rapidly enhance mutual security and allow revival of the Palestinian economy;
- Talks between the Palestinian leadership and the Israeli government, sponsored by a reinforced Quartet, on the core political issues that stand in the way of achieving a final status agreement;
- Parallel talks of the reinforced Quartet with Israel, Syria and Lebanon, to discuss the foundations on which Israeli-Syrian and Israeli-Lebanese agreements can be reached.

Since the Palestinian elections in January 2006, we have been working under these assumptions:

- The democratic process should be respected and dialogue with the elected representatives, Hamas, should take place. Dialogue by definition is called for when there are differences.

- Isolating the democratically-elected PA is giving the Muslim/Arab world a dangerous signal that the West isn't interested in true democracy but in people making choices of which they approve. The Muslim/Arab world feels that freedom and democracy are only for those the West approves.
- When the boycott began, some governments wanted to channel the aid money through churches and NGOs to bypass the government. I advised the Norwegian and Swedish foreign ministries that churches should not do what the government is meant to do; it would be inefficient and immoral. Undermining the government makes churches look like agents of the West; governments should continue their aid to the Palestinian government or increase giving through church development and educational funds only.
- The boycott, the West's attempts to oust Hamas, and Israel's disproportionate use of force are all increasing extremism in the Arab world.

I believe that in addition to the above, a solution should include these actions:

- Revive the Declaration of Principles of Mutual Recognition between Israel and the PLO of 1993;
- Include a role for religious leaders to advise negotiators on religious issues;
- Hold an international conference to deal with the core problems of the Palestinian-Israeli conflict.

Today's world is crying out for leadership, and the church must stand up and reclaim its public and prophetic voice as Jim Wallis of *Sojourners* says:

> It's time to reassert and reclaim the gospel faith – especially in our public life. When we do, we discover that faith challenges the powers that be to do justice for the poor, instead of preaching a 'prosperity gospel' and supporting politicians who further enrich the wealthy. We remember that faith hates violence and tries to reduce it and exerts a fundamental presumption against

war, instead of justifying it in God's name. We see that faith creates community from racial, class, and gender divisions and prefers international community over nationalist religion.

In our context as Palestinian Christians, living prophetically means that we:

- condemn all forms of violence and sin;
- uphold a prophetic vision of a just peace;
- uphold a prophetic vision of a modern, civil, democratic society;
- seek common values of mutual respect and human dignity with other faiths;
- work ecumenically and globally for the sake of humanity and justice;

To be prophetic is to expose and condemn sin of all kinds:

As Dietrich Bonhoeffer wrote, "It is part of the church's office of guardianship that she shall call sin by its name and that she shall warn against sin; if the church did not do this, she would be incurring part of the guilt for the blood of the wicked" (Ezek 3:17).

Today, we find that the sins that are tearing our world apart are largely corporate sins such as domination, injustice, racism and violence. Salvation today must go beyond the freed and forgiven individual to bring God's liberation and healing to communities trapped in oppression, injustice and fear. Justification by faith must go beyond eternal salvation to set free and to restore right relations in this world. This globalized world is hungry for the message of *salaam* and *shalom* which the Risen Christ brought to the disciples locked in their upper room behind doors of fear.

Occupation is a sin against God and against humanity which deprives people of their human rights and dignity. It demoralizes first the occupier and then the occupied. Ending the occupation means liberating both Palestinians and Israelis from the evils of occupation and assuring justice to both. The churches have condemned all violence and terrorism, including suicide bombings, targeted assassinations, incursions or home demolitions. All human life is sacred and must be protected.

To be prophetic is to uphold a vision of peace with justice:

Our vision of justice advocates the liberation of Palestinians from occupation and a viable, contiguous Palestinian state within the 1967 borders according to international law, living side by side with Israel in peace, equality, justice and reconciliation. We call for a political solution for the right of return for refugees, a solution to end the illegal settlements and sharing of resources such as water.

The heads of local churches in Jerusalem issued a recent statement on the status of Jerusalem, concluding that these elements must be present for a lasting peace in Jerusalem:

- "The human right of freedom of worship and of conscience for all, both as individuals and as religious communities" (Memorandum 1994).
- Equality of all her inhabitants before the law, in coordination with the international resolutions.
- Free access to Jerusalem for all, citizens, residents or pilgrims, at all times, whether in peace or in war. Therefore Jerusalem should be an open city.
- The "rights of property ownership, custody and worship which the different Churches have acquired throughout history should continue to be retained by the same communities. These rights which are already protected in the Status Quo of the Holy Places according to historical *firmans* and other documents, should continue to be recognized and respected" (Memorandum 1994).
- The various Christian Holy Places in the city, wherever they are, must remain united in geography, whatever the solution envisaged.

Jerusalem is the core of this core conflict of the Middle East. There will never be peace in the Middle East until there is peace with justice in Jerusalem. The security of Israel is dependent on freedom and justice for Palestinians, and freedom and justice for the Palestinians are dependent on the security of Israel. Only when we understand this symbiotic relationship will a just peace be realized.

We want the Palestinian to see God in the face of the Israeli, and the Israeli to see God in the face of the Palestinian. Only when we accept one another's humanity, will we recognize one another's human, civil, political, national and religious rights. Only then will the Holy Land become the promised land of milk and honey for both Palestinians and Israelis.

To be prophetic is to uphold a vision of a modern, civil, secular, democratic Palestinian society:

In our new political environment, it is now more important than ever to work for justice, freedom and equality for all, especially freedom of speech, religion and equal rights for women. Our emerging state must have a modern, democratic, civil society that lives out the premise that justice begins at home.

EDUCATION

Palestinian churches are deeply committed to community-based education focused on teaching peace, co-existence and democratic principles. Muslim and Christian students, boys and girls, learn side by side to live with one another. Quality holistic education inspires our children to develop themselves in order to build their hearts, homes and a new nation with the values of a modern civil society with human rights for all. We are teaching our children how to live together without walls, fences or barriers, without occupation or violence, to turn anger into love, fear into healing and animosity into community while struggling for their liberation in a non-violent way.

CONSTITUTION

As Christians, we realized that there were several serious flaws in the proposed Constitution, which specified that Islam was to be the official religion of Palestine and that *Sharia* (Islamic law) was to be the main source of legislation. Palestinian Christians, together with secular Muslims, wrote to the President of the Palestinian Authority to say that this is the Holy Land – a land for all religions – and all must have equal rights and responsibilities. It is simply not acceptable to have one "official" religion, making the others "unofficial."

We also told him that neither the Bible nor the Holy Qur'an (*Sharia*) can be the source of legislation in a democracy, for that promotes theocracy. A democratic state must follow the principles of modern democracy such as equal rights for men and women and for all religions and beliefs. Finally, we emphasize that Christians are an integral part of the Palestinian society and that 'secular' means equal respect for the three monotheistic faiths in the Holy Land. The letter to the President makes clear that Christians are citizens with equal rights and equal responsibilities in Palestinian society, and it is incumbent upon us to help shape our society so that it reflects the values we hold dear. As King Abdullah II of Jordan told a group of Muftis and Muslim scholars in Amman in 2005, Arab Christians are the "glue" of Arab society and guarantee the presence of a civil, democratic society.

A prophetic voice seeks common values of mutual respect and human dignity with other faiths:

Nowhere have Holy Writings been so abused and twisted as in the Middle East conflict. While each religion points the finger at the other's extremist behavior, each one has its own work to do. We Christians must clean our own kitchen before going on to others. Hans Kung said there is "no peace among nations without peace among religions and no peace among religions without dialogue." This dialogue ought to be a dialogue of life that seeks the common values for justice, peace, reconciliation, love, forgiveness, mutual respect, human dignity and living together.

As the Norwegian study, "*Vulnerability and Security*" notes, "Respect for plurality and diversity is put to the test in a special way in worldviews and beliefs that hold – each independently and in its own tradition – that they know the Truth itself. The credibility of religious convictions is put to the test in their desire for peace."

In Jerusalem, the heads of local churches, the chief rabbinate and the chief judge of the Islamic court are in the process of forming an Inter-Religious Leadership Council for the Holy Land to dialogue about important issues of faith and life. One of the issues we have been exploring is whether the root cause of our conflict here is terrorism (the Jewish position) or occupation (the Muslim and Christian perspective). We have been examining what our holy writings say about both issues. The goals of this council are to:

- Speak out jointly on any desecration of holy places, scriptures or symbols of any religion;

- Combat ignorance and stereotypes of religions and increase awareness of religions as they want themselves to be known;
- Seek to explore possible solutions to the main core problems between Israelis and Palestinians;
- Work jointly on social, ethical issues;
- Serve as a reference group for negotiators about religious issues.

Interfaith cooperation was evident during the Cartoon Crisis in the spring of 2005. Christian leaders immediately denounced the inflammatory depictions of the Prophet Muhammad and worked with Islamic leadership to defuse the tensions and anger of the Muslim community in Palestine, knowing that our 1400 years of common history had laid a good groundwork and trust from which to calm the communities. The Muslim community contacted the political leadership in Gaza on our behalf and Hamas made it known that anyone who harmed Palestinian Christians or churches would be punished.

Because of our closeness, Christians have a special role as interpreters in the midst of these crises, both of European society to the Muslim community and of the Muslim perspective to secular Europeans. To the Europeans, we explained that freedom of speech is to be respected, but that freedom of speech does not give permission to demonize, damage or desecrate holy symbols, writings or places.

Christian Zionism is one of the worst kinds of extremism we face as the Christian community of the Holy Land. A modern theological and political movement that interprets the Bible literally and uncritically, it identifies God's blessings solely through the Jewish people while ignoring and alienating the Palestinian Christians – and Muslims – and the underlying issues of injustice and oppression they face. In this theology, the Gospel is identified with the ideology of empire, colonialism and militarism. For most Christian Zionists, dividing the land here would be unacceptable and in its extreme form, it places an emphasis on apocalyptic events leading to the end of history rather than living Christ's love and justice today.

This extremist theology, then, creates a backlash and extremism on the other side. Some Palestinian Muslims might begin to see Christians as an enemy, feeding into the extremism cycle. We moderate Christians must speak out so that our society knows that not all Christians believe in this sick ideology.

In summer 2005, four Jerusalem church heads issued the *Jerusalem Declaration against Christian Zionism*, which denounces "the contemporary alliance of Christian Zionist leaders and organizations with elements in the governments of Israel and the United States that are presently imposing their unilateral pre-emptive borders and domination over Palestine. This inevitably leads to unending cycles of violence that undermine the security of all peoples of the Middle East and the rest of the world."

The Declaration rejects Christian Zionist teachings that are "polarizing our conflict and making political issues into religious wars" and that "advance racial exclusivity and perpetual war rather than the gospel of universal love, redemption and reconciliation taught by Jesus Christ." It urges Christians everywhere to pray for Palestinians and Israelis who suffer from Occupation and militarism and "to break their silence and speak for reconciliation with justice in the Holy Land." It concludes with these principles:

- We affirm that all people are created in the image of God. In turn they are called to honor the dignity of every human being and to respect their inalienable rights.
- We affirm that Israelis and Palestinians are capable of living together with peace, justice and security.
- We affirm that Palestinians are one people, both Muslim and Christian. We reject all attempts to subvert and fragment their unity.
- We call upon all people to reject the narrow world view of Christian Zionism and other ideologies that privilege one people at the expense of others.
- We are committed to non-violent resistance as the most effective means to end the illegal occupation in order to attain a just and lasting peace.
- With urgency we warn that Christian Zionism and its alliances are justifying colonization, apartheid and empire-building.

The Palestinian Christian Churches have denounced intolerance and extremism no matter which religion, and believe it is our calling as ministers of reconciliation to raise up a new generation of the faithful who will urgently seek to see God in other religions and cultures and who will urge all to seek common values of respect for all human life, justice, forgiveness, and healing. We Christians must challenge one another with a firm theology of creation and redemption, knowing that God's son, Jesus Christ, on the cross, saved the whole world equally. God created and redeemed us to live as brothers and sisters in grace, sharing with one another, doing justice and loving kindness.

A prophetic voice calls us to work ecumenically and globally for the sake of justice and humanity:

Some ask whether right now the Middle East needs democracy or justice. As much as I believe in democracy, with our situation right now, we need justice!

Once justice is implemented, democracy will come naturally. This is not only a mandate for Palestinians, but for the world. The world helped create our conflict and it is God's call to the world to be honest brokers and solve it. Christians everywhere have a vocation to keep a Christian witness in the Holy Land. As Pope John Paul said, "Peace cannot be without justice, and reconciliation cannot be without forgiveness."

We are thankful for what so many are doing to support us, especially those who go beyond making statements but come to live among us and stand with us. This chain of solidarity increases our strength here and our advocacy all over the world.

One such program is the Ecumenical Accompaniment Program in Palestine/Israel of the World Council of Churches, begun in 2001. These accompaniers live in Palestinian communities and become our eyes, our ears, and our voices to the world. It creates a human chain of justice, peace and reconciliation. This and other initiatives are complementary, composing a symphony for justice and for peace and disturbing those who promote injustice.

People often ask, "What can we do to help Christians stay in the Holy Land?" In their Easter message of 2005, the Roman Catholic, Anglican and Lutheran churches issued a statement calling on internationals to help Christians stay in Jerusalem and the Holy Land by:

- Supporting community-based education through Christian schools and educational institutions;
- Stopping the emigration of Christians by job creation;
- Providing low-cost housing because housing is a social right, not a luxury.
- Strengthening Christian social institutions that provide services to all in Palestinian society regardless of religion, gender or political affiliation.

We are thankful for the support we receive from the churches in the West, but we hope that they will do more. We believe that keeping Christians in the Holy Land will only happen if we all work together.

It is time to liberate our world from the extremism and hate that seeks to dominate and distract us from promoting common values of love, justice, peace and human dignity.

It is time to help make religion the driving force for reconciliation and healing that it should be rather than a part of the problem.

It is time for us to realize that there has been enough hate, enough violence, enough occupation!

How many more deaths, shattered cities, walls of concrete will it take before we refuse to further destroy one another?

If ever there was a time to transform our swords into ploughshares, our hatred into love, our oppression into freedom, our occupation into liberation, it is now!

May God continue to use the Palestinian church to be peacemakers, instruments of His healing, ministers of reconciliation and brokers of justice.

THE IDENTITY CRISIS
OF ARAB CHRISTIAN ISRAELI CITIZENS

Bishop Giacinto-Boulos Marcuzzo

With great joy I greet all of you from Palestine and from many different countries of the world. The whole point is that we don't know each other, but our common faith already unites us and we are united by one love, one Gospel, one Jesus Christ. That is marvelous.

We are in Nazareth! We are in Nazareth, brothers and sisters. Can you imagine, Nazareth, the very point where the Word of God became man. Here he was incarnated. There are so many countries in the world with so many parts, so many points. Among all of them, this one place was the very point chosen by God to put His hand among men. Here started the new kingdom of God. Here started the new man. Here started the new church. Here started everything anew. We are in Nazareth. We are in the very point where God dwells with us. And if you are Christians in the United States, in England, in any place in the world, it is because once something came down from heaven to Nazareth, and from Nazareth spread all over the world to your countries and to your towns and to your churches. We are in Nazareth, where we experience that remarkable thing, where we are in the very central point of that wonderful mystery, the mystery of the bond of the covenant, of the union of man with God, one with Him.

We are in Nazareth where Jesus Christ said, "Go before me. I shall see you there in Galilee. Then you can see me." Can you now see Jesus in Galilee? Yes, you can because His community is in Galilee. There is a church, there is a Christian community and that Christian community, now, today, wants to be the living presence of Jesus in Galilee. According to the Gospel of St. Matthew, Chapter 4:

When Jesus heard that John had been put in prison, he turned
to Galilee. Leaving Nazareth, he went and lived in Capernaum,
which was by the lake in the area of Zebulun and Naphtali to
fulfill what was said through the prophet Isaiah, "Land of
Zebulun and land of Naphtali, the way of the sea, along the
Jordan, Galilee of the Gentiles, the people living in darkness
have seen a great light. On those living in the land of the shadow
of death, a light has dawned." From that time on, Jesus began to
preach, "Repent for the kingdom of heaven is near."

The Galilee of Gentiles! This is the Galilee of Gentiles! The word
"Galilee" itself comes from a Semitic root which means "to go around." Galilee
is the circle, the district of the Gentiles, because in history, the Jews were not
always there. It was the country of the pagans, of the Romans, of Greeks, of
the Canaanites even earlier. It was a mixture of many peoples, a mixed
population, and even now we have a mixed population in Galilee. Today's
population is different from the historical population but still mixed.

In Galilee, we have a Christian community like that in the Palestinian
territory but even bigger. In some ways we are like them and in some ways
different because there are different categories of Christian communities within
Israel. First of all is the local Palestinian Christian community. The second
Christian community is the Hebrew-speaking community, which is very small,
numbering about 300. While very small, it is a very significant community.
The third category is made up of the foreign workers, who number almost
60,000 Christians living and working in Israel, not counting foreign workers
who are not Christians. The fourth community is the Russian Christian
community. It is a challenge to know exactly how many are here, but at least
150,000. It is a special community, in a unique situation in Israel.

Finally, we have another "special" community, the pilgrims. This is a
country of holy sites that draw pilgrims. An average of between 6,000 and
8,000 pilgrims visit the Holy Land each day, although the number varies
according to the immediate situation. Thus we have both a permanent and a
changing community of Christians. A Benedictine Father who lived in Tabgha
by the Lake of Tiberias and was an expert in theology and in history of the
holy sites once said, "Five Gospels record the life of Jesus. Four you will find
in books, the four Gospels. And one you will find in the land they call 'holy.'
Read the Fifth Gospel and the words of the four will open to you." To

understand the Gospels, please read the Fifth Gospel, which is the **land**. It is another Gospel which presents a wonderful opportunity to understand and to appreciate better the message of Jesus Christ.

The first category of Christians, the local Palestinian community, is the one we must explore. How many years have they been here? Many, many years - indeed since the time of Jesus. Our community is composed of the descendants of the first community founded by Jesus Christ himself. That fact is our greatest joy. We are proud to say that we belong to the community founded by Jesus Christ himself. We are today the actual community of Jesus, not a community founded by a holy father of the church in later centuries. No, our community is the first community of Jesus and today is composed of the descendants who have transmitted the same faith, the same reality, the same facts central to that first community. We are the Church of Jerusalem. We are the Mother Church, and all the churches in the world originated from that Mother Church of Jerusalem. This is why the best definition of our community, especially in Galilee, is that it is the living memory of the story of Jesus. By our own existence, we can witness and speak about the story of Jesus in a very living way.

What else is this community exactly? First, it is an Arab community. We speak Arabic. We are Arabs. Our country is Arab. We find ourselves part of the Arab world. The Arabic language is a wonderful, very fascinating language. Next, our community is Palestinian. It belongs to that country called Palestine, to that history called Palestinian history, to that culture called Palestinian culture. There is something which is called Palestine, Palestinian, and you know that the word itself, "Palestine," "Palestinian," comes from the Philistines. The people of Palestine descend from all the peoples who were in the land of Canaan: the Canaanites, the Amorites, the Nabateans... all the people who were here in the land and who in the Bible were called "the people of the land." Little by little they merged into the melting pot of history and of culture and they formed the Palestinian people.

Our Christians are Palestinians and they are, at the same time, citizens of Israel. Does that make everything perfect? No. That is exactly the problem. It is not always easy to put together those four elements: Arab, Palestinian, Christian, citizen of Israel. It is not easy; it is one of our major problems. As citizens of Israel, we are not directly involved in the conflicts within the Palestinian territories, and yet we are involved because we live in Israel. Everything which concerns Israel involves us, too. And because we are

Palestinian, everything which concerns Palestinians involves us, too. We are engaged in what is happening to our fellow Palestinians but we have another kind of conflict ourselves. It is an inner question, a philosophical problem, a theological problem, a pastoral problem, an anthropological problem. We don't know exactly what we are. That is the problem. We ask ourselves: What should I be? What should I do? What exactly is my mission? Defining ourselves is a problem of identity, and many, if not all, of our problems come from the identity issue. Who am I exactly? I am Palestinian. What does it mean to be Palestinian in Israel today? I am an Arab. What is the meaning of being an Arab in Israel? I am Christian. What does it mean to be a small Christian minority of 2% within a minority of Arabs, who make up about 18% of the population of Israel, where almost 6 million Jews comprise the vast majority? What is the meaning of being Christian in that situation of being a minority inside a minority inside a majority? We have a big problem of identity.

Our Christians are distributed into different churches. We have the Latin Catholic Church, which abroad is called the Roman Catholic Church. We have the Greek Catholic Church, the Maronite Church, the Anglican and the Baptist churches and other small communities. Where are they? They are in Galilee, of course with the great majority in and around Nazareth. We live among Jews, Muslims and Druze. Only two villages of the Galilee are completely Christian: Fasouta and Mia'ilya. All the other Christians live in mixed communities among the Muslims and the Druze. Interestingly, Muslims and Druze do not live together without Christians present. They don't live together but they each live with Christians. There are villages with Muslims and Christians, Druze and Christians and even Druze, Muslims, and Christians but never Druze and Muslim alone. That is a very important social and historical point. Living in such situations, in mixed communities, is difficult in terms of social life, work, and education of the children.

Like other Palestinian Christians, we face the emigration problem. When problems arise, people leave or try to leave the country. Pope John Paul II, who was a very good friend of the holy sites and of the holy community within the Holy Land, said that the universal church cannot imagine that one day there might be holy sites without Holy Living Stones, without "living community." It is the responsibility of the universal church to take care of that community, because that community is the patrimony of all the universal church as well as the patrimony of history, the living memory of the story of

Jesus. So, humanity, and especially the universal church, must not accept the idea of losing that patrimony, of losing that living presence of the living community in the holy places.

What is this community like? It is a community which is very much alive. It is a living community and a great source of joy. Everyday we thank God that the living community of Jesus is still here, that it is maintaining the holy places and acting as a living testimony and witness to the presence of Jesus Christ today. We pray that in spite of its difficult history, in spite of the many troubles the community faces today, it will remain strong.

Some years ago, the churches in the Holy Land celebrated what was called a pastoral synod, which included nine years of meeting together, of praying together, of reading the Bible together, of disciplining our work together, of programming together. It was nine years of problems, because trying to solve problems leads to more problems. Nevertheless, it was a time of the Holy Spirit. We were touched by the Holy Spirit, and we were touched by the presence of the Holy Spirit in the Church, in the Holy Land, and in the broader community. It was a wonderful, spiritual, pastoral experience. It brought to life the Gospel of St. Luke in which Jesus, here in Nazareth, quoted the prophet Isaiah: "The Spirit of the Lord is upon me because he anointed me to preach the Gospel to the poor. He has sent me to proclaim release to the captives and recovery of sight to the blind, to set free those who are downtrodden, to proclaim the favorable year of the Lord." Just as Jesus said, we in Nazareth today experience the presence of the Spirit upon us all the time.

What is life like for the Christian community within Israel rather than in Palestine, where our fellow Christians are the same people with the same language and the same history, but with a totally different experience? We officially have freedom of religion, of movement, of expression. We have the right to vote and we even have three Christian members in the Knesset who are involved even in the parliament as Christians, not just as legislators. We have many social rights, including legal protection of the law for minorities. However, what happens in reality is quite different because we are second class citizens.

The fundamental principle of Israel is that it is a Jewish state, so those people who are not Jewish are citizens in another category or class. Of course, a second fundamental principle claims that Israel is a democratic country. Therefore, there is an ongoing conflict between Israel's being Jewish and democratic. Sometimes the first prevails and sometimes the second prevails, but many times it is the principle of Jewishness which prevails over the principle of democracy. We have a problem of inequality, for we are not exactly the same as Jewish citizens. For example, in 1993 the Catholic Church and the State of Israel signed a "fundamental agreement" to settle the problems between the two communities. It is a diplomatic agreement, neither specifically religious nor political but one that asserts major principles governing church-state relations. However, these principles are rarely carried out in practice. This, unfortunately, is the general situation of our community here in Galilee. Practically speaking, we have many problems with the State relating to our schools and hospitals as well as to problems with visas and permission for our church people to stay in the country and to travel in Palestinian villages. We have daily practical administrative and social problems.

Finally, we must ask the critical question: are we forgotten? The answer is both "no" and "yes." The answer is "no" because without the solidarity, the help, the prayers, and the contributions of the universal church, we would be unable to work. We have many institutions, many schools, many hospitals, many centers for handicapped and blind people that our small community could never support without help and we are grateful for the contributions of the broader church. We feel that solidarity. So I would say that ecclesially, we are not forgotten.

Yet politically, we are forgotten. Some special Christian communities, especially in the United States, support the Zionist movement and forget or deny the existence of Palestinian Christians. For example, an evangelical preacher from the United States recently brought twenty million dollars, not for the Christian community here but for the so-called "Zionist" movement. It is a problem less because of the material help than because of their way of reading the gospel.

Another way we are forgotten politically is that when leaders raise a new problem or speak about a new plan or a new project for the Holy Land, we wonder if they think about the presence of the Christian community. The answer is usually "no." This is generally true throughout the Middle East, where politicians seldom take into consideration the presence of the Christian community in Lebanon, in Iraq, or even here in Israel. And because politically we are forgotten, we suffer and are exposed to many problems, especially problems such as identity, integration, and emigration.

We should change the political inequities. Is it possible to change? Can we do that? I don't know. But something that we can do together is not to be afraid. Here in Nazareth the voice of the angel said to Mary when she was frightened by the strange news he had brought to her: "Don't be afraid, Mary. The Holy Spirit will be upon you." It is our hope, it is our strength, it is our unity, it is our challenge to face these problems together and not to be afraid. We must remain united, unafraid, and very close to our Lord Jesus Christ of Nazareth.

THE FUTURE OF PALESTINIAN CHRISTIANITY

Naim Ateek

INTRODUCTION

This is a very difficult topic to address because ultimately only the omniscient God knows the future of Palestinian Christianity. It cannot simply be an academic topic to be discussed. At the same time, we live in a scientific world. God has given us knowledge, wisdom, and reason to study, analyze and make scientific projections. As people of faith, even when we do this, we place our trust in God's love and mercy towards us. Indeed, our future and destiny lie in God's gracious hands.

As a Christian community in the Holy Land – Israel and Palestine – we look around us and we see certain dangers that face us. We must confront these dangers and threats with courage and faithfulness to God. We cannot sit passively around. It is our responsibility to study and to analyze the potential threats to our community. It is essential to carry out surveys and to make projections. It is important to assess the movement of history and all possible trends and do whatever one can to effect positive change in the future.

There are some red warning lights. Many of our people are aware of them. There are internal as well as external dangers. The difficult questions are: What can we do to alleviate these dangers? What can we do at the grassroots level? What can our religious leaders do? What must our political leaders do? The answers to these and many other questions are not contained in this short paper. They need more thorough investigation and study to be done as soon as possible. It is mandatory that we be comprehensive. We must rise above our petty church interests in order to work for the good of the Christian community of the land.

The purpose of this paper is to stimulate our thinking regarding the future of Palestinian Christians. It is only an introduction to highlight and to make us aware of the impending dangers. It is our responsibility to ask, what must we do? And what can we do?

Here are a few important introductory remarks:

1. I want to apologize if any of my words seem insensitive or offensive to any one church or religion. This is not my intention. At the same time I would like to stimulate and stir up people's thinking so that together we can find radical and effective remedies to the serious problems that face us. It is easy to take words out of context, twist them, and to reject and condemn the whole presentation because of one little remark and forget the overall objective and the spirit in which these remarks are made.

2. It is important to point out that this paper will not be complete until it appropriates the ideas that have been put forth by many of the other authors of this book. We need to collate all the important points in order to have a clear strategy for the future.

3. The challenges facing our community are so great they demand earnest and dedicated action. Unless we are self-critical, no change can take place. If we continue to deny or gloss over the problems, no change will take place and we will wake up one day when it is too late. We must rise to the challenges before us. We need to discern the guidance of the Holy Spirit. What must be shed and what must be clung to are essential questions today. We must not be afraid of change. Theologically speaking, the Incarnation is God's way of adopting change for the sake of us humans. God was not satisfied with the old theology developed by human beings. The Incarnation was God's way of contextualization. This meant change. God does not accept theological fossilization. God meets us in our new life contexts.

4. Paramount in my mind, therefore, is the survival and vitality of the Christian community of the Holy Land. This must be our primary focus.

In my paper on the history of Palestinian Christianity, I outlined the factors that have impacted Palestinian Christians throughout the last 2000 years. It was clear that Christians faced three formidable challenges to their existence. These challenges and dangers are still with us and make the life of our community quite precarious. Every one of them threatens the viability and vitality of the Christian community.

1. Internal threats. In the past it was the theological controversies that fragmented the Church. Today it is represented not only by denominational divisions and internecine problems, but by difficulties that affect us from some extremist fundamentalist Christians, especially Christian Zionists.
2. External threats that come from Jewish and Islamic religious extremists.
3. Political threats coming from the territorial ambitions of Israel and the rising impact of global empire represented by American Empire and its Israeli extension.

DEMOGRAPHY

Dr. Bernard Sabella estimates the number of Palestinian Christians to be between 400,000 and a maximum of half a million scattered throughout the world. In the Holy Land itself, i.e. Palestine and Israel, there are approximately 160,000. Of those, 110,000 live in Israel and the rest, about 50,000, live in the West Bank, including East Jerusalem and Gaza.

IN ISRAEL

Looking at demographic trends, some people predict the eventual extinction of Christianity in the Holy Land. Others are more optimistic. By and large, young men and women are doing their university education within the country or in countries closer to home rather than venturing to the United States as they used to do. Due to growing anti-Arab feelings, the West is not anymore as attractive to some people as it was before. In addition, the economic standard of Christians in Israel is higher than before and there is greater political stability than in the occupied territories. These factors help to keep people in their homeland. However, recent events in some villages (like Mughar) have shown the fragility of the Christian presence in the land. Obviously, the gravest grievance of most Israeli Arabs is that of discrimination. The Israeli Arab community – Christian and Muslim – continues to struggle for total equality with its Jewish counterpart. The obstacle, however, is the nature of the state of Israel. It is a Jewish state and not a state for all its citizens. If this problem is resolved, I would like to believe that the lives of the Arab citizens, Christians, Muslims, and Druze, would improve greatly and the need for emigration would decrease even further.

IN PALESTINE

Given the situation of Palestine today in which there is no movement in the peace process and there is no Palestinian state, the Israeli occupation continues with its oppressive measures against the Palestinians, and there is growing religious extremism. Many people attribute this to a one-sided pro-Israel American foreign policy that lacks the will to implement a just solution to the conflict. In light of this, there are realistic dangers that may affect the presence of Christians demographically.

Based on what we know today:

1. It is probable that the presence of Christians in Gaza will continue to decrease until it disappears. There are approximately 2500 Christians within an estimated population of one and a half million in the Gaza Strip.
2. In the West Bank, it is likely that we will gradually lose our Christian presence in the northern part of the West Bank. With the exception of Zababdeh and Rafidiah that have a small number of Christians, it is only a matter of time when the few scattered Christians in the various villages would move out. Christians from rural areas will move to live in areas where they can find a larger Christian community, better employment, and better schooling for their children.
3. The viability of the Palestinian Christian presence is very much dependent on the end of the Israeli occupation of the West Bank and the establishment of a fully democratic state in Palestine.
4. It is not farfetched to dream of the return of a good number of Palestinian Christians to Palestine when there is political stability and democratic rule.

It is not a hopeless situation. In fact, I am one of those who are very hopeful about the future. It is not the demography that worries me but rather the vitality of our presence. There is much that we and our religious leaders can do if there is coordination and proper planning. At the same time, there is much that our friends abroad can do. One of the objectives of the Sabeel International Conference is both to highlight the dangers and at the same time to point to some remedies that can contribute to the strengthening of the Christian presence in Israel and Palestine.

Christian institutions and international non-governmental organizations (NGO's) can do much. We are thankful for the presence of these western institutions and all the help they extend to Palestinians, whether Muslims or Christians. In fact most of the help goes to the larger segment of the community which is Muslim; we are not against that. Our theology is to help those who are in need regardless of their religious background. They are all our brothers and sisters.

Having said that, we have a responsibility to our people: "Do good to all and especially to the household of faith" (Galatians 6:10). We need to challenge international NGO's and especially Christian ones to apply a policy of affirmative action and give closer attention to the needs of the Christian community in light of the dangers that face it. In light of the Palestinian Christians' precarious position as well as the fragility and vulnerability of their presence in the land, there is a great need to hold a conference for international Christian NGO's that will lay down policies and strategies for help.

Since political changes defy scientific trends and predictions, all the above projections can become worthless with the turn of political events. Both political as well as religious upheavals could impact the population enormously and cause sudden drastic demographic changes. But that is not an excuse for doing nothing. It is important to plan well.

INTERNAL CHALLENGES

There are many issues that need to be addressed although space does not allow going into detail. Nine areas must be highlighted briefly:

1. **The need for a renewed and transformed mentality:** Frankly, one of the disadvantages under which we work is the presence of a mentality

that is both very conservative and, at the same time, past-oriented in its culture, theology, and tradition. There is a general dichotomy between some of our religious leaders and some of our laity. Some hierarchies believe that in order to preserve and protect the church and the Christian community, they need to freeze its traditions. Many Christians have become disenchanted with the church because they see it as obsolete and irrelevant. They see it representing the past and unable to address the present. They turn to the church for certain services (marriage and burial) not out of faith but out of perfunctory habit and because they do not have other alternatives. At the same time, some clergy and laypeople believe that in order for the church in Palestine and Israel to be relevant, it must undergo certain changes. These are future oriented. We cannot continue to live only in the past. It fossilizes us and will kill and destroy us. At the same time, we cannot shed and throw away the past. There is significance and beauty in the past. We are in a dilemma. We must change what must be changed for the sake of the church. Christ meets us not only in the past; Christ is ahead of us. Christ meets us in the future because he is not only the Christ of yesterday but the Christ of today and of tomorrow. We cannot rigidly hold on to the past and hope to be relevant. History can be one of our worst enemies and can stifle our vitality.

Indeed, there is a past that we must cling to and remember with fondness and gratitude to God. We cherish our Christian heritage, the life of our Savior and Lord Jesus Christ, his death and resurrection, the establishment of the Church by the power of the Holy Spirit. Yes indeed, these are the historic foundations of our faith. But when it comes to the ministry of God's people with which we have been entrusted, we must be up-to-date, relevant, and organized. We need to distinguish between the past that must be shed because it obstructs the work of the Holy Spirit and the past that we cherish. We cherish the treasure, the heart of the Gospel, the Lord Jesus Christ. But the vessels, the equipment, the methods, and the techniques must continuously change and be renewed to fit the time and today's context of ministry (2Cor. 4:7).

2. **A more dynamic relationship among patriarchs and bishops and the importance of servant leadership:** There is a great need for a new dynamic relationship among the hierarchies of the churches in the Holy

Land. We thank God for the closer relationship that one observes since the first *intifada*. But this is not enough. The needs are immense. There is a great need to meet together not only to find solutions to immediate challenges but also to address age-old frustrations and resentments. We need to accept that history has moved on. We cannot afford to continue to hammer past wrongs and grievances. Every church has made mistakes. Every denomination has sinned against the other. All of us have grieved the Holy Spirit of God. All of us are guilty of fragmenting the Body of Christ. Both hierarchy and laypeople have committed blunders against Christ. There is a need to repent and ask forgiveness of God and of each other.

At the same time, we need to accept history. We need to thank God for the mosaic of the church in the Holy Land. We need to recognize the contributions that each of the churches has made to the building of the Body of Christ in this land. A rethinking about servant leadership and a collegial relationship between bishops and patriarchs is needed. A greater involvement of the hierarchy with the people is needed in all aspects of their life.

We need to begin to view history in a new way. Obviously, we acknowledge that the church in the Holy Land was planted by the Holy Spirit through what became known as the Orthodox Church. We thank God for all our Orthodox Churches that have played a great role in establishing the Church on the foundation of the Apostles and prophets, where Jesus Christ is the Cornerstone (Ephesians 2:20). At the same time, we can say today that we thank God for the coming of the Latins (Roman Catholics) and Protestants for nourishing, watering, and strengthening the Christian community of the land. I realize that this is not the way we interpreted history in the past. And obviously we can always debate history. Today, there is a need to recognize the valuable contribution rendered by all churches to the survival of the Christian Faith in the Holy Land under excruciating and abominable circumstances. For the sake of the vitality of the Christian presence in the land, we must move on. The present generation of Christians is not responsible for the divisions of the past. For their sake and for Christ's sake, we need a renewed commitment on the part of the hierarchy to servant leadership of their flock.

3. **Unity through Ecumenism:** We have to recognize not only intellectually but also emotionally that we cannot go back to a period before the 4th century, before Nicea or before the Crusades. Indeed, we continue to pray for the unity of the church, but we know that humanly speaking it is very difficult to achieve. What is possible to achieve, as Christ has asked of us, is greater love for one another and the tearing down of the barriers that separate us. We have to realize today the importance of working ecumenically. The future of Palestinian Christianity lies in our unity not by physically becoming one church, but by becoming more united ecumenically. Indeed, we must preserve the rich mosaic of our churches. We thank God for the liturgical richness of all the traditions that we have – the Orthodox, whether Byzantine or Armenian, Coptic, and Syrian. We also thank God for the Latin and Protestant traditions. While preserving these significant traditions, we must continually rise above denominationalism and relate to each other ecumenically. We can be one spiritually, in our love and in our witness. We can witness to the One Lord Jesus Christ who died and rose again for us. I believe that Christ calls us to work together ecumenically. There is no future for the Christian community without the full commitment of our hierarchy to Ecumenism.

4. **Indigenization and closer relations between Orthodox and Catholics:** The Orthodox Church is the original church of the Holy Land. For most of us, it is the church of our ancestors. It is the church that we love and for whose well-being we care. The relationship between the Greek hierarchy of the church and the Palestinian clergy and people must be addressed if we ever hope to strengthen the Christian presence and witness. So long as the issue of indigenization is postponed and not confronted candidly and in the spirit of love, there will be bitterness and resentment among many Orthodox Christians. Our Christian responsibility towards one another demands a resolution of this issue. Christians in the Holy Land are a tiny community. We are less than 2% of the total population. The slightest problem can affect our delicate Christian witness. We cannot put our heads in the sand and think that such problems will go away. It must be addressed. One cannot deny the importance and the contribution of the Greek Orthodox hierarchy of the church. At the same time, however, the fact persists that most of

the local Orthodox clergy have not had the benefit of a proper theological education and their role in building up the Body of Christ in the land has been limited. It is not enough these days only to baptize, marry, and bury people. The Church desperately needs to provide pastoral and spiritual care for the people of God. There is so much that needs to be done, not least a deeper spirituality that can only be developed through spiritual formation and religious education. Generally speaking, such education is lacking. When I think of the future viability of the Church in Israel and Palestine, this issue must be on top of our priorities.

There is another urgent need that must be addressed. This has to do with the importance of closer relationship between the hierarchy of the Orthodox Church and that of the Melkites (the Greek Catholics). They are two branches of the same original eastern church and together they comprise the largest Christian community of the land. On the grassroots level the relationship among many parishioners is good, but on the hierarchical level it is lukewarm, to say the least. The vitality of the Christian witness would be greatly enhanced when the two branches enter into greater cooperation with each other.

5. **Pilgrimage:** Another matter of great importance for the future of Christianity in the Holy Land relates to pilgrimage and the holy places. Here, I want to register our gratitude as indigenous Christians to those expatriate and local Christians who had the foresight to care for, control, and protect the holy places for Christian posterity. The two major communities that have achieved this are the Franciscans and the Greek Orthodox Church.

There is a great need for local Christians and the guardians of the Holy Places to work more closely together in this area. We need to reflect together on how to make pilgrimage a more spiritually enriching experience for visitors while involving the local Christians more actively. The holy places are a great asset to the Christian presence in the Holy Land but I do not think that we have maximized their value to the benefit of both pilgrims and local Christians. In fact, pilgrimage can create a bond between Christians in the West and local Christians and help boost their economic situation. I believe that this is an area worthy of thorough investigation. A conference that focuses on this important topic could prove very beneficial for the future of Palestinian Christianity in the land.

6. **The question of the Status Quo:** In light of the changing circumstances of the last 150 years, there is an urgent need to review the whole question of the Status Quo. In 1852, the Ottoman Turks managed to organize the troubled relations between the major churches in the land through what became known as the Status Quo. Due to periodical frictions among various church members especially during feast days and the misbehavior of some monks, this arrangement has become both embarrassing and scandalous to local Christians as well as vis-à-vis Muslims and Jews. It definitely mars the witness of the Church in the Holy Land and it should not be ignored. There are important issues that need urgent solutions in this regard; and some of our church leaders have lacked the spiritual will to find solutions and make decisions. I realize the sensitivity of this topic, but it is mandatory that our religious leaders arrive at the needed solutions in the spirit of Christian love and for the sake of the present and future witness of the church. It is inconceivable that such matters keep dragging on.

    Sometimes we have a tendency to become slaves to certain historical documents. They become rigid fixtures that no one wants to tamper with, even when their usefulness has long passed. We must retain the beauty of the liturgical celebrations of the various feasts that the Status Quo governs while changing some of the antiquated regulations and restrictions that have become obsolete and scandalous.

7. **Ministry and pastoral Care:** Of very great importance is caring for the needs of the people of God. The closer relationships among the patriarchs and bishops must produce a better organizational system that can coordinate the wider ministry of the church. The future of our presence in the land demands more ecumenical cooperation of the churches. I am not referring at all to the liturgical life of a denomination, which must continue within every Church. Our ecumenical work must aim at making the Orthodox member a more faithful and committed Orthodox Christian; and the same with the Catholic and the Protestant. It becomes easier then for the hierarchies of the Church to trust the ecumenical spirit in which the work is done. We can rise above denominationalism and work together. It will then be possible for most of the youth work to be done ecumenically with qualified people as

leaders. Actually, many of our churches are doing very little for their children, youth, and young adults. We lack trained young men and women that can do the work. Through ecumenical cooperation, it is possible to train the necessary leadership that we need. The same applies to the pastoral care of our people. With more sharing of resources, we can do things not only ecumenically but also professionally. There is a need for a Christian counseling center that can meet the increasing problems our families and marriages face. One can think of dozens of areas of ministry that are neglected and that we can work on together ecumenically. If we are concerned about the future of Palestinian Christianity, we have to stop thinking denominationally and start thinking ecumenically. We are Christians first and we belong to Christ before we stamp ourselves with the denominational label.

8. **Christian Institutions:** Another matter that is crucial to the future of Palestinian Christianity is the important witness of our Christian institutions. We thank God for the Christian institutions of all the churches. It is to the credit of these churches and religious orders that we have wonderful institutions serving in so many various capacities. These range from hospitals to schools, from orphanages to homes for the elderly, from charitable organizations to retreat centers and pilgrim hostels. These institutions have faithfully served the Palestinian community of the land and beyond, regardless of religious affiliation. It is of utmost importance to raise the standard of all our institutions. We need to offer the finest services, the best quality education, and the highest standard of excellence. With better ecumenical cooperation, our institutions can become exemplary. The witness of our institutions not only benefits our Christian people but can also be our window for other faith communities in the land. Through our institutions, they can really know who we are and what we stand for and this can contribute to the creation of greater openness, tolerance, and goodwill.

9. **Messianic Jews and Evangelical Christians:** It is equally important for the Church in the Holy Land to reach out as much as possible to the small independent groups of Evangelical Christians, Messianic Jews, and Russian Christians that are scattered around different areas in the country. We have a responsibility for them as our brothers and sisters in Christ and as much as possible it is important to relate to them. Again here, there is a need for a strategy that must be developed vis-à-vis these groups.

EXTERNAL CHALLENGES

There is no future for us in isolation or in passivity. Our future is linked with others.

1. **Inter-faith Relations:** There is an urgent need for the Church in the Holy Land to articulate a theology and a strategy for relations with other faiths and especially with Islam. Within the Palestinian Christian community, we have people qualified to do that. The well-being of the Christian community depends on good relations with their Muslim brothers and sisters. Relatively speaking very little is done on the Christian leadership level to maintain regular relations with Muslims. In fact, not until recently did Christian religious leaders host an *Iftar* meal, the breaking of the fast at the end of each day of Ramadan, for their Muslim counterparts. There is a great need to set up a Standing Committee that maintains direct relations with Palestinian Muslim leaders and nourishes understanding, respect, and acceptance between the two communities.

   Due to the political conflict over Palestine, it has been difficult to develop inter-faith relations with Jews. There is a need for a strategy in this regard and in spite of, and maybe because of, the political conflict, it is important to initiate some form of relations that can address certain aspects of our religious faiths as it pertains to issues of justice and peace.

2. **Relations with the state of Israel:** The most important objective on the political level continues to be the achievement of a just peace in the Israel-Palestine conflict. There is no possibility for peace without the end of the Israeli occupation of all the occupied Palestinian lands in accordance with UNSCR 242 and 338 and the establishment of a Palestinian state alongside the state of Israel. Furthermore, the City of Jerusalem has to be shared by the two states, and a just solution found for the Palestinian refugees in accordance with International Law. This prophetic voice must not die, and if pressure needs to be put on Israel, it must be done through nonviolent means and methods in line with the way of Jesus Christ. There is no peace while oppression and domination exist. Yet as I always say, the achievement of peace is not the end of the journey. Reconciliation is the ultimate goal. It is peace based on justice that opens the way to reconciliation between

Palestinians and Israelis. This is what the church should strive for.

3. **The indispensability of democracy:** The best climate for the survival of Palestinian Christianity is that of democracy. With democracy, the numbers might even increase and some Christians who emigrated might consider coming back. A climate of discrimination and religious extremism would, undoubtedly, adversely affect Christians of the Holy Land and increase their emigration. Only true democracy can guarantee their freedom and rights. As much as possible, we must avoid a minority complex. We need, with our Muslim friends in Palestine and Jewish friends in Israel, to push for the drafting and ratifying of constitutions for both the state of Palestine and the state of Israel. We cannot depend on the good will of people in power. We are living in the 21st century. We refuse the Muslim concept of Ahl-Athimma for non-Muslims, the status of protected people, as we refuse the biblical status of the Ger, the resident alien in the land. We want to be protected by a Constitution that guarantees our rights and responsibilities under the law with full equality. We believe that citizenship and nationality for all the people of the land must be combined. This is the best guarantee for the future well-being of our community. Only the presence of a fully democratic constitution for Palestine and a fully democratic constitution for Israel can guarantee that all citizens will be treated equally under the same rule of law. The future of Palestinian Christians in their land depends, to a large extent, on this process.

RELATING TO THE CHURCH IN THE WEST

What can Western Christians do to help?

1. Educate your churches about the roots and presence of Palestinian Christians in Israel and Palestine and challenge the myths that have been concocted by people of power.
2. Seek out Palestinian Christians in your countries and in your midst and relate to them.
3. Be aware of our concerns as we have outlined them in this conference
4. Continue to work with us for the achievement of a just solution to the political conflict so that we can work for the reconciliation of all the

people of the land.

5. Support projects that can contribute to the strengthening of Christian witness and presence in the land.
6. Forge closer links between churches, institutions, and organizations in your country and in the Holy Land.
7. Challenge Christian Zionism in your country through sound biblical and theological education starting from Sunday School level.
8. Think of other creative ways to stay connected.

FUTURE OF PALESTINIAN CHRISTIANS

It is possible to glean from the Gospels a few words that can characterize the life and witness of Christians everywhere and are especially apt for Palestinian Christians. In its beginnings, the Jesus movement was very small. It started with a small band of disciples and friends who loved Jesus and were loyal to him.

On more than one occasion Jesus addressed his followers with such challenging words as "Fear not little flock"; "you are the salt of the earth...you are the light of the world..." For Palestinian Christians in particular (although appropriate for all Christians) these two words – salt and light – capture the essence of what should characterize the life of Palestinian Christians. The challenge for us Palestinian Christians today is to be salt and light in our communities. You do not need a large amount of salt or light to give taste and to brighten the area around you. We are salt in our penetration and involvement in the community. We are salt because we are an integral part of the Holy Land. We are salt when we give flavor and taste to the societies where we live. We are salt when we live the love of Christ in humility and service. To be salt is to effect change. Salt is an active ingredient. It cannot be passive. We must be active in all that contributes to the health and well being of society.

The same applies to us when Jesus challenged us to be the light of the world. This is a global challenge for us. It is not to be a light in the Holy Land only but in the whole world. Our light must be seen clearly so that glory is given to God. This means that because we have been dealt with unjustly, we must forever champion justice for other oppressed people. Because we have been dominated, we must work for the liberation of others. Because we have been humiliated, we must forever stand for the dignity of human beings. We must dedicate our energy to working for peace and reconciliation of all the people of our land. We must emulate Christ in honesty, integrity, and truthfulness.

Our faith and trust must be rooted in God. Above all we need to learn to walk the way of the cross in the footsteps of our Lord and Savior Jesus Christ. This is the Sabeel of faithfulness, the Sabeel of loving our neighbor as our selves, the Sabeel of justice, peace, and reconciliation. This is the Sabeel of Christ that leads to resurrection and life.

Some people may ask what the future holds for Palestinian Christians. We do not know what the future holds, but we know and we trust the One who holds the future. With this kind of faith we venture on with God into the future and we labor on with God for the sake of our fellow human beings and for the honor and glory of God. Amen

MEDITATION ON PENTECOST

Archbishop Paul Sayah

And when the day of Pentecost had come, they were all together in one place. And suddenly there came from heaven a noise like a violent, rushing wind, and it filled the whole house where they were sitting. And there appeared to them tongues as of fire distributing themselves, and they rested on each one of them. And they were all filled with the Holy Spirit and began to speak with other tongues, as the Spirit was giving them utterance. Now there were Jews living in Jerusalem, devout men, from every nation under heaven. And when this sound occurred, the multitude came together and were bewildered, because they were each one hearing them speak in his own language. And they were amazed and marveled, saying "Why, are not all these who are speaking Galileans? And how is it that we each hear them in our own language to which we were born? Parthians and Medes and Elamites, and residents of Mesopotamia, Judea and Cappadocia, Pontus and Asia, Phrygia and Pamphylia, Egypt and the districts of Libya around Cyrene, and visitors from Rome, both Jews and proselytes, Cretans and Arabs – we hear them in our own tongues speaking of the mighty deeds of God."

And they continued in amazement and great perplexity, saying to one another, "What does this mean?" But others were mocking and saying, "They are full of sweet wine." But these men are not drunk, as you suppose, for it is only the third hour of the day; but this is what was spoken of through the prophet Joel: And it shall be in the last days ," God says, "That I will pour forth of my spirit upon all humankind; and your sons and your daughters shall prophesy, and your young men shall see visions, and your old men shall dream dreams." *(Acts 2:1 – 17)*

The experience of Pentecost which took place in this great city of Jerusalem 2000 years ago has been, is and will always be a determining event in the life and growth of the Church of Jesus Christ. So what is the Spirit telling us 2000 years on? As I read the account of this event again three features stand out:

- This is an event marked by two vivid signs coming together, violent wind and fire! What a combination! This is anything but a wishy-washy, lukewarm kind of an encounter. This is "the power from on high" promised in Luke 24:49. She, the Spirit, (in our Maronite Syriac tradition the Spirit is feminine) gave the Apostles "the power to express themselves AS SHE directs them."
- This is an event marked by an ontological unity, a unity at the level of being, among the various members of that small Community of Apostles: "the same tongues as of fire separated and came to rest on the head of each one of them." This is a deeply unifying event.
- Lastly, it is an event distinguished by the greatest possible diversity of people who witnessed it, as "there were devout men living in Jerusalem from every nation under heaven."

This whole scenario points out three challenges which our Churches both here and all over the world are called upon to face at this particular juncture of history.

FIRST: THE CHALLENGE TO ACCEPT GOD'S SPIRIT AND SURRENDER TO HIM

God, the Father, in the Son, by the power of the Holy Spirit, comes to each one of us personally to challenge us, to shake us up strongly and give us new power from on high (strong wind and fire). Do I really agree to engage with Him, to enter into real communion with Him and become a part of the Holy Trinity? Do I accept inclusion in the realm of the Spirit to allow the Spirit to cry in me "Abba," Father…Dad? I have been called to be an integral part of His household, as Saint Paul says. Am I really aware of my true identity, and even more, do I dare to accept truly and fully this acceptance of my Creator and Savior for me? Of course, says I! Who would be such a fool as to reject such a fantastic offer? But this fantastic offer of adoption and integration carries with it an equally special and demanding call "to speak as the Spirit gives me the power to," to actually echo the voice of God, to be prophetic all the way, to say a blind and lasting "yes" to God, to His people, to life and to His creation. When Mary said her "yes" she didn't have a clue that it would lead her all the way to the cross. Neither did the Apostles know all that would be involved in their total surrender. Incidentally, when I catch myself saying, "Oh, we are only a small minority and can't really do much," then I remember that they were only 12 initially and not one of them was a great hero by human standards. But when they accepted the Spirit, when they took things seriously and surrendered to God, then the sky became the limit. Do I dare accept my new identity as a Christian, as "the Temple of the Holy Spirit" and surrender to that spirit and live by it? This is the first challenge put to every Christian by the Holy Spirit: **come alive again, get up, be renewed and work with God.**

SECOND: THE CHALLENGE TO ACCEPT THE CALL TO UNITY

The challenge is to allow the Spirit to unite us as Christians, as adopted daughters and sons of the same God and Father! The very same tongues of fire separated, we are told, from a single flame and came to rest on the head of each one of them, the fathers of each and every believer in Jesus Christ. Every Church claims to be born from the same Spirit, the same Word of God and yet we remain divided. We all claim to be nourished and constantly renewed by the same sources of life, the Eucharist, the Scriptures and the Traditions of our early Fathers, yet we still fail to grow into Him and become one with Him and with each other. We dare to remain divided while we know clearly that the express will of Jesus Christ in his prayer for us is to be one. "Father may they all be one, just as you Father are in me and I in you, so that they also may be one in us, so that the world may believe." Our divisions are first of all an obstacle to our communion with God. We cannot say that I am OK with God and you are not! I am well in with God but it is all still ahead of you! As long as we remain divided, each one of us bears the weight of this great sin! Furthermore, our divisions are a scandal, a stumbling block to the world's believing in Jesus Christ. What is really at stake in our divisions is the authenticity of our fidelity to our very identity, and of course, the credibility of our witness. This is the second challenge: **let each one of us repent and let all come together and be united.**

THIRD: THE CHALLENGE OF DIVERSITY

"There were devout men (not just any men but devout men!) living in Jerusalem from every nation under heaven and at this sound (the violent wind and fire) they all assembled and each one was bewildered to hear the men speaking in their own language and they were amazed and astonished." Clearly the Holy Spirit came upon each and every one of them without distinction as to race or religion (The Holy Spirit does not allow herself to be possessed or monopolized by anyone in particular!) as we often would like to think. Overwhelming was the impact on them. Listen once again to the four verbs used: "at the sound of the Spirit they were **assembled**, they were **bewildered**, **amazed** and **astonished**." The Spirit made them move and come together. The Spirit unites, brings people closer into dialogue and even into communion. The fruits of the Spirit, according to Saint Paul, are nothing but a deep expression of communion, a real encounter. They are "love, joy, peace, patience, goodness, truthfulness, gentleness and self control." (How handy to keep these in mind when it comes to dialogue!) No wonder each and every one of those people was touched at the very core of his or her being, so much so that they were bewildered, amazed and astonished! All those devout men (and women, I am sure as well), coming from such diverse religious and ethnic backgrounds, lived such a wonderful experience of unity within diversity. Once again, their religion mattered to them; they were devout people, taking things seriously. They lived such an experience thanks to the unifying action of the Spirit of God upon them, mediated by the Apostles from whom we have inherited "this great Ministry of Reconciliation"! Is the Spirit sufficiently present in us and alive to carry on such unifying power as they experienced? I need not emphasize the great need for such ministry nowadays, for there is no country, not even a small community, where several religious or ethnic groups are living, that can claim to be immune to problems! Our challenge is to be able to repeat this miracle and touch the hearts and souls of different factions, perhaps not amaze and bewilder them, but at least assemble them, bring them into dialogue and allow the Spirit to do her work. This is the third challenge put to us as individuals and to our churches as communities: **openness to diversity and work towards a ministry of reconciliation.** But, of course, nobody would believe us unless as individuals we project an image of real seriousness about our own commitment to our Christian identity and as communities we show forth a true spirit of unity.

My brothers and sisters, you have come from all over the world to reflect with us on the future of Christianity in this Holy Land. Let me tell you something you know very well. Christianity is the religion of the Cross and Resurrection and like her Master, the Church here has to know how to embrace the Cross, how to be aggressive in accomplishing the work of the kingdom by witnessing to God's love, and then she will truly live. She is the grain of wheat, and unless she knows how to die just like her Master, how to sacrifice herself in the service of all the people of this land, she will never live and prosper and yield a rich harvest. In as much as the future of Christianity in this land depends on us, it will depend on our ability **to allow the Spirit to work in us and to be free of fear and full of love.** Full of love in this context means not only to endeavor to eliminate prejudice, eradicate discrimination and abolish all injustice but also to learn to celebrate ethnic and religious differences as real and precious gifts that we all exchange and treasure.

My Sisters and Brothers,

Let me conclude my reflections with these simple and straightforward words of Saint Paul to the Galatians: "Since we are living by the Spirit let our behavior be guided by the Spirit (Simply stated, let us put our action where our mouth is!) and let us not be conceited or provocative and envious of one another." When you come to think of it, these are really the fruits of the Spirit put in a different form. That is what I hear the Spirit saying both to us here in the Mother Church of Jerusalem and perhaps also to some of your Churches as well. But the main thing that remains for us to do now is that all those who can hear should listen to what the Spirit is saying to the Churches. Amen.

CULTURAL UNDERSTANDING OF THE PARABLE OF THE PRODIGAL SON (LUKE 15:11-31)

Kenneth E. Bailey

The late famous world-class theologian Lesslie Newbigin spent more than two decades of his life in India and became a Bishop of the Church of South India. He wrote:

> Many times I sat with groups of Indian pastors and evangelists to study together a passage of Scripture.... Many times I had to confess that my reading of the text, which I had hitherto taken for granted, was wholly shaped by my own intellectual formulation in what we call the modern scientific worldview. My Christianity was syncretistic, but so was theirs. Yet neither of us could discover that without the challenge of the other... We do not see the lenses of our spectacles, we see through them, and it is another who has to say to us, "Friend, you need a new pair of spectacles." (Newbigin, *The Gospel in a Pluralistic Society*, p. 192)

Elsewhere Newbigin comments, "You cannot push the bus in which you are riding."

The Gospels are collections of stories from and about Jesus. Conceptual theology requires a good mind, the ability to think rationally and an awareness of the philosophical underpinnings of the age. With these tools one can think about and engage in serious conceptual theology. But if theology is attached to stories about people, then the interpreter must penetrate as deeply as possible into the total intellectual and cultural world of the people who appear in those stories.

N.T. Wright says that to penetrate any system of thought one needs to examine four things:

1. The stories the movement tells to encapsulate its world view
2. The ideas it extracts from those stories
3. Their praxis; how they live out their world view
4. The symbols they choose to invoke that world view

It is significant that Wright places the story at the top of this list. But stories are not suspended in air, and the interpreter inevitably looks at the story through the spectacles of the interpreter's world view, as Newbigin has so succinctly stated. The interpreter is not a disembodied eye looking down on the world from a height of 100,000 miles. Each of us comes to the text with "plausibility structures" which are influenced by language, culture, faith commitments, history, economics, politics and the military industrial complex.

How can any of us escape this dilemma? How can we escape the bondage of our own cultural particularity? How can I become aware of the glasses on my face and replace them with better lenses that will give me a clearer focus? Surely the best answer is to ask, "How have Middle Eastern Christians understood the text of the Gospels across the centuries?"

In approaching this question, however, it is evident that three dense curtains have divided Middle Eastern Christians from Christians elsewhere in the world:

- **The Council of Chalcedon** (451 AD) divided Semitic-speaking Christians of the Middle East from the Greek and Latin Christians. From that time onward Christians in the West have been obliged to interpret Scripture in isolation from Armenian, Syriac and Coptic Christians.
- **The Islamic conquests** (early 7th century) cut off Christians in the East and West from each other.
- **The linguistic curtain:** while the languages of the Semitic-speaking Christians of the Middle East are Arabic, Syriac and Coptic, serious Biblical study typically involves learning Greek, Hebrew and Latin along with the modern languages of German, French and English. Who among us has pressed on to master Arabic, Syriac and Coptic? And for what purpose?

George Graff, a German Catholic scholar, dedicated his life to producing a dictionary of Arabic-Christian literature, entitled *Geshichte der christlichen arabischen Literature*. This set was published in five weighty volumes. Most of the authors Graff cites remain unpublished, untranslated, unknown, unread, unhonored and unsung.

After Greek and Latin, Arabic has the right to be seen as the third great ancient classical Christian language. It is widely known that from the 9th to the 14th centuries there was a brilliant flowering of Islamic literature. What is often overlooked is the fact that there was a parallel outpouring of Arabic-Christian literature during the same period.

My own 35 year search has led me to a few great names in New Testament commentary from the 7th through the 20th centuries:

- Musa Bar Kefa (7th century)
- Abu al Faraj Abdallah Ibn al-Tayyib al Mashreqi (11th century)
- Hibat Allah ibn al Assal (13th century)
- Ibn al- Ebri (13th century)
- Dionesius Ibn al-Salibi (13th century)
- Ibrahim Sa'id of Cairo (died 1975?)
- Matta al-Miskeen, a Coptic orthodox monk of the monastery of St. Makarious in Wadi Natrun (died summer 2006)

Beyond these commentators on the Gospels are the Arabic and Syriac versions of the New Testament. The ancient churches worked hard at translating the New Testament and in the early centuries produced the great classical versions of their various language traditions. These include Armenian, Syriac, Coptic and Latin translations that have stood the test of time and blessed the churches that produced them. This movement ended with the Harclean Syriac completed about 614 AD. After that, for nearly a thousand years, the pens of the translators were for the most part dry. Beginning in the 16th century their inkwells were replenished as the Bible was translated into German and other languages.

For almost 1000 years, however, from the 6th to the 16th centuries, only the Arabic-Christian tradition labored tirelessly to keep the translations of the Bible alive and vital for the Church. Perhaps even before the rise of Islam and certainly shortly after the Islamic conquests, Middle Eastern Christians translated the New Testament into Arabic from Greek, Coptic and Syriac.

These versions have been labeled "corrupted" by textual critics because of interpretive flourishes added to the text. If one is looking for evidence for establishing the original text, this judgment is fair, but if the goal is to understand how Arabic-speaking Christians have understood the New Testament, these versions are a gold mine of interpretation although the evidence from them is unknown.

Beyond the commentaries and the translations remain the exegetical efforts embedded in longer theological works and in shorter sermons and essays called *mayamir*. I have worked extensively in the first two categories but have, as yet, not touched the *mayamir* (singular: *maymar*).

For a thousand years Christian Arabic has served as a great lake into which various Middle Eastern Christian literary traditions have flowed. Behind all of them is the still observable pattern of archaic traditional village life depicted on the walls of ancient tombs and experienced in isolated villages. From such village life, one can find a standpoint to formulate new questions in search of deeper levels of meaning.

What is the result when evidence from all of these sources is put together and focused on a single story? I wish to look briefly at the famous parable of the Prodigal Son and focus on those aspects of culture that need clarification in order to unlock the meaning of the parable in its Middle Eastern cultural world. The parable is well-known and appears in Luke 15:11-31.[1] The following critical cultural points are important to the story:

The request

In the story, the prodigal asks for his inheritance while his father is in good health. This request is an unthinkable breach of traditional culture. Simply stated it means he cannot wait to receive his inheritance and his request makes clear that he is eager for the death of his father. The parable opens, therefore, with an unspeakable breach with traditional cultural attitudes.

His father's gift

The father is expected to fly into a rage, strike the boy across the face and drive him out of the house with nothing. Instead, the father violates the code of an Oriental

---

[1] For a full description of this story see Kenneth E. Bailey, *Jacob and the Prodigal*, InterVarsity Press, 2003.

patriarch. New Testament authors are often accused of taking an Oriental patriarch and using him as a metaphor for God. This is not the case. At five points in the parable the father does things no Oriental patriarch would ever do. Namely:

a. The father grants the request.

b. He allows the son to sell his assets.

c. On the prodigal's return the father runs down the road, kisses him and orders a celebratory banquet.

d. When the older son refuses to enter the banquet, the father, humiliated in public, goes out to him.

e. When insulted by the older son, the father pleads for joy rather than ordering punishment.

A hurried sale

The text informs the reader that "after not many days" the prodigal "sold all that he had." The key verb here is often translated "gathered together." This is a banker's term that means "sold." Jewish law forbade a son to acquire possession of his inheritance while his father was still alive and thus denied the possibility of the son selling that inheritance. The inheritance clearly involved land, buildings and herds of goats and cows, all of which are mentioned or implied in the story. As the prodigal moves around the village to sell his inheritance, he advertises his break with his father and in so doing triggers the anger of the community. He realizes he must leave town quickly and does.

The kezaza ceremony

Early Jewish literature (the Babylonian Talmud and the Midrash Rabba) speak of an early Jewish tradition that existed in the first century in the Holy Land. If a Jewish boy lost the family inheritance "among the Gentiles" and if he dared return home, the village would break a large pot in front of him and cut off all relations with him. As the prodigal leaves town, this threat hangs over him. He must not lose the money among the Gentiles because if he does, he cannot return home.

Expensive living: Not **riotous** (KJ), nor **loose** (RSV), nor **dissolute** (NRSV), nor **wild** (NIV)

Many Western translations, as noted, imply that the prodigal lived an immoral life in the far country. Indeed, his brother makes some pointed remarks on this subject at the end of the story. But is the older son being fair? The Greek word that describes the lifestyle of the prodigal in the far country is *asotos*, which is literally *a* + *sozo*, i.e. without saving. The word itself carries no hint of immorality and is properly translated "expensive." The prodigal wastes his money "in expensive living." The Arabic and Syriac versions (with one exception) clearly translate "expensive living." At the end of the story the reader knows that the older son is manufacturing an accusation of life with "harlots" out of thin air in order to make the younger son appear in as poor a light as possible. When the prodigal's life-style is characterized as "riotous" or "wild" or "dissolute," this finely tuned contrast is lost.

The search for employment

The prodigal must find a paying job so he can repurchase his father's land. The reader does not know where the prodigal is living but knows it is a "far country" where the leading citizens have herds of pigs. He is in a Gentile city and it is among the Gentiles that he loses his money. He knows, consequently, that he has broken the code of honor that holds the threat of the *kezaza* ceremony. After this kind of loss, if he dares return home, he will be faced with the pot being broken and the community shunning him. Naturally, he tries to find employment in order to earn enough money to be able to buy back the property he sold and regain the money he squandered. But alas – the only job he can find is feeding pigs. The prodigal feeds carob pods to the pigs and longs to eat them himself but they are too coarse for his stomach. His abasement is so total that he longs to become a pig in order to eat their food. A second problem is that he is fed but not paid. The plan does not work.

The Pharisees went to Jesus complaining, "This man receives sinners and eats with them." (Lk 15:1). Jesus does not trivialize the problem of sin. Instead, he describes as repulsive an image of a sinner as can be imagined by the audience. From this point on the Pharasaic audience is drawn into the story because its point of view is authentically represented therein.

A self-serving plan

This is one of the critical traditional misunderstandings of the parable. Does the prodigal "repent" in the far country? The popular mind in the Church says "yes." If that line of reasoning is followed, an irreconcilable conflict is created within the heart of the three parables of Luke 15. The question at stake is: Can a sinner return to God unaided or does God need to come to us and find us?

In the first two stories Jesus affirms that God must come after us. The Good Shepherd (a symbol of incarnation) does not wait for the lost sheep to struggle home alone. Rather, the shepherd goes out into the wilderness to find the lost sheep and carry it home (Lk 15:3-7). The good woman does not sit musing to herself, "I wish that lost coin would hurry up and jump out of its hiding place in the cracks of the floor and land beside me on the kitchen table!" She knows the coin cannot and will not find itself but that she must pay a high price to find it (Lk 15:8-10). Are we to understand that in the third story Jesus reverses his views and the prodigal makes it home alone without any assistance? The first two stories follow the theology of the New Testament and of St. Augustine. The traditional assumption that the prodigal returns to his father (repents) alone, without any help, represents the view of Pelagius, the opponent of Augustine who argued that return to God did not require God's grace. Is Jesus confused or is he blatantly contradicting himself by affirming one view in the first two stories of this trilogy and setting forth an opposing view in the third? Surely not.

Perhaps the Church has long imagined that the prodigal repents in the far country because he plans to tell his father, "I have sinned before heaven and in your sight and am no more worthy to be called your son. Fashion out of me a craftsman." (My translation) Granted, this sounds like "repentance" except for the fact that the prodigal states his motive. He wants to eat! He wants "bread enough and to spare." In his reflection on his predicament he expresses no remorse. Furthermore, the statement "I have sinned before heaven and in your sight" is almost a word for word quote of Pharoah's speech to Moses after the ninth plague when Pharaoh is trying to "work" Moses to get the plague lifted. Pharaoh is not "repenting" and the reader knows it. The same is true of the prodigal. The speech is crafted to convince the father to send the son off for job training so that he can obtain a good job and have "bread enough and to spare." One day he will have enough saved to buy the land back and return home – or so he hopes. He is planning to return as an obedient servant, not as a son.

Turning point

The costly demonstration of unexpected love: the son steels his nerves to enter the hostile village and "while he was yet far off," his patient and watchful father ran to meet him and did so in front of the village that would judge his actions as undignified and inappropriate. The costly love was offered before the son's speech was given. This is the critical point. Paul stated the same theology with the phrase "God showed his love for us in that while we were yet sinners Christ died for us" (Romans 5:8). Without that costly demonstration of love the son would have become one more self-serving, law-abiding servant, but the father would not have a reconciled son.

A father who behaves like a mother

Middle Eastern culture expects the father to wait in the house, isolated and withdrawn, to discern what the son has to say for himself. The mother can run down the road and shower the dear boy with kisses. The picture painted in the parable is, therefore, of a father who acts with the tender compassion of a mother. God is spirit and is neither male nor female but the hero of this parable. This is the finest metaphor for a compassionate self-giving God known in the history of religious imagery, as far as I have been able to trace.

Revised speech

Not an interruption but a picture of authentic repentance: the son is not interrupted, but does change his mind. He "accepts to be found" which is the definition of repentance set forth in the parable of the Good Shepherd and the Lost Sheep. The prodigal can refuse and insist on finishing his speech with its implied hope of earning the money and paying it back. His acceptance means that at last he accepts that he has broken a relationship that he cannot mend. He can only accept to be found as did the lost sheep and in that acceptance is his salvation.

Christology: Incarnation and atonement meet

The shepherd, the woman and the father must be seen as a troika. Each of the three pays a high price to find the lost. Each is a symbol of God in Christ who comes offering costly love which alone can save and restore.

The meaning of the banquet: Three views

What is the meaning of the banquet? The parable offers three views. The first two are in harmony with each other while the third stands in stark contrast to the other two. These are:

a. The Father orders his servants to prepare a banquet, "for this my son was dead, and is alive again; he was lost, and is found." These are divine passives. The father is really saying "My son was dead, and I have brought him to life; he was lost and I have found him." The father does not say, "He was lost and has returned." Rather, "He was lost and is found." Although at the edge of the village the son was physically close to home, spiritually he was so far away from his father that he believed he could work, earn money and compensate for having fractured the family's tranquility and broken his father's heart. The agony of rejected love cannot be eradicated with the proceeds of a well-paying job. In front of his father the son states his unworthiness and offers no solution to their ongoing relationship. For the father the banquet is a celebration of the success of his costly efforts at restoring his dead son to life.

b. Later in the story a young boy (*pais*) reports to the older son and tells him that the banquet is happening, "because he (the father) received him (the prodigal) with peace (*hugeino = shalom*).

c. In the final scene of the parable the older son shouts at his father and says, "You killed for him the fatted calf." But that was not the case. The banquet was in honor of the father, not the prodigal. It was not a celebration of the prodigal's return. It was a joyful occasion to celebrate the success of the father's costly efforts at restoring his son to the family. The village does not like the prodigal and it will not attend a party to honor him. But it attends a celebration to congratulate the father for his extraordinarily successful efforts at restoring his lost dead son to the family.

Older son's anger at grace

Grace is not only amazing – for certain types it is also infuriating. You get what you pay for, don't you? The older son's attitude is: "Throw the bum out until he pays!" When he discovers that the father has "received him (the prodigal) with peace," the older son is furious. His anger leads him to insult his father publically by refusing to enter the banquet hall. This insult is worse than the insult the prodigal leveled at his father at the beginning of the parable.

Father's response

Once more, on the same day, the father must offer even more costly love to a wayward son. Instead of demanding obedience and ordering appropriate punishment for the insult, the father goes down and out to offer love, to plead for joy and to defend grace.

Older son's final reaction

The parable concludes without any hint as to how the older son will respond. By this point the Pharasaic audience is "on stage" in the role of the older son and must "finish the play."

What was the parable created to convey to its listeners and readers? I find a cluster of interlocking themes which together form a house in which the listener/reader is invited to take residence. The "rooms" of that house are twelve:

THE PARABLE OF THE TWO LOST SONS - THE THEOLOGICAL CLUSTER

1. SIN: The parable exhibits two types of sin. One is the sin of the law-breaker and the other the sin of the law-keeper. Each centers on a broken relationship. One breaks that relationship while failing to fulfill the expectations of family and society. The second breaks his relationship while fulfilling those same expectations.
2. FREEDOM: God grants ultimate freedom to humankind, which is the freedom to reject His love. Humankind is free to choose its own way even if that way causes infinite pain to the loving heart of God.
3. REPENTANCE: Two types of repentance are illustrated dramatically. The first is earning acceptance as a servant/craftsman; the second,

accepting the costly gift of being found as a son.

4. Grace: A freely offered love that seeks and suffers in order to save.
5. JOY: For the father, joy in discovery. For the son, joy in being found and restored to community.
6. FATHERHOOD: The image of God as a compassionate father is given its finest definition in all Scripture. That definition includes the offer of costly love to law-breakers and to law-keepers.
7. SONSHIP: Each son returns to his father either defining (the older son) or intending to define (the prodigal) his relationship to the father as that of a servant before a master. The father will not agree. He offers costly love to each from his determination to have sons responding in love rather than servants obeying commands.
8. CHRISTOLOGY: The father twice takes upon himself the form of a suffering servant who, in each instance, offers a costly demonstration of unexpected love. The woman and the shepherd do the same on a lesser scale. There is dramatic "self-giving" in each case. The third parable embodies an implied one-to-one relationship between the actions of Jesus and the actions of the father in that each welcomes sinners to table fellowship. This unity of action affirms some form of unity of person.
9. FAMILY/COMMUNITY: The father offers costly love to his sons in order to restore them to fellowship in the context of family/community. The family is Jesus' metaphor for the Church.

10. INCARNATION AND ATONEMENT: The father humbles himself and goes down and out to meet the sons where they are (incarnation). In the process he demonstrates costly redeeming love (atonement). Because of who he is, these acts generate incalculable atoning power. Some of the deepest levels of the meaning of the incarnation and the Cross are revealed.
11. EUCHARIST: The son(s?) who partake of the banquet in the parable sit and eat with the one who offered costly love to win them to fellowship with himself. The heart of the Eucharist is thereby clearly affirmed. The mood of the banquet/Eucharist is that of a celebration, not a funeral. The price paid by the shepherd, the woman and the father is not forgotten at the banquets that conclude each parable. But the atmosphere at the banquet is one of joy at the success of the costly efforts of discovering the lost.

12. ESCHATOLOGY: The Messianic banquet has begun. All who accept the father's costly love are welcome as his guests. Table fellowship with Jesus is a proleptic celebration of the Messianic banquet of the end times. The parable of the Great Banquet in Luke 14:15-24 precedes this parable. Luke (or his source) presents the reader with the former parable where "to eat bread in the Kingdom of God" finally means to accept table fellowship with Jesus. The same theme is woven into this parable as well.[2]

In conclusion, it is clear that when this parable is seen from the heart of Middle Eastern traditional culture, rich treasures emerge. As all of the sources noted at the beginning of this essay are applied, new layers of meaning are uncovered. Fifteen hundred years of separation will take many lifetimes to overcome. The "forgotten faithful," the Christians of the Middle East, need to be remembered, not so much for their sakes as for ours.

---

[2] Revised from Kenneth E. Bailey, *Finding the Lost*, St. Louis, Concordia, 1992, pp 190-192 and from *Jacob and the Prodigal*, Downers Grove, InterVarsity Press, 2003, pp 115-117.

THE MINISTRY OF RECONCILIATION

Jonathan Kuttab

> So if anyone is in Christ, there is a new creation; everything old has passed away; see, everything has become new. All this is from God, who reconciled us to himself through Christ, and has given us the ministry of reconciliation; that is, in Christ, God was reconciling the world to himself, not counting their trespasses against them, and entrusting the message of reconciliation to us. So we are ambassadors for Christ.
>
> (II Corinthians 5:17-20a).

I feel particularly privileged because the subject of the sermon today, as set out in Paul's letter to the Corinthians, is the whole ministry of reconciliation. Perhaps this is what Sabeel has been about all along. Sabeel has been an experience of reconciliation. It has been a ministry and a mission of bringing together, first of all, the Palestinian community. For us Palestinians, this is a message we needed to hear: the different parts of the body of Christ need to be reconciled, need to be one in Him, need to be part of a ministry of bringing people together in Christ for a better purpose. Perhaps there is nothing that is more needed in this part of the world than a ministry of reconciliation. This part of the world is torn apart by hatred, by violence, by separation, by divisions, by fragmentation, much of which is deliberate and institutionalized as a program.

Somehow we Christians are to bring a new message into this situation: a message of reconciliation. I must emphasize, however, that for Christians this is a distinctly Christian and spiritual message. Our involvement in issues of peace and justice is not merely an attempt to quiet down a situation. This is not about peace-keeping or about everybody being "lovey-dovey" together. We see too many people who talk about peace and the peace process and who create programs for bringing Jews and Arabs together without ever touching the core of the problem. I understand that in Germany there are more than 400 groups that are dedicated to bringing Jews and Arabs together. So they bring school children and teenagers together to sing songs that are partly in

Hebrew and partly in Arabic and it is all good and nice and wonderful and "lovey-dovey" but they do not touch the core of the problem which separates and creates enmity and hatred between Jews and Arabs in Palestine.

The Christian message of reconciliation, however, is very specific, and as I understand it, has three very important elements. The first element, of course, is that it requires **a change within us**. It is a message of reconciliation of people through Christ where God reconciles us to Him first. It requires a change of heart. We cannot expect enemies to become friends without a change of heart. There needs to be a fundamental change within every individual being. I know this seems very religious and very spiritual, and it is not at all what you hear in the secular press or in the secular world where they have conferences and conventions and shuttle diplomacy and U.N. resolutions and grand attempts by politicians to bring peace. These attempts fail. And they fail again and again. And we, as Christians, should not be surprised. We should expect this failure because unless there is a change of heart, there will be neither peace nor reconciliation.

This is not a message you usually hear. Very often we Palestinian Christians are accused of being involved in politics. We are not. We are involved in God's work and God's ministry of reconciliation, which impacts politics, which impacts this situation, which is very deeply involved at a basic level in what is happening here. We are deeply involved out of our Christian love and because of the ministry of reconciliation that has been delegated, assigned to us, as we heard in the letter to the Corinthians. Such involvement starts with a change of heart.

A second element in that ministry of reconciliation is **forgiveness**. As we saw in the scripture, part of the ministry of reconciliation is God's willingness to forgive and forget our past transgressions. In the political arena, forgiveness is a very, very difficult message to bring. It is very hard for Palestinians to forgive or to forget all the deprivations, all the violence, all the tragedies that have befallen them, starting with the ethnic cleansing of the *Nakba* in 1948: all the losses of property, of land, of loved ones, of freedom, of potential, of dreams. So much has been done to us. Only through God's grace will we ever to be able to forgive what has been done to us as Palestinians. And yet, to get to healing, we must experience forgiveness. But it is not only us, the Palestinians, who need to learn about this balm of forgiveness, this healing power. I think that Jews also need to learn forgiveness. Oh, I know, what was done to Jews throughout millennia and particularly through the Holocaust is horrendous beyond belief. And yet, if healing and reconciliation are ever to come to them and to this part of the world, they need somehow to learn the message of forgiveness, the healing power of forgiveness without which their lives and their entire worldview will forever be poisoned by the failure to reach reconciliation.

Yes, forgiveness is necessary for the past. A change of heart is necessary in the present. But we also need the future. The passage about reconciliation also speaks about a **new creation**. The old things have passed away; all things must now become new. In Christ we know that new creation is an absolute necessity and in politics we know that this is also true. We cannot talk about reconciliation while massacres continue everyday. We cannot speak about peace when there is a structural system in place that is based on injustice. To try to do so is simply not an option. And all those who preach peace without justice, peace without change, peace without an end to the occupation, peace without challenging the ingrained integral discrimination and racism on which this whole system is built, are totally missing the boat. Any of us who give credence or acceptance to any peace proposal or peace activity just because we want everything to be nice and simple and quiet and wonderful, any of us who urge others to "just say no; just don't do anything; just stop fighting and resistance; just stop struggling" fail to understand this central message of reconciliation. Reconciliation involves change. It involves putting away the old things and creating a new reality. This is where our message needs to be strongest because all those attempts to deal with the Palestinian/Israeli situation without thinking about a new reality, without a future, without a vision, without justice that will continue and bring a new thing into this part of the world, are doomed to failure. We need to stop being apologetic about wanting change. We are not looking to be "**peacekeepers**" in order to maintain quiet. We are "**peacemakers**"! We must create and build a new thing, and sometimes that involves rocking the boat, sometimes that involves upsetting people, sometimes that involves challenging much of the conventional wisdom. Sometimes — and for this we need to ask God's forgiveness — we have failed because we got caught up in the peace process. We wanted to give the Oslo process a chance. We wanted to allow the politicians to work it out, and they made a huge mess of it. Both Palestinian and Israeli politicians, not to mention U.S. politicians, have made a huge mess out of this place under the guise of this so-called peace process, and most of us went along. Many of us allowed that process to continue because we wanted peace. We wanted to give peace a chance. No. Our faith tells us that a ministry of reconciliation requires change, requires us to rock the boat, requires us not only to ask forgiveness for the past, but to seek a fundamental change of heart and bring about a new reality in the future.

That pulls us all together. That brings us together in this ministry of reconciliation. Then we will see the fruits that come out of it. I am afraid we continue to live in a situation of being torn apart. I am afraid that we will be facing in this land, particularly in the Occupied Territories, a determined effort to set in motion a process that is much more invidious than *apartheid*. Apartheid, as you know, was the ideology of separation in South Africa. We now have a new policy called *hafrada* in Hebrew, which also means "separation." It is built on keeping people apart, not only keeping Palestinians apart from Israelis, but fragmenting the Palestinian community into little enclaves, each separate and divided from the other. There is a separate road system, one for Jews, one for Arabs. There is a horrendous wall being put within and between the different communities. There are Jewish settlements that are only for Jews. There are new restrictions requiring permission to move from Israel into the Occupied Territories and from one portion of the Occupied Territories into the other areas. Soon even people in East Jerusalem will not be allowed to go to Ramallah or to Bethlehem without a permit. Such restrictions already prohibit those in Ramallah or Bethlehem from entering Jerusalem without a permit. This fragmentation and separation is going to be promoted by some as a good thing: the Arabs here and the Jews there. They cannot get along together, so we have to keep them apart. In fact, we will be told that this is a helpful thing. It is a step towards a Palestinian state, towards creating a two-state solution. That is the lie that is being sold to the world.

We need a Christian voice somehow to come in and say there is something fundamentally wrong with a process that is built on *hafrada*, on separation, on walls, on keeping people apart. We are called to a ministry of reconciliation, of bringing people together, not of dividing them. This is a very difficult message, but it is the message that Christ has entrusted to us. In the Biblical passage today we heard that we are now being called to be ambassadors, to be in charge of this new ministry of reconciliation.

At Sabeel, we stand foursquare behind the message of Christ in reconciliation. It is one that includes forgiveness, that includes a change of heart, but, most important, it is one that requires a new creation as people are reconciled to each other in Christ. They leave the old things apart and they move to a new beginning. Amen.

PILGRIMAGE FROM A LOCAL POINT OF VIEW

Kevork (George) Hintlian

Many European travelers mention that in the 16th and 17th centuries, whenever a group of pilgrims arrived at the gates of Jerusalem, they were met by Franciscan friars who led them in procession to St. Saviour's monastery, where the Custodian washed their feet. Similarly, the Armenian monks received pilgrims at the gates of the City, led them in procession to the church of St. James and then had the doors of the Church of the Holy Sepulcher opened at night so pilgrims could offer their prayers at the tomb of the Lord. Pilgrims were housed in dormitories and offered free meals for three days as initial hospitality.

Pilgrimage throughout the centuries has been the lifeline of the local churches. The Armenians serve as a model of what the local community has gained from pilgrimage over time. Although Armenians are not native to this land, they are one of the most ancient communities living in Palestine. People often wonder why there is an Armenian Quarter. There is a single answer: pilgrimage. Armenian pilgrimage dates back 1600 years. Armenian kings, queens, princes, monks and peasants came on pilgrimage. They came to be inspired, seeking redemption; they came to be transformed spiritually. They offered their gifts of gold, silver, and embroidery. They donated their money for building, and with their donations, a whole quarter was developed to accommodate future waves of pilgrims. For them it was of supreme importance to leave an inscription, a chalice, a holy painting so that they might be remembered by future generations. They took back with them the tidings of the gospels, the liturgy, the lectionary, the calendar of the feasts of the Holy Land, along with ideas of how to establish monasteries. Many were totally transformed: some pilgrims decided to stay on to become monks or simple deacons serving in the holy places; others fell in love with the land and settled here, establishing the Armenian community and the Armenian Quarter of Jerusalem. Income generated from pilgrimage also provided for the upkeep of the holy places, and in the last centuries, pilgrimage income was used to buy income-producing property.

The Armenian example holds true for all Christian groups, including the Greeks, Latin Catholics, Ethiopians, Copts, and Syrians. The bond between the Jerusalem church and the Christian world is as old as the beginning of the Christian faith. The most important feature of pilgrimage was the encounter between the pilgrim and the Mother Church. This encounter with the Holy Land, the holy places, the Church, and members of the local congregations was overwhelming, traumatic, transforming and, in short, extremely fruitful for both sides.

The pilgrim became the messenger to the rest of the world. He took back the images, the legends, the traditions and the spirit of the Holy Land. For long centuries the pilgrim was an intermediary, a cultural and spiritual mediator who took back the manuscripts, the teachings of the desert fathers, the hymns of the Holy Land, and, most important, the spiritual traditions of the land.

The term **pilgrim** was always associated with the insecurity of travel. Pilgrims braved the storms of the seas and weathered the attacks of pirates and highwaymen, but in the end, they reached their destination. Access to the Holy Land has never been easy. It had to be negotiated and won, but despite all these obstacles, the dream was fulfilled. Despite wars, epidemics and perennial hazards of the voyage, pilgrims throughout history achieved their goal.

Pilgrims have contributed considerably to knowledge of the Holy Land. Most of our information on Palestine throughout the centuries comes from pilgrim travel literature. During the 19th century alone, 5000 travel accounts about the Holy Land were produced in English.

Modes of travel were revolutionized in the 19th century and transport facilities like shipping and railways facilitated the flow of pilgrims. The number of Russian pilgrims reached extraordinary proportions. Annually as many as 15,000 Russian pilgrims came to wander on foot around the Holy Land singing hymns. Photographers have immortalized these images of piety and profound faith as the pilgrims were dipped into the waters of the Jordan River.

How does pilgrimage manifest itself today? New patterns are emerging, especially since the collapse of the Soviet Union. We are witnessing a dramatic revival in Russian pilgrimage even in low seasons. The level of piety and veneration of the Holy Sites exhibited seems to compensate the pilgrims for all the years they lost under Communist rule. We are also witnessing development of new traditions and new legends among Russian guides and pilgrims.

The depth of Russian piety is matched by that of eastern European pilgrims, and we are also seeing increasing numbers of Nigerians, Sri Lankians, and people from the Philippines and the Far East. On the other hand, "unconventional pilgrimages" undertaken by fundamentalist Christians from abroad tend to reject local Christians, and in turn, these groups are rejected by the historic churches of the Holy Land.

The Israeli Ministry of Tourism issues an annual report which categorizes the various groups of tourists, including pilgrims. The Christian Information Centre of Jerusalem also makes a rough yearly estimate of the number of Christian pilgrimage groups visiting the Holy Sites. It is important, however, also to look at some of the lesser-known and frequently overlooked issues of pilgrimage. Very few talk about the total disruption of pilgrimage from the Middle East during the past 40 years. Already several generations of pilgrims have been unable to visit the Holy Land. In local eyes, this type of overland pilgrimage from neighboring countries was a genuine and traditional form of pilgrimage. Individuals and families still come from Jordan and Egypt. But gone are the days when during Holy Week over 30,000 pilgrims came from all over the Middle East, including Syria, Lebanon, and Iraq.

For the eastern Christians this was an essential encounter, a family reunion, and today their presence is greatly missed, leading to a deepening sense of the isolation of the local church. Pilgrimage from the Middle Eastern countries produced many benefits: some of the young were recruited for priesthood; others settled here as partners of the local community.

Like other rights, the right of pilgrimage is an absolute and inviolable right as is the right of access to Holy Places. These rights are complementary. In the last few years, we have become deeply concerned about our brother and sister Christians beyond the Separation Wall. Their rights of pilgrimage and access have become rare indeed.

Sadly, the changing pilgrimage situation has caused local Christians to experience many shortcomings, although solutions are possible:

- We have lost our centuries-old faculty of hospitality, sometimes leading us to treat pilgrims as tourists.

- In the last few years, Holy Week has been marred by sad events which have been artificially provoked. The accession of Greek Patriarch Theophilos III hopefully will clear the air, allowing future Holy Weeks to be as inspiring as any pilgrim deserves.
- As suggested by Ruth and Thomas Hummel in a paper presented at a recent Sabeel Conference, local Christians should without delay set up a Christian Heritage Center in Jerusalem or Bethlehem as a witness of our collective experience.
- The number of Christian guides has dropped sharply. Some young Christians should embrace this important profession to convey the Christian narrative competently.

To conclude, we need to remember that the classic pilgrim was a messenger and an intermediary to the broader Christian world. Is this still true today? Have we created adequate conditions of encounter between the local church and the pilgrims? This is an open question. In the name of the local Christian community, I salute all who came from afar to the Sabeel Conference as the new pilgrims of solidarity and thank you for your familial support and commitment to this land and to the forgotten Christians.

PILGRIMS' NARRATIVES: HONING THE ETHICAL EDGE OF THE SACRED JOURNEY

Henry Ralph Carse

Ambrose Bierce wrote that "a pilgrim is a traveler who is taken seriously." This is a very questionable definition. Many pilgrims are not even aware of their own serious intentions, if they have any, and those who watch them are far from serious in their observations. Many of our contemporaries think of pilgrims as religious vacationers, perhaps nothing more than tourists on a holy spree.

Richard Niebuhr provides one of the better serious definitions of pilgrimage or, more precisely, of pilgrims:

> Pilgrims are persons in motion,
> passing through territories not their own,
> seeking something we might call completion,
> or perhaps the word clarity will do as well,
> a goal to which only the spirit's compass
> points the way.

But do Christian pilgrims to the Holy Land really have a goal of clarity or completion? When we read the ancient journals of pilgrims of long ago, we sense that their intentions were unpretentious: to understand the Bible (Mileto of Sardis), to visit the places where Christ once walked (the Pilgrim of Bordeaux), to participate personally in the gospel narrative "in the very places" of the original events (Egeria of Spain). Or simply to pray, as if in response to the poetic exhortation of T.S. Eliot:"You are here to kneel where prayer has been valid." The oldest Christian pilgrim graffito in Jerusalem is perhaps the

"DOMINE IVIMUS" inscription under the Church of the Resurrection, which simply reports: "Lord, We Have Arrived!"

Later Christian theology of Holy Land pilgrimage ranges from the obvious to the ambiguous. Some of the great theological minds of the Christian world (including heavy-weights like Gregory of Nyssa, Jerome, Calvin and Luther) all roundly condemned the practice of pilgrimage, and scoffed at the idea that it could have any spiritual merit:

> Look closely at the matter and you will see that it is bound to do moral harm to those who have begun to lead the stricter life…What advantage is to be gained by the one who reaches those famous places themselves? One cannot suppose that Our Lord lives there today in the body, but is absent from us foreigners! Or that the Holy Spirit is fully present in Jerusalem but cannot travel so far to reach us! (Gregory of Nyssa, *On Pilgrimage*).

Fortunately thousands of Christians throughout the ancient world ignored the moral proscriptions of Gregory and others who espoused the "teaching of restraint." There is plenty of evidence that pilgrimage remained popular in the Byzantine period, and thereafter whenever travel conditions allowed it. Egeria, at the end of the 4th century, is a model of the pilgrim who marvels at the opportunity to read the Gospel in the actual original setting, and she was deeply touched by the emotional engagement of her fellow pilgrims during the memorials of Christ's passion in the Holy City:

> What I admire and value most is that all the hymns and antiphons and readings they have, and all the prayers… are always relevant to the day which is being observed and to the place in which they are used…. It is impressive to see how the people are moved by these readings, and how they mourn….You could hardly believe how every single one of them weeps…because of the manner in which the Lord suffered for us. (*Egeria's Travels*)

Being touched and moved by the place and by the sacred text is still a genuine hallmark of pilgrimage today. In their landmark anthropological study of pilgrimage in the Christian world, Victor and Edith Turner show that the essence of the experience is the "inner movement of the heart" (*Image and Pilgrimage in Christian Culture*). This sentiment is echoed by Cynthia Ozick when she writes: "a visitor passes through a place; the place passes through the pilgrim."

The point is that the pilgrim must be moved, must be engaged, must be changed. Somehow, encounter with the Holy Land is intended to be transformational, even revolutionary. **But is it?** Each Christian pilgrim today will answer that from a very different point of view. Glenn Bowman's study (in *Contesting the Sacred*) of the "three traditions" of Christian pilgrimage is helpful here, but only partly so. Some (but not all) Orthodox pilgrims surely come to Jerusalem to prepare for a holy death. Some (but not all) Roman Catholic pilgrims make the journey for renewal of moral commitment. Some (but not all) pilgrims from reforming (including Protestant) traditions come to the Land of the Bible with a critical mind and an awakened conscience, ready to ask probing questions about faith and contemporary realities.

In over 30 years of experience guiding and listening to Christian pilgrims of all types, I have noticed an emerging pattern which contrasts remarkably with the ancient prototype. The essential "meaning" of a pilgrimage to the Holy Land is gradually but surely being changed by the evolution of ethical engagement, specifically with the struggle for freedom, peace and justice in the "Land Called Holy." This is a remarkable and unprecedented development, and needs to be noted and encouraged.

When I read the diary of Egeria, I am struck by the fact that she totally ignores the contemporary social scene around here. I cannot believe that there was no oppression or injustice in the Jerusalem of her time. Gregory himself goes out of his way to say that the residents of Jerusalem are constantly "pouring out each others' lifeblood for the sake of lifeless property." Egeria, however, seems immersed in her holy agenda. The only "mourning" she notices is the drama of the re-enacted passion of Christ in the shrines of the city. She does not once mention a beggar, an oppressed minority, a conflict or even an unpleasantness. Her pilgrimage takes place in a holy bubble largely devoid of contemporary meaning. The same can be said for most of the conventional pilgrim reports from the Byzantine and the Crusader period, up to the dawn of modernity.

Today, there are Christian pilgrims who follow suit, and somehow maintain a near-total ignorance of the systemic violence, the injustice, and the sheer suffering of many of the people who live in this land today. But it is getting more and more difficult to keep up the imposture of the "oblivious pilgrim." My conversations with many pilgrims over the last several years have provided many examples of a deeper ethical awareness, and the trend is deepening even as the realities are becoming more brutal. Of course, we can always find pilgrims who simply don't get it, like the lady who told me: "I absolutely hated it. . . dashing from place to place. . . . Today is Monday; it must be Bethlehem. . ." and so forth.

And there will always be Christian pilgrims for whom every other faith and culture is simply an abomination, like the pilgrim who refused to go into the Dome of the Rock (when it was still usual for pilgrims to go inside). She claimed that she saw Jesus weeping because of the pagan disbelief of those "Muslim idolaters"! Religious bigotry concerning other faiths is not the monopoly of one era, as we know too well!

However, a growing number of Christian pilgrims whom I have interviewed have had a truly eye-opening and heart-opening encounter here. Their narratives speak of a deep moral courage and humility, as they prepare to re-invent their theological priorities in the light of encountering the divine, not in shrines and rituals, but in the "suffering body" of Jerusalem's **contemporary Christs**. Listen to these pilgrim narratives and voices carefully, for they bring hope and clarity, perhaps even a form of redemption:

"I expected to walk in the footsteps of Jesus. I didn't expect to come face to face with Israeli and Palestinian tension, intolerance, inequality, diminishing human rights. . . ."

"The passion and the power and the pain of the Lord [are] everywhere. There's the same intolerance where I live and work. And I see it in myself."

"But God hears the oppressed. God hears the cry of a child suffering and responds. God cares not only for the blood line of Abraham and Sarah, but also for Hagar and Abraham's child [Ishmael]. . . . God cares for all people. God is even in the rejection and humiliation. . . ."

Although I must quote these insights anonymously, I can assure you that they reflect very personal, very real theological and moral developments.

I believe that once these seeds of conscience have been sown in the Holy Land pilgrimage experience, they will eventually grow into a new pilgrimage ethic, more sensitive to the shared divine image in all faiths, and less apathetic about the cry for justice and peace:

> "At Dominus Flevit
> Here is the God of humanity
> Reaching out to gather in the chicks
> Of his creation....
> In the Holy Land of today
> We see another God,
> The image of God at a checkpoint
> Where the people are oppressed,
> An image of God at Yad Vashem
> Where memories try to rest."

CALLING A SPADE A SPADE: THE 1948 ETHNIC CLEANSING OF PALESTINE

Ilan Pappe

For many years, the term *Nakba* – a human catastrophe – seemed a satisfactory term for assessing both the events of 1948 in Palestine and their impact on our lives today. However, it is time to use a different term, "The Ethnic Cleansing of Palestine." The term *Nakba* does not indicate directly any reference to who is behind the catastrophe – anything could have caused the destruction of Palestine, even the Palestinians themselves. Not so when the term **ethnic cleansing** is used. It implies a direct accusation and reference to culprits, not only in the past but also in the present. Far more importantly, it connects policies such as the ones that destroyed Palestine in 1948 to an ideology. And when this ideology is still the basis of Israel's policies towards the Palestinians wherever they are, the *Nakba* continues or more forcefully and accurately, the ethnic cleansing rages on. In this 59th commemoration of the *Nakba*, it is time to use openly and without hesitation the term **ethnic cleansing** as the best possible term for describing the expulsion of the Palestinians in 1948.

Ethnic Cleansing is a crime and those who perpetrated it are criminals. In 1948, the leadership of the Zionist movement, which became the government of Israel, committed a crime against the Palestinian people. The crime was **Ethnic Cleansing**. This is not a casual term but an indictment with far reaching political, legal and moral implications. The meaning of this term was clarified in the aftermath of the civil war in the Balkans during the 1990's. Any action by one ethnic group meant to drive out another ethnic group with the purpose of transforming a mixed ethnic region into a pure one is Ethnic Cleansing. Such action becomes part of an ethnic cleansing policy regardless of the means employed to obtain it. Every means – from persuasion and threats to expulsions and mass killings – justify the attribution of the term to such policies. Moreover, the act itself determines the definition, and therefore certain policies were regarded as ethnic cleansing by the international community, even when a master plan for their execution was not found or exposed. Consequently, the victims of ethnic cleansing are both people who left out of fear and those expelled forcefully as part of an ongoing operation. The above definitions and references can be found on the websites of the American State Department and United Nations. These are the principal definitions that guided the establishment of the international court in The Hague to hold responsible those people who had perpetrated crimes against humanity by planning and executing ethnic cleansing operations.

The Israeli objective in 1948 was clear and was articulated without any evasions in Plan Dalet, which was adopted in March 1948 by the high command of the Hagana (the main Jewish underground in the pre-state days). The goal was to take over as much of the territory of Mandatory Palestine as possible and to remove most of the Palestinian villages and urban neighborhoods from the coveted future Jewish State. The execution was even more systematic and comprehensive than the plan anticipated. In a matter of seven months, 531 villages were destroyed and 11 urban neighborhoods emptied. The mass expulsion was accompanied by massacres, rape and imprisonment of men (defined as males above the age of ten) in labor camps for periods over a year. From the vantage point of the year 2006, all these characteristics can be only attributed to an ethnic cleansing policy, namely a policy that according to the UN definition aims at transforming a mixed ethnic area into a pure ethnic space by means which are all deemed by the perpetrators as justified. Such a policy is defined in the international law as a crime against humanity; the US State Department believes such crimes can only be rectified by the repatriation of all the people who left, or were expelled, as a result of the ethnic cleansing operations.

The political implication of such a statement is that Israel is exclusively to blame for the making of the Palestinian refugee problem and bears legal as well as moral responsibility for the problem. The legal implication is that even if there is obsolesce, after such a long period, for those who committed a deed which is described as a crime against humanity, the deed itself is still a crime for which nobody ever was brought to justice. The moral implication is that indeed the Jewish State was born out of sin – like many other states of course – but the sin, or the crime, was never admitted. Worse, among certain circles in

Israel the sin is acknowledged, but in the same breath, is fully justified in hindsight and affirmed as a future policy against the Palestinians, wherever they are.

However, all these implications were totally ignored by the Israeli political elite and, instead, a very different lesson was derived from the 1948 events: as a state, Israel could expel half of Palestine's population, destroy half of its villages and get away with these actions without a scratch or criticism. The consequence of such a lesson was inevitable – continuation of the ethnic cleansing policy by other means. There are quite well-known landmarks in this process, including the expulsion of tens of villages between 1948 and 1956 from Israel proper; the forced transfer of 300,000 Palestinians from the West Bank and the Gaza Strip and a very measured, but constant, cleansing from the Greater Jerusalem area.

As long as the political lesson is not learned, there will be no solution for the Israeli-Palestinian conflict. The issue of the refugees will repeatedly cause the failure of any attempt, successful as it may be in any other parameters, to reconcile the two conflicting parties. This is why it is so important to recognize the 1948 events as an ethnic cleansing operation, so as to ensure that a political solution will not evade the root of the conflict; namely the expulsion of the Palestinians. Such evasions in the past are the main reason for the collapse of all the previous peace accords.

As long as the legal lesson is not learned, there will always remain retributive impulses and revengeful emotions on the Palestinian side. The legal recognition of the 1948 *Nakba* as an act of ethnic cleansing would enable a restitutive justice. This is the process that has taken place recently in South Africa. The acknowledgement of past evils is not done in order to bring criminals to justice but rather in order to bring the crime itself to public attention and trial. The final ruling there will not be retributive – there will be no punishment – but rather restitutive: the victims will be compensated. The most reasonable compensation in the particular case of the Palestinian refugees was stated clearly in December 1948 by the UN General Assembly in its Resolution 194: the unconditional return of the refugees and their families to their homeland (and homes where possible).

As long as the moral lesson is not learned, the state of Israel will continue to exist as a hostile enclave at the heart of the Arab world. It will remain the last reminder of the colonialist past which complicates not only Israeli relationships with the Palestinians, but with the Arab world as a whole. And very importantly, because the moral lesson has not been taken in, today in Israel there are both a hindsight justification for the past ethnic cleansing and a real danger of yet another attempt to bring it about more completely.

When and how can we hope for these lessons to be learned and to be absorbed into the efforts to bring peace and reconciliation in Palestine? First, of course, not much can be expected to happen as long as the present brutal phase of the Occupation of the West Bank and the Gaza Strip continues. And yet alongside the struggle against the Occupation – with the positive development of the BDS (Boycott, Divestment and Sanctions) option being adopted as the main strategy put forward by the civil society in the occupied territories as well as by supportive international movements – the effort to locate the 1948 ethnic cleansing at the center of the world's attention and consciousness must continue.

The work can not be limited to one place. Unfortunately, the place where the ethnic cleansing of 1948 occurred – Israel of today – is almost totally excluded from this enterprise. The work inside the land of the *Nakba* should be coordinated and included in the overall effort wherever there are Palestinians and those who support them. With the help of Badil and other organizations, including leading Palestinian NGOs, the internal refugees inside Israel have begun to cooperate with a group of Jewish activists. Their goal is to initiate a serious attempt to bring to public attention the historic and ongoing ethnic cleansing and to argue forcefully and without any hesitation for the implementation of the Palestinian right of return.

In two conferences supporting the right of return, Palestinian and Jewish researchers and activists aired in public their findings about the ethnic cleansing from 1948 until today. They presented their ideas on how best to move forward in educating public opinion about the disastrous implications – for Palestinians and Jews alike, indeed for the world at large – for the continued denial of the 1948 ethnic cleansings and the refusal to accept the internationally recognized Right of Return.

On the 59th anniversary and in preparation for the 60th anniversary of the founding of the modern state of Israel, we – Palestinians, Israelis and whoever cares for this land – should demand that the 1948 crime against humanity be included in everyone's history books and that, before it is too late, there be a worldwide campaign to prevent the present crimes from continuing.

MEMORY AGAINST FORGETTING:
THE CHURCH AND THE END(S)
OF PALESTINIAN REFUGEE RIGHTS

Alain Epp Weaver

Milan Kundera, in his novel, *The Book of Laughter and Forgetting*, writes that "the struggle of people against power is the struggle of memory against forgetting." In contexts where the victors seek to erase the textual and material traces of the vanquished and to obscure the bloody means by which victory was obtained, acts of memory can become political acts, disturbing and challenging dominant narratives. Thus, when Palestinians make pilgrimage to the ruins of their ancestral homes in places such as Bir'am, Mujaydil, and Suhmata, walking around the remaining stones and narrating the life of the village and its destruction by the Israeli military, they re-create landscapes from which Palestinian presence has been removed, and name as a *Nakba*, or catastrophe, what prevailing Israeli narratives call redemption. Or when communities of Palestinian refugees in Lebanon, Syria, Jordan, or elsewhere in the Diaspora compile "memory books" for their villages, collecting the history and folklore of places like Ein Hawd, Beit 'Itab, or Lifta, they put the more than 500 destroyed Palestinian towns and villages back on the map, thus sustaining the hope that exile will not be forever, that the day of return will not be postponed indefinitely. These acts of memory are embodiments of what the German Jewish thinker Walter Benjamin termed the historian's task of brushing against the grain of history, of disturbing the tapestry of official accounts and state narratives in pursuit of silenced lives and voices; the historian's vocation is thus a political vocation, to be an agent of memory against forgetting.

My goal in this paper is to examine how Western churches have related to the desire of Palestinian refugees, both Christian and Muslim, to return home. One thesis will be that Western churches, by maintaining a strange silence concerning Palestinian refugees and by refusing to undertake a theological engagement with and critique of Zionism, are complicit with those who would put an end to the Palestinian refugee issue, to Palestinian refugee rights, by a simple denial of Palestinian rights of return and restitution. After examining the reasons for this silence, I'll then discuss why the church should be concerned about the end, as in the *telos*, or the goal, of Palestinian refugee rights.

In describing Western Christian approaches to the Palestinian-Israeli conflict, the simple thing to do would be to contrast two phenomena. On the one hand, one has Christian Zionism, with its luminaries, political action committees, and pop culture, all informed by a particular theology that reads the biblical story as pointing towards an apocalyptic end of history in which the founding of the State of Israel and the in-gathering of the exiled Jewish people play decisive roles in precipitating the last battle of Armageddon in which Satan is decisively defeated. Not surprisingly, Palestinian aspirations and rights are at best irrelevant in such a theological vision; at worst, Palestinians are obstacles to apocalyptic triumph, obstacles to be removed.

To Christian Zionism one could contrast efforts by various Christian bodies to explore "selective divestment" as a tool to pressure Israel to end its military occupation. These Western churches have ties to the Palestinian church and have been moved by their Palestinian co-religionists to work for justice. Or one could contrast Christian Zionism with the efforts of an ecumenical advocacy organization such as Churches for Middle East Peace (CMEP), which comprises a variety of Protestant, Catholic, and Orthodox bodies: while Christian Zionists insist that all of Palestine is the exclusive patrimony of the Jewish people, CMEP advocates for an end to occupation and a just two-state resolution of the Palestinian-Israeli conflict (although CMEP, unlike some of its member churches, has assiduously avoided association with divestment initiatives, perhaps fearing that promotion of such initiatives would harm CMEP's effectiveness in its "inside-the-Beltway" context).

This contrast, however, would fail to get at root questions that Western churches need to address. In comparison to the lurid and arguably heretical theology of Christian Zionism, the lobbying of Christian groups like CMEP for an end to occupation and in favor of a two-state solution, and the tentative engagement of Christian churches with divestment initiatives, are of course preferable. What is missing from CMEP advocacy work or from much of the tentative talk in church circles about divestment, however, is any sustained discussion of Palestinian refugees. For churches captivated by dispensationalist theologies for which Zionism and the founding of the State of Israel represent key events in the unfolding of apocalyptic scenarios, Palestinian refugees do not represent a particular moral problem; like all Palestinians, they are viewed as interlopers onto and usurpers of the territory rightly belonging to the Jewish people. For the so-called mainline churches, however, those churches that have been engaged in various forms of peace advocacy related to the Palestinian-Israeli conflict, Palestinian refugees do represent a problem, for their very existence raises questions and issues that Western churches would rather avoid. One finds precious little mention of Palestinian refugees, let alone refugee rights of return and restitution, in CMEP's writings or in the Middle East resolutions of mainline Protestant churches. The reasons for this omission are various, but I would suggest that a fundamental reason is that facing the Palestinian refugee issue forces the church to determine what it thinks about Zionism and about Israel as a Jewish state.[1]

Support for a two-state solution is comfortable for many Western churches, because it allows them to say: "We affirm Israel's right to exist, we affirm Israel's legitimacy as a Jewish state, we're simply against the occupation." Calls to end the occupation fit easily into this framework; advocacy for refugee rights complicates the picture. Palestinian refugees thus fade from view (as do Palestinians inside Israel).

Two recent statements arising from Christian-Jewish dialogue initiatives exemplify the reticence of Western churches to undertake a thoroughgoing critique of Zionism. One comes from a Catholic-Jewish conference held in Buenos Aires in July 2004; the other is a May 2005 report emerging from a

---

[1] A point of nuance is in order here. CMEP and, for the most part, the mainline churches, are on record as officially endorsing the right of return of Palestinian refugees. The churches' uncritical embrace of the rhetoric of the two-state solution, however, time and again means that refugee rights are de-emphasized or qualified, Geneva Initiative-style, by a virtual affirmation of an abstract "right" of return coupled with a contention that any concrete realization of that right would be severely restricted. To the extent that the churches respond to the call of Palestinian civil society to engage in boycott, divestment, and sanctions (BDS) initiatives, grappling with the refugee issue will become urgent, and unquestioned commitment to a two-state solution will come into question. After all, the Palestinian civil society call for BDS explicitly names refugee return as one of the major goals of the campaign.

series of Jewish-Protestant conversations at the University of Chicago.[2] Both statements follow the same line of reasoning: to question Israel's military occupation, with its attendant human rights abuses, might be legitimate, but what falls beyond the pale of acceptable criticism are questions concerning the justice of the State of Israel's founding or about the Zionist project of establishing and maintaining a Jewish state. The Buenos Aires statement declares a "rejection of anti-Semitism in all its forms, including anti-Zionism as a more recent manifestation of anti-Semitism." The report emerging from the conversations at the University of Chicago cautions that "those who criticize Israeli policies should take care to ensure that such criticism not threaten Judaism, the Jewish people, or the legitimacy of the State of Israel." The Christian participants in the Chicago dialogue–whose liberal theological orientation is far removed from the fundamentalist orientation of Christian Zionism–proceed to affirm as an "act of justice the establishment of a Jewish state after two thousand years of Jewish exile, wandering, and homelessness." The document thus draws on biblical imagery concerning the pain and anguish of exile, affirming the "Jewish state" as the antidote to homelessness. Such an approach both mirrors the standard Zionist "negation of the diaspora" (*shelilat ha-galut*) and appears to assume without question that the only political alternative to "exile" is exclusivist, nationalist sovereignty.

Both statements thus warn that critiques of Zionism and of the "legitimacy of the State of Israel" are akin to anti-Semitism. While "anti-Zionism" is left undefined, Zionism is implicitly defined by these statements as the movement to establish "a Jewish state," so anti-Zionism must therefore be understood to be a theological or political position that at least questions if not opposes the justice of establishing and maintaining a "Jewish state." Recognizing the State of Israel's "legitimacy" is bound up, from this perspective, with recognizing it as a "Jewish state." A reader of these documents is left with the understanding that Christians, while they might criticize particular Israeli policies or actions, should affirm Zionism and recognize the justice of "the establishment of a Jewish state."

---

[2] The "Joint Declaration" of the 18th International Catholic-Jewish Liaison Committee Meeting can be found at http://www.vatican.va/roman_curia/pontifical_councils/chrstuni/relations-jews-docs/rc_pc_chrstuni_doc_20040708_declaration-buenos-aires_en.html. The Chicago document, "What We've Learned from Each Other: A Report on a Jewish-Protestant Conversation about the Israel-Palestinian Conflict," can be accessed at http://divinity.uchicago.edu/news/spring_2005/jewish-protestant_conversation.pdf.

What "Jewish state" means in these types of claims is often left undefined and ambiguous, the key issues at stake unarticulated. The key issue that often goes unstated in these claims is demography. In contemporary Israeli political discourse, the question of the Jewishness of the Israeli state is repeatedly tied to questions of demography. Proponents of the "disengagement" plan and of the Wall argue that "separation" from Palestinians is required in order to project Israel's Jewish majority from the demographic threat represented by Palestinians in the Occupied Territories. Israeli officials, meanwhile, when arguing against Palestinian refugee return, routinely describe calls to allow refugee return as attacks on Israel's character as a "Jewish state." Israel's identity as a Jewish state, on the terms of this political discourse, was and is thus tied to creating and maintaining a Jewish demographic majority within particular territorial boundaries.

This project, many Israeli demographers warn, is under threat. Haifa University demographer Arnon Soffer has been the most prominent of many Israeli voices warning of demographic disaster for Israeli Jews. The number of Palestinians between the Jordan River and the Mediterranean Sea (that is, in both Israel and the Occupied Territories, or the boundaries of British Mandate Palestine), Soffer has warned, will equal the number of Jews in that land by 2010. Israeli politicians from across the political spectrum view this demographic reality with alarm. Israeli public-opinion researchers Ephraim Yaar and Tamar Hermann have found that "the strong desire for a separation, even a unilateral one, is connected to a fear among the overwhelming majority of the Jewish public regarding the emergence of a de facto bi-national state." The fear of an emerging bi-national reality has been put most pointedly by Israeli Labor politician Avraham Burg. "I am not afraid of weapons and terrorism," Burg notes. "I am afraid of the day that of all them [Palestinians] will put their weapons down and say 'One man, one vote.'"

Demographic fears, coupled with a commitment to Zionism understood in terms of a linkage of demographic hegemony and territorial control, explain why nearly all Israeli Jewish politicians concur in rejecting any significant return of Palestinian refugees to homes and properties inside Israel, arguing that this would threaten the Jewish character of Israel. That the PLO has continued to call (at least on paper) for Palestinian refugees to be allowed to return to their homes and properties if they so choose has been taken as a sign that the Palestinians reject Israel as a state. It is not sufficient, the argument goes, to recognize Israel (as the PLO did in the Oslo accords); one must recognize Israel as a **Jewish** state, its right to maintain a Jewish majority.

If "Jewish state" and Zionism are understood as projects to create and maintain demographic and political hegemony over a particular territory, then the following conclusions would flow from the Chicago and Buenos Aires critiques of anti-Zionism and affirmations of the "justice" of Israel as a "Jewish state." First, the expulsion of hundreds of thousands of Palestinians (Christians and Muslims) from their homes and villages in 1948 was, if tragic, also necessary. If Zionism meant creating a state with a Jewish majority in historical Palestine, and if one affirms Zionism as a just vision, then one must view some form of "transfer" of Palestinians from their homes as imperative, even just. Second, it follows that any return of these Palestinian refugees that would undermine this Jewish majority must be prevented. The logic of the Chicago and Buenos Aires documents thus falls in line with the Israeli characterization of calls for refugee return as anti-Semitic threats to Israel's Jewish identity.

Western churches need to question this logic which links the Jewishness of Israel to exclusivist discourses of demographic and territorial control. Part of breaking this logic would mean for the churches to become much more vocal than they have been regarding support for the rights of Palestinian refugees. Such support will mean being prepared for the charge that one is anti-Semitic for supporting refugee return: by supporting refugee return, the argument will go, one opposes Israel as a Jewish state, and this is equivalent to anti-Semitism. Such charges are, of course, frustrating and painful in their unfairness, but this frustration and pain do not, to my mind, constitute reasons for avoiding a critique of Zionism or for being quiet about the rights of Palestinian refugees. However, even if the Western churches continue to ignore Palestinian refugees, realities on the ground will make a critical examination of Zionism more difficult to avoid. Championing the two-state solution has, one could argue, allowed mainline churches to avoid a serious evaluation of Zionism as an ideology and a practice. The two-state solution appeals to liberalism's sense of fairness: there are two peoples, so there should be two states. It also appeals to the Christian concern for reconciliation: when the two peoples each have their own states, the logic goes, enmity will be transformed first into good neighborliness and then into friendship. The unilateral separation plan, however, writes the epitaph for a two-state solution based on the 1949 Armistice Line and shows how the State of Israel has effectively hijacked the rhetoric of the "two-state solution" to create an apartheid reality in the Occupied Territories. With the demise of the two-state solution, Western churches serious about working for a future of landed security for

Palestinians and Israelis alike will have to move beyond advocacy for two states towards advocacy for the dismantling of discriminatory laws and institutions throughout Palestine/Israel, including the dismantling of the legal and political structures that prevent refugees from returning home.

For Christians, rights are not ultimately ends in themselves. Rather, they make sense within a teleological framework, within, that is, a vision of the broader political good to be nurtured and developed through the securing and implementation of these rights. The political *telos* towards which Christian action should be directed is a holistic vision of reconciliation in the context of landed security. This vision is captured well by two portions of Scripture: first, the prophet Micah's vision of a day in which God's people will live secure under vine and fig tree, with no one to make them afraid (Micah 4:4); and second, the proclamation by the writer of Ephesians that in Christ Jesus the dividing wall of hostility between Jew and Gentile has been broken down (Eph 2:15). Christian concern about refugee rights is not about retribution and not even solely about restitution – rather, Christian concern about Palestinian refugee rights is driven by a concern for future Palestinian-Israeli reconciliation.

After the horrors of the Shoah, it is understandable that the idea of Israel as a safe haven with a Jewish majority would be so important to many Jews. But must such a safe haven be tied to a project of maintaining and protecting a Jewish majority by any and all means? Might not a bi-national future in one state be one in which Palestinians and Israelis alike both sit securely under vine and fig tree? Such questions, as difficult and sensitive as they may be, will prove unavoidable in future Jewish-Christian conversation.

STRATEGIC DIMENSIONS OF ISRAEL'S UNILATERAL SEGREGATION PLANS IN THE OCCUPIED PALESTINIAN TERRITORIES

Jad Isaac

In June 2002, the Israeli government began implementing its policy of unilateral segregation between Israel and the Occupied Palestinian Territories (OPT) by creating a Separation Zone in the western part of the West Bank. The Separation Zone runs from north to south in the West Bank, grabbing the most fertile agricultural lands, isolating Palestinian communities into enclaves, undermining territorial contiguity between the Palestinian villages and cities, taking control of the natural resources, and annexing most of the Israeli settlements.

What Israel is implementing in the OPT is known as the Apartheid or Separation Wall, which takes two forms. The first and most prevalent consists of a 40-100 meter wide double-layered solid fence complex comprised of barbed wire, trenches, military roads and footprint detection tracks, as well as a 4-5 meter high electrified metal fence with security control cameras. The other form, in densely populated areas or those near the Green Line, consists of a concrete wall 6-8 meters high and 30-40 meters wide with military watchtowers 250 meters apart. Attempting to legitimize the route of the Apartheid Wall in the West Bank and ignoring the decision of the International Court of Justice (ICJ) issued on 9 July 2004, Israel made minor changes "for humanitarian reasons" in the path of the Wall rather than dismantling the structure and compensating those affected. The last amendment, announced 30 April 2006, focused on the path of the Wall in areas that create obstacles to Israel's expansion. Changes made in the route of the Wall since the commencement of its construction are shown in the table:

Table No. (1): Amendments made in the Route of the Apartheid Wall

Date	Area taken out in favor of the Wall	% of the West Bank's Area	Wall Length	On the Green Line
June 2002	1,024 km²	18%	734 km	—
June 2004	633 km²	11.7%	645 km with some exceptions	83 km
February 2005	565 km²	10%	683 km	138 km
April 2006	555 km²	9.8%	703 km	128 km

Source: Geographical Information System Unit - Applied Research Institute of Jerusalem (ARIJ)

Amendments made in the route of the Apartheid Wall aim primarily at serving, annexing and absorbing the Israeli settlements despite the negative psychological, economic, and social impact on the Palestinian people and despite the fact that they constitute grave violations of international law.

In the final plan, the Apartheid Wall will extend 703 kilometers from north to south, of which only 128 kilometers (18.2% of the total) are located on the Green Line. Upon completion, the Wall will append to Israel an area of 555 km² (9.8% of the total area of 5,661 km² in the West Bank) and annex some ninety-nine Israeli settlements, with a total population of 37,500, while isolating approximately 60 Palestinian localities with a total population of 90,000 Palestinians.

A follow-up study of the status of the route of the Wall by the Applied Research Institute of Jerusalem (ARIJ) disclosed that the Israeli occupying forces have completed construction of 307 kilometers of the Wall in the West Bank, 91 kilometers are under construction, and 305 kilometers are planned for completion by the end of 2007 as shown:

Table No. (2): Status of the Apartheid Wall in the West Bank

Apartheid Wall	Length (km)	% of the Total Wall Length
Existing Wall	307	43.7%
Planned to be built	305	43.4%
Under construction	91	12.9%
Total Wall Length	703	100%

Source: Geographical Information System Unit - Applied Research Institute of Jerusalem (ARIJ)

In September 2004, the Israeli Ministry of Defense issued new military orders for the creation of a Buffer Zone with a depth ranging from 150 to 200 meters on the eastern (Palestinian) side of the Wall, precluding all new construction and making an additional 252 km^2 (4.4%) of the total area of the West Bank (5,661 km^2) inaccessible to Palestinians.

THE EASTERN SEGREGATION ZONE: THE JORDAN VALLEY

Besides seizing land for the Wall, Israel has made the Jordan Valley part of its security and settlement expansion plans. This policy has negatively impacted the land and people of the Jordan Valley since 1967 as Israel has continuously supported construction of settlements there. Successive Israeli governments have consistently enforced this major policy of control and have declared large areas of Palestinian lands as "closed military areas" to which Palestinians are denied access for agricultural, housing and other economic purposes.

Following the closure of the Jordan Valley, Israel issued Military Order Number 378 on October 2, 2003, declaring the "Seam Zone" behind the Wall a closed area in which the only Palestinians allowed to enter are those over age 16 with proven residency. Such persons had to apply for special permits to remain in the area and were allowed to enter and exit only at specified passages. Further military orders give the process by which long-term residents over age 12 can obtain a permit and by which non-residents with special reason to enter the Separation Zone can apply for permits to enter at specific "control points."

After the order was issued, former Israeli Prime Minister Ariel Sharon said, "I do not envision a Wall as necessary in the eastern area. We will prevent access to the eastern zone by erecting military checkpoints." There are now 25 at the main entrances connecting the Jordan Valley to the West Bank and at the roads connecting Palestinian communities inside the Jordan Valley with each other. Israel's closure policy and the erection of military checkpoints in the Jordan Valley are integral parts of its segregation policy, aimed at strangling and forcing Palestinian citizens to leave, and set in motion the plan for full Israeli control of the area and of passages to the western Segregation Zone.

The Jordan Valley or eastern Segregation Zone represents 29.4% (1,664 km²) of the total area of the West Bank. Some forty-two Israeli settlements with a total population of more than 12,000 Jewish settlers have been established in an area totaling 38 km² (2.3% of the total area of the eastern Segregation Zone) in addition to Israeli military camps. According to the Palestinian Central Bureau of Statistics, over 52,000 Palestinians live in 42 Palestinian localities in the Jordan Valley. The following table shows the land distribution of the area:

Nature of Land Utilization - 2002	Area in km²	% of the Total Area of the Eastern Segregation Zone
Israeli Military Camps	30.80	2%
Israeli Settlements	34.97	2%
Palestinian Residential Areas	10.48	1%
Agricultural Land	863.88	52%
Forests & Natural Reserves	721.00	43%
Limited Surface Water	0.69	0.04%
Excavations & Quarries	2.23	0.13%
Total	1,664.05	100%

Source: Geographical Information System Unit - ARIJ Institute, 2005

ISRAELI BYPASS ROADS & PROPOSED ALTERNATIVE ROADS

Israel has intensified its colonization activities in the West Bank & Gaza Strip over decades of Occupation. Approximately, 80 km² (1.4%) of the West Bank have been taken to build a network of bypass roads (around 795 km) that fragment and isolate Palestinian communities. Additionally, the Israeli army creates so-called "Buffer Zones" of approximately 75 meters on either side of each road, thereby confiscating more land.

The term "Bypass Roads" emerged with the signing of the Oslo Agreement between the Israelis and Palestinians in September 1993 to indicate roads built by the Israelis in the OPT to connect Israeli settlements with Israel and Israeli military camps in the West Bank as well as connecting settlements to one another. There are three types of Israeli bypass roads:

- Roads for exclusive Israeli use, which Palestinians are completely prohibited from using;
- Roads which Palestinians are allowed to use with special permits issued by the Israeli Civil Administration;
- Roads which Palestinians can use but which are subject to military checkpoints at their entrances.

Israeli bypass roads are part of a racist segregation plan which Israel seeks to impose in the OPT. Since the beginning of the First Intifada in 1987, Israel has imposed strict restrictions on the movement of Palestinians in various ways:

- Imposing full closure on the OPT and preventing movement of Palestinians into Israel for work except with special entry permits;
- Imposing curfews that prevent people from leaving their houses in a particular town or village;
- Closing roads leading to a particular town or village by erecting iron barriers, cement blocks, or earth-mounds or trenches, thus violating international rights and conventions, such as article (13) of the Universal Declaration of Human Rights which states that everyone has the right to freedom of movement and residence within the borders of each state.

Furthermore, Article (12) of the International Covenant on Civil & Political Rights (ICCPR) states:

- Everyone lawfully within the territory of a State shall, within that territory, have the right to liberty of movement and freedom to choose his residence;

- Everyone shall be free to leave any country, including his own;
- The above-mentioned rights shall not be subject to any restrictions except those which are provided by law, are necessary to protect national security, public order, public health or morals or the rights and freedoms of others, and are consistent with the other rights recognized in the present Covenant;
- No one shall be arbitrarily deprived of the right to enter his own country

The right to freedom of movement is an important condition on which other conditions are based and which are stated in other international covenants such as the International Covenant on Economic, Social & Cultural Rights (ICESCR) which stipulates:

- Article (6) the right of everyone to work;
- Article (10) the right of everyone to protection and assistance;
- Article (11) the right of everyone to an adequate standard of living for himself and his family, including adequate food, clothing and housing, and to the continuous improvement of living conditions;
- Article (12) the right of everyone to the enjoyment of the highest attainable standard of physical and mental health;
- Article (13) the right of everyone to education.

ISRAEL'S VISION IN THE OCCUPIED PALESTINIAN TERRITORIES

Proposed Alternative Roads:

On October 28, 2004, Israel disclosed plans to complete connections of Israeli settlements to each other by building a network of alternative roads designated especially for Palestinians. These roads - 500 km in length - are side roads of inferior quality with limited capacity for traffic and situated in such a way as to deny Palestinian use of Israeli bypass roads. These alternative roads are part of Israel's unilateral segregation plan in the OPT, built under the pretext of protecting Israeli citizens. In addition to building a network of alternative roads, Israel has built 18 underground tunnels and passage ways costing, according to the Israeli government, approximately $1,581,000. Israel seeks to mobilize support from the EU and the US to fund these plans, thereby gaining international legitimacy for its undertaking.

As a follow-up to the segregation plans in the West Bank, Israel issued on December 15, 2005, a military order "regarding closed areas - Judea & Samaria (no. 34) 5727 – 1967." It prohibits "non-Israelis" from the West Bank from entering or leaving Israel except through border crossing points currently being created by Israel. A number of crossing points have already been established. The order explicitly exempts Israeli citizens and all soldiers and security forces. An Israeli citizen is defined as anyone who has the right to immigrate to Israel in accordance with the Law of Return 5710 – 1950, which explicitly excludes non-Jewish citizens.

Palestinian residents of the West Bank who have a valid permit to enter Israel are prohibited from using the Israeli bypass roads. Furthermore, Israelis are prohibited from using the bypass roads to transport "non-Israelis," even those who have valid permits.

Israeli Border Crossing Points

In December 2004, Israel declared its intention of establishing ten border crossing points and 23 secondary crossings along the route of the Apartheid Wall, replacing Israeli military checkpoints erected at the entrances of the Palestinian cities and villages. The aim of these Israeli crossings, according to the Israeli government, is to improve the humanitarian conditions of Palestinians by reducing the contact of Palestinians with Israeli soldiers at the checkpoints.

The Israeli government's decision to establish border crossings has a number of political implications. The most important reason to establish border crossings along the path of the Wall, particularly around the city of Jerusalem, is to define the final borderline between Jerusalem and the West Bank as well as between Israel and the OPT. Israel has thus unilaterally redrawn the Green Line established by the United Nations in 1949.

Settlement Expansion and Construction of Thousands of Housing Units

ARIJ's analysis of satellite pictures and field activity reveal that Israel has carried out recent settlement expansion throughout the West Bank that differs from previous expansion by increasing the number of housing units in settlements west of the Apartheid Wall. During 2002 and 2004, Israel established 32,632 housing units in 58 Israeli settlements in the West Bank, of which 26,816 units lie in 30 Israeli settlements situated west of the Apartheid Wall. In addition, 720 new housing units were built in 10 settlements across the Jordan Valley, and 5,096 units were built in 18 settlements in the central area of the West Bank.

This analysis shows that the East Jerusalem and Bethlehem settlements, which are part of Israel's 'Greater Jerusalem' Plan and include the settlement clusters of Ma'ale Adumim, Gush Etzion, Giv'at Ze'ev, and Binyamin, have witnessed the largest amount of expansion and construction. More than 15,400 new housing units were added to East Jerusalem's settlements (constituting 47% of the total housing units in the West Bank), and 10,500 new housing units were added to the Bethlehem settlements (constituting 32% of the total housing units in the West Bank).

3,550 of the 4,000 housing units constructed in 2005 in the West Bank fell west of the Apartheid Wall, accounting for 89% of the new construction. This clearly strengthens Israeli settlements west of the Wall and places them de facto within the planned final borders of Israel. The increase in the number of housing units in the western settlements thus is a preliminary step for receiving settlers to be evacuated from areas between the western Segregation Wall and the eastern Segregation Zone. As for activities in the settlements due to be evacuated, Israel intends to strike a bargain in which settlers depart from the internal settlements in exchange for Palestinian acceptance of the Apartheid Wall as the border of the state of Israel.

Israeli Settlement Outposts

1996 witnessed the launching of the first Israeli settlement outpost in the West Bank with indirect support of the Israeli government and the backing of Ariel Sharon, who later became Prime Minister of Israel. He repeatedly called on settlers to take elevated Palestinian lands close to existing settlements. Outposts help to deter criticism of Israel's settlement policy in the OPT as Israel from time to time dismantles an outpost. However, new outposts, supported by the Israeli Finance and the Infrastructure Ministries which provide electricity and water, are rampant in the Palestinian territories.

The Geographical Information System Unit (GIS) at ARIJ confirms that 217 outposts were established between 1996 and 2005: 158 outposts in random locations in the West Bank and 59 settlement outposts within the boundaries of existing settlements.

The Roadmap called for removal of the outposts, particularly those established after March 2001. However, Israel tried to legitimize them through the Sasson Report, which concluded that one-third of the existing outposts were illegal (did not have government approval); the second third were unclassified (had been transferred to settlers after being evacuated by the army); the final third were government approved. The government expressed willingness to dismantle only the third considered illegal and declared the others valid, although article (49) of the Fourth Geneva Convention of 1949 stipulates the illegality of transferring the citizens of the occupying state into occupied territory. Peace agreements between the Israelis and the Palestinians also call for the cessation of all forms of settlement activity in the OPT, the dismantlement of outposts, and the restoration of land to its Palestinian owners.

Annexation of Large Settlement Blocs to Israel

Israel has often sought to implement its plans unilaterally. It considered the concessions made in the West Bank and Gaza Strip as giving up its legitimate rights in Palestine. Since 1993, Israel has unilaterally and deliberately made geographical changes on the ground, in violation of agreements that neither Israelis nor Palestinians should initiate any step that might affect the final status issues: Jerusalem, settlements, borders, water and refugees. Israel has continued its settlement activities in the West Bank and Jerusalem, imposed new political borders with the Apartheid Wall by incorporating large areas of Palestinian land, annexed groundwater resources in the West Bank, and renounced the right of Palestinian refugees to return to their homeland. The withdrawal from Gaza is another example of unilateralism, which is often supported internationally.

In 2005, the Israeli government proposed a draft law which would annex to Israel large settlement blocs, including Ma'ale Adumim, Ariel, Giv'at Ze'ev, Gush Etzion and Modi'in Ilit, by including their land inside the Wall and making them an integral part of the state of Israel. As former Israeli Prime Minister Sharon said to President George Bush on April 11, 2005, this action was a "good decision for maintaining its security, its political status, its economy, and the demography of the Jewish people in 'the land of Israel.'" When the Apartheid Wall is completed in 2007 as planned, Israel will be able to incorporate these large settlement blocs with an approximate population of 150,000 settlers, as well as some 60 Israeli settlements located on the western side of the Wall, producing a total of 99 settlements annexed to Israel.

The 'Greater Jerusalem' Plan

The construction of the Apartheid Wall on large areas of the West Bank, especially around Jerusalem, the acceleration in the pace of settlement activities encircling the city with a series of Israeli settlements, and the construction of border crossings around the city are measures taken by Israel within the framework of its 'Greater Jerusalem' Plan. The Plan began in the early seventies when the Israeli government expanded the Israeli settlement area located outside the municipal boundaries of Jerusalem in order to connect the Israeli settlements in Jerusalem and, at the same time, to cut off Palestinian communities on the eastern side of Jerusalem from the city, thereby denying their residents the right of residence. The Plan includes four Israeli settlement blocs (Ma'ale Adumim, Giv'at Ze'ev, Gush Etzion & Binyamin) out of six which Israel seeks to annex.

The Israeli 'E1' Plan

Because of its location inside the boundaries of Jerusalem and its proximity to East Jerusalem, the Ma'ale Adumim settlement bloc is one of the most dangerous as it blocks contiguity between the northern and southern parts of the West Bank and isolates East Jerusalem from the West Bank, destroying the Palestinian people's aspirations to establish an independent state with Jerusalem as its capital. Given Ma'ale Adumim's proximity to East Jerusalem, the committee in charge of the route of the Wall developed a new "E1" plan which calls for:

- Building a new housing complex connecting the settlement to the heart of the city;
- Denying Palestinian villages and towns (Abu Dis, Al-Izzariyya, At-Tur, Al-Issawiyya & 'Anata) their historical rights to expand;
- Creating an Israeli housing belt that will block the geographical contiguity between the northern and southern parts of the West Bank.

The 'E1' Plan includes the construction of 3,500 new housing units northwest of Ma'ale Adumim settlement, on an area totaling 12,000 dunums (1 dunum= 1/4 acre).

The Sea Barrier in Gaza and the Security Zone

With the aim of strengthening Israel's control over the borders of the Palestinian area of the Gaza Strip, Israel deliberately expanded the scope of its siege to include Gaza's seashore. It extended the construction of the Wall along the northern borders of the Gaza Strip 950 meters into the Mediterranean Sea. The first 150 meters of the sea barrier consists of cement pillars embedded in the seabed, while the rest - 800 meters in length - consists of a floating security fence at a depth of 1.8 meters below water.

Israel also seeks to strengthen its control over the Israeli security belt stretching across the northern Gaza Strip, along the eastern borders (72 km), and ending at the Rafah border crossing in the south. Announced in December 2005, this plan creates a new security zone with an area of 8 km^2 in the northern part of the Gaza Strip in addition to the above-mentioned security belt, which cuts out 53 km^2 of Gaza's total area, leaving 61 km^2 of the Gaza Strip (16.7%) under Israeli control, despite Israel's alleged withdrawal from Gaza.

Sharon's Unilateral Segregation Plan

Former Israeli Prime Minister Ariel Sharon's vision, which was expressed fully and clearly in the Disengagement or "Gaza Pull-Out Plan," was not surprising but consistent with positions declared over decades of Israeli occupation of the Palestinian territories. The Plan makes no mention of a Palestinian state but envisions Palestinian communities as islands isolated from each other, separated by Israeli-controlled areas. This makes the establishment of a "viable Palestinian state with geographical contiguity" impossible.

The Israeli Convergence Plan

Israel's Convergence Plan, the final stage of unilateralism, affirms the racist nature of the Israeli state. Its primary goal is to preserve and maintain an Israeli state with a Jewish majority regardless of the methods and approaches required to achieve this goal.

The Apartheid Wall constitutes one key factor for ensuring the Jewish identity of the state of Israel. In addition to stealing and annexing to Israel 555 km² (9.8%) of the Occupied West Bank, the Wall will annex to the Israeli side the largest settlement blocs in the West Bank as well as in Occupied East Jerusalem, with its population of 230,000 Jewish settlers. This annexation confirms Israel's plan for the 'unification of Jerusalem' which was originally issued in 1981 but rejected internationally.

In addition, Israel's Convergence Plan seeks to strengthen the presence of the Israeli army along the Jordan Valley by enhancing agricultural settlements and tightening the Israeli army control over all the roads leading to the Jordan Valley. The Israeli army has erected scores of military checkpoints along the Jordan Valley which isolate the valley from the rest of the West Bank. Restricted movement of people and goods around Israeli areas in the Valley and West Bank also increase the possibility of arrest and detention by the Israeli army.

The Israeli Convergence Plan claims that movement of Palestinians between the Gaza Strip and the Palestinian-controlled areas in the West Bank will be through a "safe passage," but the Israeli army will retain security control of the roads and of movement procedures between the two. Thus, the Convergence Plan is a violation of all peace agreements signed between the Israelis and the Palestinians from 1993-1999, each of which stipulates that the status of the Gaza Strip and the West Bank cannot unilaterally be changed or freedom of movement between the two be curtailed.

The Broad Outlines of Israel's Strategy in the OPT

The Israeli government's strategy has made clear to everyone that it never sought a just peace nor intended to restore the rights of Palestinians. Instead, Israel has implemented facts consistent with its strategic vision:

- Substituting conflict management for long-term solutions to the conflict while pursuing its greedy goals;
- Substituting the concept of unilateral action for the principle of negotiation by declaring a lack of a suitable negotiating partner;
- Ignoring agreements stating that "none of the conflicting parties should impose facts on the ground with the aim of changing the outcomes of the conflict, including Occupied East Jerusalem" while steadily imposing such facts;

- Attempting to give international legitimacy to its plans in violation of the peace agreements signed with the Palestinians: unilateral withdrawal from the Gaza Strip, the construction of the Apartheid Wall, the annexation of large settlement blocs, and other measures;
- Adopting the "non-solution policy" for the conflict by creating false pretexts such as lack or non-compliance of a peace partner, maintaining the security of Israel, and Palestinian resistance to occupation;
- Destroying the Palestinian dream of establishing a viable, united, independent Palestinian state and replacing it with West Bank communities lacking geographical contiguity to each other and to the Gaza Strip, except through areas under Israeli security control;
- Refusing to acknowledge UN Security Council Resolutions 242 (1967), 338 (1973) & 478 (1980), which confirm that Israel's occupation of the West Bank and Gaza Strip and the annexation of East Jerusalem violate international law, and refusing to implement the international and humanitarian laws applicable to the OPT, such as the Fourth Geneva Convention of 1949;
- Retaining full control over the Palestinian economy, including the natural resources, by controlling the terrestrial, naval and aerial borders, and subjecting the Palestinian market to repressive laws and measures such as taxes, customs and restrictions.

Scenarios of the Israeli Plans
to Solve the Palestinian-Israeli Conflict

Israel's actions in the OPT provide a picture of its solution to the Israeli-Palestinian conflict: facts on the ground will determine the final solution. Four major scenarios suggest its vision:

Scenario 1: Palestinians will control 54.5% of the total area of the West Bank while Israelis will control the eastern Jordan Valley and the Segregation Zone west of the Apartheid Wall, in addition to five safe passages, three of which are located in the north of the West Bank, and two in the south of the West Bank, keeping East Jerusalem under the Israeli occupation. The Israeli government will dismantle 20 Israeli settlements, with a total population of 7,000 settlers.

Scenario 2: This is the same scenario except that it has four safe passages, increasing the Palestinian-controlled area to 56% of the West Bank and increasing the number of Israeli settlements to be dismantled to 25, with a total population of 8,000 settlers.

Scenario 3: This scenario is an extension of the previous one, eliminating another safe passage, increasing the Palestinian-controlled area to 57% of the West Bank and increasing the number of Israeli settlements to be dismantled to 29, with a total population of 10,500 settlers.

Scenario 4: This proposal differs from the others in that Palestinians will be given control over East Jerusalem, except for the settlement of Ma'ale Adumim and Israeli settlements within the municipal boundaries of Jerusalem. Palestinian-controlled areas increase to over 60% of the West Bank, including East Jerusalem for the first time.

It should be noted that none of the Israeli proposals include any reference to Palestinian control over the terrestrial border crossings, the safe passage leading to Gaza Strip, or the naval and aerial borders.

INTERNATIONAL LEGAL STATUS OF THE APARTHEID WALL

In July 2004, the International Court of Justice (ICJ) in The Hague provided its advisory opinion regarding the legality of the construction of the Apartheid Wall. In its opinion, the ICJ cited the rules and principles of international law, the Fourth Geneva Convention of 1949, the Hague Treaty, and a number of international human rights conventions and UN Security Council resolutions.

It found that the Apartheid Wall is a violation of human rights, especially the rights of self-determination, freedom of movement, labor, health, education, appropriate living standards, and visitation of holy places. The ICJ decision urges Palestinians to assert their rights, especially the right to self-determination, despite being deprived of practicing them as a result of Israel's construction of the Apartheid Wall. Furthermore, the court declared that Israel has no right to use such terms as "self-defense," "provide protection" and "security" to justify its violations of Palestinians' basic human rights and of international laws and conventions. It called for construction of the Apartheid Wall to cease and for other countries to stop supporting Israel's efforts. Finally, it declared that the establishment of the Segregation Zone is a violation of all peace agreements signed between the Israelis and the Palestinians, and a violation of Article 31, paragraph 7 of the Oslo Interim Agreement, which asserts that "Neither side shall initiate or take any step that will change the status of the West Bank & Gaza Strip pending the outcome of the final status negotiations."

CONCLUSION

What Israel has undertaken over the 40 years of its ongoing Occupation of the OPT disregards international law: its refusal to withdraw from the territories it occupied in 1967, its construction of settlements, its demolition of Palestinian houses, its restriction of Palestinians' freedom of movement, its violation of Palestinians' basic human rights to reach holy places, and its construction of the Apartheid Wall in the West Bank. These are an inevitable result of the failure of the international community to exert any form of pressure on Israel to abide by international law and UN Security Council resolutions.

The international community must insist upon the implementation of such resolutions, including Security Council Resolution no. 452 (1979), which calls on "the government and the people of Israel to cease the construction and establishment of Jewish settlements in Arab land occupied since 1967, including Jerusalem" and Security Council Resolution no. 446 (1979), which stipulates that "Israeli polices and measures with regard to establishing settlements in the OPT and other Arab land occupied since 1967 are not based on any legal foundation, and constitute a dangerous obstacle to achieving a just, comprehensive and lasting peace in the Middle East."

THE OPEN BETHLEHEM CAMPAIGN

Leila Sansour

The Open Bethlehem Campaign was launched in November 2005 to respond to the state of emergency in Bethlehem, and the context in which this campaign was created is very important to understand. From the beginning of the Oslo Agreements, the settlement building in Bethlehem has increased dramatically. These settlements are usually built on land confiscated from Bethlehemites, either from private owners or from municipal public property. Today the Bethlehem district is almost completely surrounded by these settlements, which occupy every hilltop and require the uprooting of thousands of trees, damaging the environment and depriving many local families of their main source of income.

The latest development in Bethlehem is the Wall. The route of the Wall splits Bethlehem into two separate ghettoes, the urban ghetto in the East and the agricultural ghetto in the West. Urban Bethlehem will have only two exit gates to the outside world, one of which can only be used by tourists while the other one will be used by us Bethlehemites. It will not be possible for local people to use this second gate unless they are granted permits by the Israeli authorities, but these are very difficult to obtain. We will also be connected to our outlying villages by a different set of gates with yet another system of permits, thus severely hampering exchange between the two territories.

The Wall already separates Bethlehem and Jerusalem, which have historically formed one single region and whose communities are totally interdependent when it comes to trade, social facilities, families and religious ties. The Wall confiscates most of Bethlehem's agricultural lands and landmarks and leaves the district with no room for expansion.

In the last few years Bethlehem has witnessed an unprecedented level of emigration. Members of the Christian community are the first to leave as they are the main beneficiaries of Bethlehem's tourist industry and have a long history of family ties and opportunities abroad. Reports warn that in a matter of one generation Bethlehem's Christian community might become unsustainable.

It was in response to all these grave developments on the ground that Open Bethlehem was created. We feel that we can still reverse the clock but only if we act decisively and if we act now. In short we have no time to lose. We know that the solution to our problem does not lie here. It is only through changing public opinion in the world, especially in countries that influence the political map, that a solution can be found. We also know that it is not enough to influence people's opinions; it is crucial to engage them proactively with our situation and to provide them with tools that will help them do advocacy work on our behalf.

So what do we do? Open Bethlehem is an international public relations campaign which aims to draw the world's attention to the plight of Bethlehem and through Bethlehem provide a doorway to the wider region. We work proactively with media, decision-makers and churches around the world to help them learn about our situation through very well-designed fact finding tours, advocacy kits and regular briefings. Visit our website *www.openbethlehem.org* to stay updated on the latest news from Bethlehem and to download our latest presentations.

Since our launch in 2005, Open Bethlehem has managed to generate more than 150 articles and TV reports and has hosted more than 70 fact finding tours for church groups, parliamentarians and academics. We have built an Open Bethlehem support group in the British parliament and inspired many people to bring events to our city to help us keep it open against all odds.

Open Bethlehem invites all people to join our efforts by sponsoring trips for their local politicians, journalists and church leaders to visit Bethlehem and see the situation on the ground. We also encourage aspiring tour leaders to get in touch to help shape new programs for pilgrims wishing to visit our city. For a very long time now, our tourist industry has been controlled by Israeli tour operators. This means that most of our visitors spend less than an hour in Bethlehem. They never get the chance to connect with our communities or explore all the spiritual and cultural experiences that Bethlehem has to offer. It also means that visitors never contribute to the local economy, which is suffering a dramatic decline. We are not asking the world for charity. By celebrating life with us, you can make history and help us save the heritage of a city that is sung by millions of people around the world.

Finally, I would like to introduce you to the idea of "the Bethlehem passport," an honorary citizenship of our city which was developed to coincide with our launch as a way of inviting all citizens of the world to take part in helping Bethlehem survive this critical moment in its history. The first Bethlehem passport was granted by our President Mahmoud Abbas to his Holiness Pope Benedict XVI. In 2007, Open Bethlehem will launch its passport program to the public. We hope that you will follow our news and that you will consider becoming one of us, a Bethlehemite.

The citation on the passport reads:

> In that the bearer of this passport is a citizen of Bethlehem: that they recognise this ancient city provides a light to the world and to all people who uphold the values of a just and open society; that they will remain a true friend of Bethlehem through its imprisonment, and they will strive to keep the ideals of Bethlehem alive as long as the wall stands; we ask you to respect the bearer of this passport and to let them pass freely.

LIVING TOGETHER:
THE EXPERIENCE OF MUSLIM-CHRISTIAN RELATIONS IN THE ARAB WORLD IN GENERAL AND IN PALESTINE IN PARTICULAR

Father Rafiq Khoury

Living together is the big issue of today during a phase of our human history in which our world has become a "small village" where it is no longer possible for any people to live apart, separate from other peoples. In that context, we are called today to reflect on Christian-Muslim relations in the Arab world in general and in Palestine in particular.

This issue is actually of particular importance now because Islam and the Muslims have unfortunately become a sort of obsession in the West, especially after September 11th, 2001. Such an obsession does not offer a sane atmosphere in which to develop positive relations among religions, peoples and cultures.

For us Christians in this part of the world, the Muslim is not an abstract or imaginary "thing," but a real and concrete person. Muslims are our next-door neighbors, the merchants where we shop, our colleagues at work, at school or in the university; we meet them routinely in political or economic or cultural or social life. They are for us concrete human beings, with their good qualities and defects, and we stand before them also with our good qualities and defects.

I would like to have a look at these relations in the past and in the present, before presenting some perspectives for the future.

EXPERIENCE OF THE PAST

When I was a child, there was always a Muslim in our home working with my father, sleeping, eating and praying in our house. We shared "bread and salt," as we say in Arabic, expressing the living together, the co-existence, of persons or communities. I am from a small village located to the north-east of Jerusalem, entirely Christian, a village surrounded by several Muslim villages; we shared the same language, the same social traditions, the same culture, the same way of life, working together in our fields, collecting our olives together, drinking the same water, smelling the same soil of the land and learning together. (In our parish school, a third of the students were from the Muslim village next door.)

Now, this personal and local experience is also a collective and historic one since it goes back thirteen centuries, with its ups and downs, as is the case with every human and collective experience.

On this occasion, I would like to focus on four elements of the past, which were definitive for both Arab Christianity and for Muslim-Christian relations in the Arab world:

- **The contribution of the Christians to the administration of the new state:** When Muslims arrived in our region, they appealed to the local Christians to help in the administration of the new state. Some of them reached very high and sensitive positions. The example of the Christian Mansour family of Damascus is well-known, since this family was called upon to organize the finances of the state in addition to serving in many other public fields. We can say that the Eastern Christians took the wise step of integrating themselves into the public life of the new society instead of remaining apart, isolated and living in the past.
- **The adoption of the Arabic language:** Several languages were used by the Christians of these areas, including Aramaic, Syriac, Chaldean, Coptic and Greek. But relatively soon, they all adopted the Arabic language in their daily life, in their liturgies, in their administration and in their religious literature. The Arabic language allowed these Christians to communicate among each other as well as with the surrounding new world which was arising.
- **The contribution to cultural life:** Eastern Christians translated major parts of the Hellenistic culture, especially philosophy, medicine, and the sciences, into Arabic. In that way they enabled the interaction between Arab-Muslim culture and the Hellenistic one and thereby contributed to the development of the formation of the Arab-Muslim culture, which became the most important one at that time. In addition to translation, they also produced results in these cultural fields. It was

very common, in that period, for a Muslim philosopher to be the disciple of a Christian one and vice versa (the case of Al-Farabi is well known).[1]

- **The formation of the Arab-Christian heritage:** Eastern Christians not only contributed to the formation of the Arab-Muslim culture but developed original Christian thought in Arabic in several religious fields. This heritage is actually being published in a collection entitled The Arab Christian Heritage.

All these factors were decisive in the formation of Arab Christianity as we know it today. This experience was summarized by the Eastern Catholic Patriarchs in these words: "We [Christians and Muslims] draw on a single heritage of civilization. Each of us has contributed to its formation according to his own genius....Christians of the East are an inseparable part of the cultural identity of Muslims. In the same way, Muslims of the East are an inseparable part of the cultural identity of Christians."[2]

Palestine was a part of that process. However, the peculiarity of the Palestinian experience was determined by further factors such as the geographical position of Palestine at the crossroads of three continents and the unique religious position of Palestine for the three monotheistic religions. In modern times, the nature of Muslim-Christian relations in Palestine has been profoundly determined by the tragic Palestinian experience, since Christian and Muslim Palestinians suffered together, were exiled together, fought together and share the same aspirations for the future. All these factors make Muslim-Christian relations in Palestine deeper than in any other part of the Arab world. That experience was summarized in the *Palestinian Declaration of Independence*, which mentions Palestine as "the land of the three monotheistic faiths," adding:

> Nourished by an unfolding series of civilizations and cultures, inspired by a heritage rich in variety and kind, the Palestinian Arab people added to its stature by consolidating a union between itself and its patrimonial Land. The call went out from Temple,

---

[1] The Royal Institute for Interfaith Studies, founded by Prince Hassan of Jordan, has started to edit a dictionary of all the Christian figures who contributed to the cultural life in that period, with a short biography of each of them. The first volume is already published, covering the first three letters of the alphabet, comprising 304 pages.

[2] *Common Pastoral Letter: The Christian Presence in the Middle East, Witness and Mission*, 1992, n. 48.

Church and Mosque that to praise the Creator, to celebrate
compassion and peace was indeed the message of Palestine....
Thus shall these principles allow no departure from Palestine's
age-old spiritual and civilizational heritage of tolerance and
religious co-existence.

When Christian-Muslim relations are studied, it must be within that
framework. Ups and downs have to be seen and considered in that context.
Otherwise, we misunderstand and deform reality.

THE SITUATION OF THE PRESENT

First and foremost, it has to be said that what happened in the past has happened
again in modern times. In the second part of the 19th century, a movement
called "The Arab Awakening" took place and constitutes the re-entry of the
Arabs into modern history. What has to be said here is that the Christians of
the Arab world not only took part in that renewal but were also the pioneers
of its cultural, economic and political life. This reality, which is still ongoing,
shows that the Arab Christians are an integral part of their societies.

However, at the same time, it also has to be said that in the past two
decades a number of events have occurred on the local, regional and
international levels which have deeply affected Muslim-Christian relations.
After the collapse of the Soviet Union, many politicians and strategists, in
search of a new enemy, started to develop the idea of the "clash of civilizations"
by looking at Islam as the number one enemy of the West. After September
11th 2001, this trend was deepened and transformed into action (the wars in
Afghanistan, Iraq and recently in Lebanon). Additionally, we must mention
the ethnic and religious "cleansing" in the Balkan areas and in other parts of
the world; the Islamic fundamentalist movements with their parallels in the
West, especially in the USA; the religious revival which often takes a
fundamentalist orientation in Islam, Christianity and Judaism; globalization
in its Western and American forms; and the chronic instability of the Arab
world with its huge political, economic, cultural and social problems, terrorism
and violence. Above all, we have to mention the ongoing international inability
to resolve in a fair way the Palestinian problem and its consequences such as
the intolerable oppression of the Palestinian people.

All these factors have created an atmosphere of tension, which affects Muslim-Christian relations locally, regionally and internationally. In that atmosphere of tension, we have witnessed some attacks on Christian institutions here and there in the Holy Land. One example is the attacks against some churches after the declarations of the Pope of Rome on Islam. I purposely raise such an example not to minimize these attacks but at the same time not to exaggerate them or generalize about them. In these cases, we have to take into account the popular and the official reactions to these acts. The Muslim passersby in Qabatia prevented the burning of the church and forced the perpetrators to flee. In the other towns where such acts occurred, they caused a general outcry from the entire population with its parties, civil organizations, popular movements, religious organizations and establishments as well as individuals, showing that these were the acts of isolated persons who did not represent the whole community and that these acts were viewed, indeed, as harming Muslim-Christian relations and creating a sense of fear in the Christian community.

PERSPECTIVES OF THE FUTURE

An experience – personal or collective - is never static. And if it were to be so, it becomes a mummified experience without life and unable to give life. An experience is always a dynamic reality which develops when it is confronted with challenges, new appeals and new needs. The Christian-Muslim experience in our region and in our land has to be permanently developing and deepening in order to ensure its future.

This sort of reflection has already been taking place in Palestine and in the Arab world, a reflection on the experience of the past in order to adapt it to the new challenges of the present. This work is done through several channels. Here in Palestine, this reflection is conducted by a number of organizations, such as Sabeel Center and Al-Liqa Center, which since 1982 has organized annual conferences and different initiatives which aim to develop Muslim-Christian relations in Palestine, including the International Forum in Bethlehem, Passia (Palestinian Academic Society for the Study of International Affairs) in Jerusalem and other forums and organizations.

Within this perspective, I would like to mention two texts which deal with Muslim-Christian relations in the Arab world. The first one is a common pastoral letter published by the Eastern Catholic Patriarchs entitled *Together before God for Human Beings and Society: the Living Together between Christians and Muslims in the Arab World* (Christmas 1994). The Assembly of the Catholic Patriarchs was created in 1990. In one of its annual meetings (1994), the Patriarchs discussed Muslim-Christian relations in the Arab world and consequently published a common pastoral letter dealing with these relations in the past and the present as well as offering many perspectives for the future.

The second document is the work of the Arab Working Group on Muslim- Christian Dialogue, which is comprised of prominent independent personalities from the different Arab countries, Muslim and Christian alike, and which has taken several initiatives to develop Muslim-Christian relations in the Arab world. In the year 2002, the group published an important document on the issue entitled *Dialogue and Coexistence: An Arab Muslim-Christian Covenant*, which is, in my opinion, one of the most important texts on this issue and which deserves to be better known and studied. It is presented as a reflection of religious believers, not only as a political perspective, and it has the courage to confront the real problems facing Muslim-Christian relations today in the Arab World.

To open the door to the future, Muslim-Christian relations in the Arab world have to face a variety of issues, such as mutual knowledge, visceral prejudices existing on both sides against the other, public discourse and its repercussions on the common people, politics and religion, the challenge of otherness, the challenge of sectarianism, the culture of dialogue, and spirituality and dialogue. This reflection aims to develop a culture of dialogue through education in the family, in the schools and in the different educational forums, such as churches and mosques.

CONCLUSION

Coexistence involves not only looking at one other, but also looking together at the poor and the marginalized. Religious dialogue can be strongly developed through a common effort on issues such as development, human rights, and social problems. In that case, coexistence becomes witnessing together. As Christians and Muslims in Palestine and in the Arab world, we are called to witness to the possibility of living together before God and humanity, a co-existence which the entire world aspires to. Living together is possible; it is decisive. This is our witness, our hope and our commitment.

A WITNESS TO LIFE TOGETHER

Mamdouh Aker

The issue that first arose in my mind in thinking about this topic of the Christian-Muslim relationship is why the fact of our life together, as Palestinian Muslims and Christians, has even become a question. Do I, as a Muslim, or do we, as Muslims and Christians, need to defend our life together? Does the "obvious" need a proof? Is it not correct that "Proofs do bore the truth" as a French artist once put it? إن البراهين تضجر الحقيقة

But on second thought, I convinced myself to see the topic from a different perspective. At certain times and under certain circumstances, societies (as much as individuals) do need to revisit certain facts of their life, not because these facts are in question, but rather to rediscover them. Certain facts are sometimes so obvious that they are taken for granted. They are too obvious to be noticed, let alone to be appreciated for the wealth they hold. Yes, every now and then, we need to rediscover ourselves and the nature of the Palestinian Muslim -Christian bonding and relationship.

This was the very experience I passed through when reflecting on the facts about our life together. It has been quite a revealing experience. I went back into my memory, looking at the Palestinian scene around me since my early childhood days. In every recollection I called up, whether it was of my school days, my social life, the early days of my involvement in the Palestinian National Movement, the cultural life, the professional career... in all these recollections, Palestinian Christians were always there. They stood as an integral component of every single aspect of the Palestinian fabric.

I grew up in my home town of Nablus, which besides being the biggest city in the West Bank is also well-known for its conservative nature, in contrast, for example, to the more liberal life in Ramallah. When I looked at my public school days, I thought of my classmates: Yousef Nicola Khouri and I sat on the same bench. Sameer Bishara Mubarak sat on the bench in front of us. Two benches behind us sat one of my earliest best friends, Farid Musallam. In the neighborhood where my family used to live, our neighbors in the flat underneath us were the family of the famous banker, Mr. Emile Talhami.

Let me share with you a couple of incidents as simple examples of the sort of life together we Palestinian Muslims and Christians enjoyed. When Mr. Talhami's elderly mother died, my father insisted on hosting the condolences in our flat. I remember the priests moving around, calling out their religious rituals. I can almost recall the smell of the incense all around the house. Carrying out Christian rituals in a Muslim house did not raise any eyebrows in our neighborhood. At the same time Mr. Talhami considered it no more than a usual and expected gesture extended between two neighbors.

Another incident is very dear to my memory. Once a burglar broke into the Talhami flat in the morning hours when Mrs. Talhami was alone. The neighbors around heard her screams and rushed immediately into the flat and took hold of the thief. Poor Mrs. Talhami was so scared and shaken that she suddenly could not breast feed her baby! My mother, who happened to be breast-feeding one of my youngest brothers, offered to breast-feed Mrs. Talhami's baby for a while until she calmed down and restored her lactation. Mrs. Talhami, without hesitation, brought her baby to my mother!

This is the essence of our life together. This is what I meant by "The Obvious" and "The Norm." When the Israeli army occupied the West Bank in 1967, many Palestinian students left their universities to join the fledgling Resistance Movement. Yacoub Dawwani was one of those who managed to cross the waters of the River Jordan and make his way into his home town of Nablus. After a while, the Israeli Army intelligence became aware of his activities and put him on the list of wanted men. So Yacoub went into hiding. One of the first places he chose for hiding was the house of a friend, which happened to be the "family house" of my wife. It was fascinating to listen to Yacoub in London, many years later, reflecting on his experience of hiding in that house!

As I mentioned earlier, whenever and wherever I look around the Palestinian scene, past and present, Palestinian Christians are always there. They are not only an integral component of the ordinary Palestinian fabric, through the types of examples I have just described, but also major contributors to the Palestinian scene, be it in education, cultural life, political life, or as historians, national leaders, musicians, artists, or professional institution builders. Some of the names that come to the mind are only examples: Khalil Sakakini, Albert Hourani, George Habash, Kamal Nasser, Nayef Hawatmeh, Edward Said, Silvador Arnita, Henry Qattan, Emile Habibi, Kamal Bullata, Ameen Majaj (who was the Medical Director of Maqassed Islamic Charitable Hospital and one of the early Palestinian physicians who contributed greatly to research in medicine). All of these individuals have made significant contributions to Palestinian life, in addition to the many educational and health institutions, including schools, universities, clinics and hospitals, spread throughout Palestine.

The Palestinian Christian-Muslim relationship is unique in the sense that no other Muslim-Christian community, even in other Arab countries, shares a similar historic context.

First of all, the Palestinian Christians are the indigenous population of the land. The Christian existence in Palestine goes back to the origin of Christianity. Every Palestinian is proud of the fact that Jesus was Palestinian.

Secondly, the Palestinian Christians do not form a different ethnic community or have their own language, but rather share the same stock as their Muslim compatriots. We are all Arabs, we belong to the same culture, and we share the same national aspirations.

Thirdly, alongside the recognition by Islam of Christianity as a religion, and Jesus as a Prophet, it is very important also to point out the very early recognition by Islam of the centrality of Jerusalem, Bethlehem and Nazareth to Christianity. This recognition was best expressed and officially formulated by Caliph Omar's commitment in the declaration known as "Al- 'Uhda Al-Omariyya," which guaranteed the safety of Christians and their holy places as far back as the year 638 AD.

Fourthly, although during the Ottoman rule, the "Millah" system recognized the autonomy of the Christian communities in running their internal affairs in religious and civil matters, this "Millah" system was superseded in the regimes following the Ottomans by the "Citizenship" system with equality of all citizens before the law. This was enshrined by the *Palestinian Declaration of Independence* of 1988, and the Basic Law of the Palestinian National Authority.

However, there is one thing still missing in the midst of this context of life together which we need and should seek in order to advance this relationship and bonding into a further dimension. It is not enough to be equal citizens; it is not enough to recognize and respect each other's religion. We should and must know more about each other's religions. The notion that: "you have your own religion, and we have our own religion" "لكم دينكم ولي دين" should not be interpreted as a call to avoid knowing more about each other's beliefs and traditions. Understanding requires knowledge. It is a pity, as much as it is a drawback, that our school curriculum does not include an introduction to basic knowledge of each other's religion. It is high time for us to work together towards that goal.

THE PALESTINIAN CONSTITUTION
AND DEMOCRACY

Ali Khashan

As secretary of the committee of local and international lawyers charged with drafting a constitution for Palestine, I know that with regard to the constitution and democracy, we must start with a preliminary question: are there possibilities for reconciliation between the Arab masses and democratic ideas and institutions? The next issue is the definition of a democratic constitution. How can we judge whether a constitution is democratic or not?

There are many theoretical principles of democracy but we must resort to the reality of our actual lives. How can we achieve genuine democracy regardless of the texts of our documents? Basically, without the good will of all concerned, any written text loses its importance and will not be applied on the ground. We should also note that in any country, the constitution is created by its own people according to agreed upon principles and mechanisms based on the sovereignty of the people. No other country, including Israel, may interfere in the drafting or establishment of the Palestinian constitution nor will Palestine accept international interference in the process.

While we were drafting the constitutional texts, I focused on the rights, freedoms and the principles of citizenship and said repeatedly that summer and winter – Islam and Christianity – must meet in the skies over Palestine.

Let me be frank with you. Without doubt there are some difficult matters that we must tackle whether we wish to do so or not. Looking at the texts of some Arab constitutions, one might feel shocked. My job is to free myself from this state of shock and do my utmost to fully ensure fundamental rights to all citizens, regardless of the visions held by one particular sector or another of the Palestinian community. I cannot and will not make myself believe that Palestinians are divided into a majority or a minority with regards to Muslims and Christians, even if many feel this way.

However, I cannot share that view of such division within the Palestinian community because I can only understand the terms "majority" and "minority" in relation to political conditions and parties. Thus, the terms majority and minority are meaningful in a political context only when we talk about the majority in the parliament with a political minority in the opposition. This use of the terms is what I understand and it is not determined by religious affiliation.

Many questions which require answers have emerged in the Palestinian arena. One has to admit that there is a kind of implicit agreement to marginalize the constitutional role and push it out of the thoughts and off the agenda of the official parties in the Palestinian political system. My perspective, based on my reading of the draft constitution, focuses on the need to provide every citizen with the right to become a partner in the social contract so that eventually we have the democracy of the ruled and not the democracy of the rulers. In developing this document, we must move from political considerations to exclusively legal considerations so that the constitution is neither a theoretical text nor the result of coercion but is an agreement establishing the minimum rules for a just political order.

Therefore, I am seeking the development of a document that protects the rights of everyone rather than one that emerges from a closed-minded constitutional vision that justifies the presence of a particular political authority but fails to protect the rights and freedoms of every citizen.

Thus, I believe that in order to be democratic, the constitution has to include the following six points:

- First, it should be based on the principle of full citizenship.
- Second, it should depend on the rule of law.
- Third, it should respect the principle of separation of powers.
- Fourth, it should protect the rights and freedoms of individuals.
- Fifth, it should recognize an orderly and democratic process for the transfer of power from the minority to the majority.
- Sixth, the establishment of the constitution should result from a democratic process and should not be imposed by one group.

Our problem in Palestine is that we are affected by the patterns that exist in many Arab countries. However, we must pay attention to fundamental rights that require protection. As I cannot mention all the kinds of constitutions existing in the world, I will elaborate here on three basic and simple kinds of constitutions:

- The first type of constitution is the secular constitution. The French and Turkish constitutions are examples. While our committee has had much discussion of this type of constitution, many parties, including religious parties, reject it and cannot coexist with such a secular approach.
- The second type of constitution uses religious law as one of a variety of sources of legislation. Examples include the Greek constitution, which is based in Orthodoxy, and those of Arab countries which use Sharia as a source for legislation.
- The third type is the religious constitution of Iran and some other countries, which depends entirely on religion as its only source for developing methods of governance.

The majority of the constitutions of Arab countries as well as those of Greece and some other countries belong to the second type. These constitutions prohibit initiation of religious laws and attacks on individual rights and freedoms either constitutionally or legally. However, political repression by the state can still occur. If such violations of rights and freedoms do occur, they are clear violations of the constitution and one can resort to the constitutional court for redress. Laws ratified by the parliament are based on popular will.

The Palestinian draft constitution can be classified as belonging to the second type, but unlike the constitutions of many of the Arab countries, it contains no text stipulating that the presidency or other posts be reserved for Muslims or other designated groups. Nor does it include language establishing differences in the rights and freedoms granted to persons either in the constitution itself or in the laws.

Moreover, the Palestinian Legislative Council passes legislation according to both a prescribed legislative process and the will of its members, regardless of whether these laws agree with or contradict the prevailing attitudes of the society. Of course, the law is always a reflection of the popular will, which is the basis for its legitimacy on condition that it does not violate the constitution.

The text which stipulates that the religion of the state is Islam does not mean at all that the rights and freedoms of others can be violated. Everybody possesses citizenship as we have mentioned before and all have equal rights and freedoms even though Muslims comprise the majority of the citizens. This text follows a precedent established by the previous Legislative Council and the Basic Laws it enacted. It is not easy to override this proviso as it has become both an independent norm and a set of enumerated regulations that maintain all rights and freedoms for each person.

With regards to the constitution, we must emphasize that the Islamic Sharia does not control the entirety of the Palestinian population. The Islamic Sharia is implemented in Palestine only in the area of personal statutes for Muslims; each Christian sect implements its own personal laws according to its religious courts. We cannot compare implementation of punitive measures in Palestine with those of Saudi Arabia or Iran because there is no implementation of Islamic Sharia law in Palestine. An article allowing the implementation of Sharia might appear in any Arab constitution but this does not make the constitution religious; therefore, all matters related to the personal or religious statutes of Christians must be implemented by their religious courts and all such matters relating to Muslims must be implemented according to the Islamic Sharia

However, some fervent parties might look at the provisions of the Basic Laws and of the current constitutional draft texts as a move away from Islamic reality and might consider it a blasphemous constitution violating the Islamic Shari'a. This is a sensitive case in which we must face the following reality. Although we might wish to include in the constitution articles that maintain the Palestinian social fabric by specifying that both Muslims and Christians have full citizenship with all rights and freedoms, that might not be a practical approach, especially because a democratic constitution must be approved by referendum. Any attempt to remove any of its provisions (such as the specification that Islam is the religion of the state) may lead to its rejection by the general public. Having worked in this reality, I understand it and have held many discussions on the topic.

The drafters of the constitution have encountered many political obstacles on the ground, including the potential rejection of the document by those who really want to create something other than a true constitution while claiming that they respect the constitution.

For example, I wrote an article on the topic of Hamas, the Palestinian Authority and Islam, in which I posed the following questions regarding Hamas:

- If Hamas fails to function as a government, will they allow for the democratic formation of a new government?
- Given that Muslim jurisprudence (*fiqh*) prohibits an Islamic government from ceding power to a secular or non-Islamic government, if Hamas loses the next election, will it relinquish power democratically just as it acquired power democratically?

In January 2006 when Hamas agreed for the first time to stand for election within an existing secular framework, the party ran under the slogan "Islam is the Solution." After achieving a majority in free and open elections, Hamas members have been asked why they do not apply this principle in governing. Their answer has been that they cannot apply it for many reasons, the economic siege being the most obvious one.

It is important to emphasize that Hamas attained the majority of the seats in the current legislature as a result of a democratic choice. Whether we like it or not, my colleagues and I cannot differentiate among voters and say that Muslims supported Hamas as an Islamic choice and that Christians voted for Hamas to try to end the corruption of the Palestinian Authority or that others supported Hamas in the hope that they would bring about reform and change along with social, health, educational and other improved programs. For whatever reasons, the majority of voters chose Hamas party members as their representatives.

In reviewing the process of drafting the Palestinian constitution in our current political climate, I must emphasize that although the draft constitution does not institute popular and societal mechanisms of governance, it does set up basic principles in the hope that the people will reach a consensus. I believe that our constitutional committee did an important task in creating this draft constitution, which has as its goal protecting the rights of all Palestinians, regardless of their religious or political affiliations.

EFFECTS OF THE LAND REGIMES
ON ARAB CITIZENS OF ISRAEL

Suhad Bishara

BACKGROUND

Palestinian Arab citizens of Israel are an indigenous group who became a national, ethnic, linguistic, and religious minority in their own homeland following the establishment of the state of Israel in 1948. The "Arab citizens of Israel" or the "Arab minority" or the "Palestinians in Israel" are a part of the Palestinian people who also live in the West Bank, Gaza Strip and the Diaspora. Arabic is their native language, and they belong to three religious communities – Muslim, Christian and Druze. They live predominantly in villages, towns, and mixed Arab-Jewish cities in the Galilee region in the north, the Triangle area in central Israel, and in the Negev Desert in the south.

The Arabs in Israel are an indigenous minority that since 1948 sees itself in a regressive process in many fields, including land and planning issues. The massive land confiscations that took place in the past, the huge decrease in the jurisdictional lands of Arab local authorities and the unjust allocation of land between the Jewish majority and the Arab minority in the state have resulted in mistrust and suspicion towards the authorities and towards any formal action in the field of land and planning, among others.

On the other hand, we have a state that sees the Arabs as a problem and that sees itself in a constant conflict with its Arab citizens in two main fields: 1) demography; 2) land and planning. Thus, the state has developed policies to reduce to a minimum land used by the Arab citizens of the state and to establish segregation based on a national basis. These policies will be illustrated later in this paper through three cases undertaken recently by Adalah Center for Arab Minority Rights in Israel. First, however, a short summary of the international law framework is required

INTERNATIONAL LAW FRAME

According to international law, national, linguistic, cultural, or ethnic minorities have the right to maintain their culture and way of life and "to prevent the imposition of assimilation."[1] The rationale behind this right, as an exception for the principle of equality, is that the minority group risks losing its identity and culture through its submission to the majority culture. Article 27 of the *International Covenant on Civil and Political Rights* states:

> "In those states in which ethnic, religious or linguistic minorities exist, persons belonging to such minorities shall not be denied the right, in community with the other members of their group, to enjoy their own culture, to profess and practice their own religion, or to use their own language".

In addition, Article 1(1) of *The International Convention on the Elimination of All Forms of Racial Discrimination* states:

> "In this Convention, the term 'racial discrimination' shall mean any distinction, exclusion, restriction or preference based on race, color, descent, or national or ethnic origin which has the purpose or effect of nullifying or impairing the recognition, enjoyment or exercise, on an equal footing, of human rights and fundamental freedoms in the political, economic, social, cultural or any other field of public life".

Article 3 of the *Convention* states: "Parties particularly condemn racial segregation and apartheid and undertake to prevent, prohibit and eradicate all practices of this nature in territories under their jurisdiction."

---

[1] Regarding this case, see the statement of Justice Barak in H.C. 6698/95, Adel Qa'dan, et. al. v. Israel Lands Administration, et. al., PD 54 (1), 258, 279.

It is not accidental that international law provides no recognition of the right of the dominant majority to preserve its culture through segregation. The principle of corrective justice actually justifies the establishment of Arab communities, but certainly cannot be invoked to justify the establishment of Jewish-only communities. In practice, Israel is applying these principles to the Majority group by managing a land regime that allows segregation for the benefit of the Jewish Majority in the state.

ISRAELI PRACTICES

Since the establishment of the state in 1948, successive Israeli governments have enacted land laws and pursued land planning, allocation and settlement policies that have resulted in the confiscation of Arab-owned land, the displacement of Arab citizens from their homes, and the unjust and unequal allocation of land resources. Through the vigorous implementation of these laws and policies, today, **93% of all land in Israel is under direct state control.** The Israel Lands Administration (ILA), a governmental body established by law, administers all "Israel lands." These lands belong to (i) the State of Israel - 71% (15.3 million dunams); (ii) the Development Authority - 16% (2.5 million dunams); and (iii) the Jewish National Fund (JNF) - 13% (2.6 million dunams).[i]

State control of land makes state land policies extremely significant to the development of the Arab minority in Israel. The **clear inequality** between Jewish and Arab citizens of Israel regarding their access to land resources, their land rights, and their abilities to use the resource of land to develop their communities is exemplified by the following data:[ii]

- Arab citizens of Israel comprise close to 20% of the total population of the state.

---

[i] See Oren Yiftachel, "Land, Planning and Inequality: Space Distribution Among Jews and Arabs in Israel," (Tel Aviv: Adva, 2000).

[ii] See Oren Yiftachel, "Land, Planning and Inequality: Space Division Between Jews and Arabs in Israel," ADVA Center, November 2000 (Hebrew); and Oren Yiftachel, "Nation-Building and the Division of Space in the Israeli 'Ethnocracy': Settlement, Land and Ethnic Disparities," 21 (3) *Tel Aviv University Law Review* 637-663 (June 1998) (Hebrew).

- Arab Local Authorities have jurisdiction over only 2.5% of the total area of the state.
- In the Galilee, Arab municipalities have jurisdiction over 16.1% of the land, while Arab citizens comprise 72% of the population. In the northern Negev region, Arab municipalities have jurisdiction over 1.9% of the land, while Arab citizens comprise 25.2% of the population.
- About one-half of the private lands owned by Arab citizens of Israel in 1948 have been confiscated by the state.
- Land allocation for public purposes in all of the Arab towns and villages is under the minimum national standard.
- In practice, Arab citizens of Israel are blocked from purchasing or leasing land in about 80% of the area of the state.
- The Arab population in Israel increased six-fold between 1948 and 2000, but in the same period, the land under its control has shrunk. The state has not allowed the Arab minority to establish new towns. As a result, the building density in Arab municipalities has increased 16-fold, and the population density 12-fold, between 1948 and 2000.
- Tens of old Arab villages are "unrecognized" and the state is trying to evacuate them.
- The Central Bureau of Statistics in Israel defines approximately 89% of all towns and villages in the state as Jewish.[iii] Arabs are not allowed to live in approximately 78% of these towns and villages, owing to the fact that admissions committees monitor applications for housing units, partly in order to filter out the Arab population. [iv]
- Arab citizens of the state are not permitted to lease or purchase approximately 80% of the land (Yiftachel and Kedar: 2000, p. 85).

Similar to the Israeli political, social and economic regimes, the land regime in Israel developed into a violent regime lacking the capability, and indeed the desire, to accept differences on the basis of ethnicity, class and communality. Hence, the regime created, and indeed continues to create, "conflicts" over space and housing, homogeneous spaces which express the vision of "land redemption," and endless spatial violence.

[iii] According to the Statistical Abstract of Israel, a settlement is defined as Jewish or Arab according to the "decisive majority" of the settlement's population.

[iv] Compilation based on data from the Statistical Abstract of Israel, 2004 No. 55, Table 2.9.

In such a spirit, successive Israeli governments have developed policies to ensure "preservation of national lands," prevent "control by foreign elements" and promote solely Jewish settlement over significant areas of the state in order "to stop the expanding settlement of Arabs." This policy led to segregated housing, established the division of the land for separate use by Arab and Jewish citizens of the state and created large gaps between the jurisdictional areas available to Arab and Jewish towns and villages.

This policy of segregation is implemented in practice by use of planning, building and land laws, as well as use of the authority granted by these laws. The cases presented below exemplify this policy at different levels and describe the different means used by the government to achieve the goals behind this policy.

CASE 1: JNF LANDS TO JEWS ONLY

Established in 1960, the ILA is the governmental agency that manages and controls over 93% of land in Israel.[2] Since 1948, large tracts of Palestinian-Arab-owned land have been confiscated, or otherwise appropriated, under Israeli law and taken into the possession of the state or Zionist institutions, such as the Jewish Agency, the World Zionist Organization and the JNF, for the exclusive use of those holding "Jewish nationality," whether they are citizens of Israel or not. Under Israeli law, this land cannot be sold to individuals, and the ILA allocates leasing rights to "Jewish nationality" holders for 49–98 years. The 19.5 million dunams of land (about 78 million acres) managed by the ILA are comprised of lands controlled by the state, the Development Authority and the JNF.[3] Israel's Basic Law: Israel Lands (1960) categorizes these lands as "Israel Lands."

According to ILA figures, as of 2003 the JNF claimed ownership over 13% of all "Israel Lands," or a total of 2,555,000 dunams.[4] To place this figure in historical context, the UN Palestine Commission reported that, as of

---

[2]   See the website of the ILA at www.mmi.gov.il.

[3]   ILA Annual Report 2003 (Hebrew), available at www.mmi.gov.il/static/p236.html.

[4]   Ibid. According to the ILA, the JNF owns: 1,031,000 dunams in the northern district; 403,000 dunams in the central district; 382,000 dunams in the southern district; 508,000 dunams in the Jerusalem district; 207,000 dunams in the Haifa district; and 24,000 dunams in the Tel Aviv district.

January 1948, the JNF held only approximately 600,000 dunams.[5] It should be emphasized that the JNF claims that it bought 1.25 million dunams of land from the state immediately after the establishment of Israel, using donations from Jews from around the world.[6] These acquisitions totaled close to 2,000,000 dunams, or approximately 78% of the total land currently held by the JNF. These were actually acquired by the JNF from the state in 1949 and 1953.[7]

The majority of this land belonged to Palestinian refugees (i.e., those people who either became refugees during the Israeli-Arab war of 1948–49 and found themselves outside of Israeli-held territory after the war, or those who were displaced from their land but remained within Israel and became citizens of the new state).[8] Those in the latter group are also known as "present absentees."

The JNF enjoys a special status under a series of Israeli laws and agreements with the state of Israel. For example, the state concluded a covenant with the JNF in 1961 declaring that all JNF-owned lands would be administered by the ILA, subject to the Memorandum and Articles of Association of the JNF (*Keren Kayemeth Le-Israel* in Hebrew). The JNF's objectives, as set forth in its Memorandum are: "To purchase, acquire on lease or in exchange, etc…in…the State of Israel in any area within the jurisdiction of the Government of Israel or any part thereof, for the purpose of settling Jews on such lands and properties." The JNF interprets the Memorandum as prohibiting the allocation of its lands to "non-Jews." This prohibition is discriminatory in its nature and effect and contributes to the ongoing conflict.

Israeli law also confers upon the fund privileges usually reserved for a public authority. For example, Article 4a of the ILA Law (1960) provides that the JNF will hold 50% of the seats on the ILA Council, the policy-making body of the ILA. This provision affords the JNF a substantial role in formulating

---

[5] United Nations Palestine Commission, "Considerations Affecting Certain of the Provisions of the General Assembly Resolution on the 'Future Government of Palestine': Control of Land Regulations," 10 January 1948.

[6] See JNF response, December 2004, to (High Court) H.C. 9205/04, Adalah, et. al. v. The Israel Lands Administration, et. al. (case pending).

[7] See Arnon Golan, "The Acquisition of Arab Land by Jewish Settlements in the War of Independence" in Catedra, Vol. 63 (1992), pp. 122-154 (Hebrew); Yifa'at Holtzman-Gazit, "The Use of Law as a Status Symbol: The Jewish National Fund Law – 1953 and the Struggle of the JNF to Establish its Position in the State" in Iyoni Mishpat Vol. 26, pp. 601-644, July 2002 (Hebrew).

[8] Ibid. A. Golan and Y. Holtzman-Gazit.

Israel's land policies over 93% of the territory of the state. Additionally, while "Israel Lands" may not be sold, the Israel Lands Law (1960) allows these lands to be transferred between the state and the JNF as an exception to this general rule. Furthermore, for the purposes of confiscating land, the JNF enjoys the same status as a Local Authority according to Article 6 of the JNF Law – 1953 and Article 22 of the Lands Ordinance (Acquisition for Public Purposes) - 1943.

Still, ILA policy and a regulation promulgated by the Minister of Finance (MOF), effectively permit the ILA's marketing and allocation of JNF lands through bids open only to Jewish citizens.

On 13 October 2004, Adalah submitted a petition to the Supreme Court of Israel against the ILA, the JNF and the Minister of Finance challenging this policy. In its written response to the petition, submitted to the Supreme Court in December 2004, Chairman of the Board of the JNF in Israel, Yeheil Leket stated on behalf of the JNF that:

> The JNF is not the trustee of the general public in Israel. Its loyalty is given to the Jewish people in the Diaspora and in the state of Israel... (p. 34) The JNF, in relation to being an owner of land, is not a public body that works for the benefit of all citizens of the state. The loyalty of the JNF is given to the Jewish people and only to them is the JNF obligated. The JNF, as the owner of the JNF land, does not have a duty to practice equality towards all citizens of the state. (p. 38)

The case is still pending.

Case 2: Atir -Umm al-Hieran

The village of Atir-Umm al-Hieran was established roughly 51 years ago, following the transfer of Arab Bedouin citizens of Israel to the area in 1956 by order of the Regional Military Governor. The village's inhabitants leased approximately 7,000 dunams of land for agricultural use. Prior to their enforced transfer, the inhabitants of Atir-Umm al-Hieran were living in the Wadi Zuballa region, where they had lived and farmed for hundreds of years. Following their expulsion from Wadi Zuballa, their land was transferred by the state to Kibbutz Shuval for agricultural use.

In August 2001, the Israel Lands Administration (ILA) submitted a report on "new and renewed" settlements to the Prime Minister's Office. The report details initiatives for the establishment of 68 new settlements throughout the state of Israel, including the settlement of Hiran, earmarked for construction in the area currently inhabited by Atir-Umm al-Hieran residents. The ILA report identifies a number of "special problems" that may affect the planning and establishment of the new Jewish settlement of Hiran, among which the Arab Bedouin inhabitants of Atir-Umm al Hieran appear. The establishment of the settlement of Hiran was approved by the National Council for Planning and Building on 9 April 2002 and by the government in its decision no. 2265, dated 21 July 2002.

In April 2004, the state of Israel filed lawsuits to the Magistrate Court in Beer el-Sabe' (Beer Sheva) requesting that evacuation orders be issued against the inhabitants of Atir-Umm al-Hieran. The lawsuits were based primarily on the claim that the inhabitants of the village are using state land without permission and that they therefore need to evacuate the territory and be prevented from using it in the future.

CASE 3: THE ADMISSIONS COMMITTEES

In August 2004, a decision No. 1015 entitled "recommendation procedures for accepting candidates to purchase leasing rights for lands in agricultural and community settlements" was made by the ILA's council.

The decision directs the Selection Committees of small community and agricultural settlements to apply a number of criteria in deciding whether or not to recommend that the ILA accept a candidate's request to live in one of these settlements. Among the criteria that the decision sets forth are that the candidate: (i) is suited to social life in a small community or agricultural settlement; and (ii) has "the financial capacity to build a house in the settlement in the period of time stipulated in the development contract with the ILA."

The decision also stipulates the composition of the Selection Committees themselves. According to the decision, a Selection Committee should be formed of the following representatives: "in a community settlement […]: a senior official from the settlement agency (The Jewish Agency or The World Zionist Organization), a senior official from the Ministry of Housing and Construction along with representatives of the cooperative association, the regional council and the settlement body – in the relevant settlements; […] in an agricultural settlement: the composition of the Selection Committee will be established by the society's governing bodies."

These criteria raise serious suspicions, which are *de facto* supported by the practice of the Selection Committees, that the residency applications of Arab Palestinian applicants and applicants of low socioeconomic status will be rejected on the grounds of their social and/or economic lack of suitability. Selection Committees currently reject applications on these bases and are expected to continue to do so.

Further, under the conditions set out by the ILA, Arab applicants have no chance of purchasing leasing rights in agricultural and community settlements because of the presence of settlement bodies on the Selection Committees, on the one hand, and the lack of Arab representation on the Committees, on the other. Thus, the above-mentioned decision will result in the continued exclusion of Arab citizens of Israel from these settlements.

Such exclusion is especially severe as the decision affects approximately 900 settlements defined as "Jewish rural settlements" in Israel, which are organized in regional councils and which jointly control some 80% of territory in Israel. Thus, the decision contravenes the principles of equality and just distribution which were set out by the Supreme Court, and the duty of the ILA as a public body to refrain from engaging in discriminatory practices.

THE PALESTINIAN IDENTITY
IN A JEWISH STATE

Jafar Farah and the Mossawa Staff

The Mossawa Center, the Advocacy Center for Arab Citizens of Israel, is a nonprofit, non-governmental organization that works to promote equality for the Arab Palestinian citizens of Israel. Established in 1997, the Mossawa Center strives to improve the social, economic and political status of the Arab citizens of Israel without sacrificing their identity as Palestinians. This paper is based on the Annual Report of Mossawa and a position paper written by Mossawa Center staff in August 2006, entitled "The Arab Citizens of Israel and the 2006 Lebanon War: Reflections and Realities."

INTRODUCTION

As citizens of the state of Israel and as an integral part of the Palestinian people, the Palestinian community in Israel is uniquely positioned to contribute to a just, human rights-based sustainable resolution of the conflict between Israel, the Palestinians and the wider Arab world. While identified as part of a wider Arab world, the Arab Palestinian citizens of Israel represent a national (Palestinian), ethnic/racial (Arab), linguistic (Arabic) and religious (Muslim, Christian and Druze) minority in Israel.[1] Moreover, the Palestinian Arab citizens of Israel are members of the Palestinian people who were dispersed in 1948 and who became citizens of the State of Israel at its establishment. As

---

[1] Yousef Jabareen. *Constitutional Protection of Minorities in Comparative Perspective: Palestinians in Israel and African-Americans in the United States* (2000)(unpublished doctoral dissertation, Georgetown University Law Center) (on file with author).

such, they share deep familial, national, religious, social and cultural ties with Palestinians in the Occupied Territories of the West Bank, Gaza and East Jerusalem and beyond. The Palestinian Arab community, about 20% of the Israeli population and 10% of the Palestinian people,[2] is a potentially formidable force for coexistence between Palestinians and Israeli Jews.

While community members preserve their Arabic language and identity, they are also fluent in Hebrew, the state's first official language. The community, constantly exposed to the dominant Jewish Israeli society and culture, adeptly navigates and understands Israeli institutions and political, social and economic systems.

Despite a growing trend of racism and systemic and institutional discrimination against the community,[3] the overwhelming majority of Palestinian Arabs in Israel wish to remain citizens of Israel,[4] and believe in future friendly relations between Jews and Arabs in Israel.[5] However, as the community forms part of the Palestinian nation, it is often seen as part of the "problem," but not as an integral part of the solution.

CURRENT STATUS OF THE ARAB COMMUNITY IN ISRAEL

At the end of the 1948 War, at the time of the founding of the state of Israel, the majority Palestinian population had been reduced to a debilitated and persecuted minority. More than 480 Arab villages were destroyed,[6] a quarter

---

[2] Central Bureau of Statistics, Statistical Abstract of Israel 2004, Table 2.1, available at <http://www1.cbs.gov.il/shnaton55/st02_01.pdf>. Arab citizens constitute 1.3 million versus 5.4 million Jews and other groups. Id. In 2002, there were 9.3 million Palestinians worldwide. Palestinian Central Bureau of Statistics, Press Release (Jan. 8, 2003), available at <http://www.pcbs.org>.

[3] Mossawa Center, Anti-Racism Program, at <http://www.mossawacenter.org/en/projects/anti_racism.html>. Legal and advocacy NGOs cite at least 17 laws which directly discriminate against the Arab citizens of Israel. See Legal Status chapter of this report.

[4] See e.g., Israel Democratic Institute, *The 2004 Israel Democracy Index Auditing Israeli Democracy Attitudes of Youth* (2004); As'ad Ghanem and Sarah Ozacky-Lazar, *"The Status of the Palestinians in Israel in an Era of Peace: Part of the Problem but Not Part of Solution"*, in *The Israeli Palestinians: An Arab Minority in the Jewish State* 276 (ed. Alexander Bligh) (2003).

[5] Summary of studies by Sammy Smooha, Professor in the Sociology and Anthropology Department, Haifa University, Israel (July 11, 2004) (in Hebrew) available a t <www.sikkuy.org.il/modiin/tzohar1/11_7_04.html>.

[6] See *All That Remains: The Palestinian Villages Occupied and Depopulated by Israel in 1948* (Walid Khaldi ed., Institute for Palestine Studies 1992). Other accounts report that about 531 communities were destroyed. See Palestinian Central Bureau of Statistics, Palestinians in Israel, at http://www.pcbs.org/abs_pal/abs_pal4/palestinian.htm.

of the remaining Arab population was transformed into internal refugees,[7] and families were divided by newly defined international borders.[8] The 1967 Israeli-Arab war created a second wave of displacement with more than 500,000 Palestinians, nearly half of whom were already refugees, uprooted again.[9]

Today, the 1.3 million Palestinian Arab citizens of Israel[10] live in three concentrated regions in Israel: the Galilee, the Triangle adjacent to the West Bank, and the Negev. Israel includes between 228,000 and 249,270 Palestinian Arab permanent residents[11] of annexed East Jerusalem as part of the total Arab population in Israel.[12] About 63% of the community lives in villages, including 8% in "unrecognized" villages in the Negev and Galilee; 29% live in small municipalities, mostly in the Triangle area; and 8% live in mixed Arab-Jewish urban centers.[13] Religious affiliation is primarily Sunni Muslim (1.1 million) with Christians numbering 113,000 and Druze 106,000.[14]

Even in the so-called "mixed cities," Arab and Jewish residents tend to live in ethnically homogeneous neighborhoods with minimal inter-communal interaction. Moreover, overall, Palestinian Arab citizens living in mixed cities suffer from poorer socio-economic conditions than the Jewish citizens in the same cities, and as compared to Palestinian Arab citizens living in Arab localities. For the past 59 years, the Arab community of Israel has been the subject of

---

[7] Mustafa Kabha, "The Conspiracy and the Victim", in Kafr Kassem: Myth and History 106 (Ruvik Rosenthal ed., 2000).

[8] As'ad & Ozacky-Lazar, supra note 2, at 263.

[9] United Nations, Palestine Refugees, at 8 at http://www.un.org/Depts/dpi/palestine/ch10.pdf.

[10] Arab citizens constitute 1.3 million versus 5.4 million Jews and other groups. Central Bureau of Statistics (CBS), Statistical Abstract of Israel 2004, Table 2.1, available at http://www1.cbs.gov.il/shnaton55/st02_01.pdf.

[11] Under the Entry into Israel Law of 1952, Palestinians living in annexed East Jerusalem are permanent residents. The immigration law permits their travel as tourists and stay as immigrants, granting authorities wide discretion to terminate their status. See B'tselem and Hamoked, *Forbidden Families: Family Unification and Child Registration in East Jerusalem* (January 2004), at 5.

[12] According to 2004 Israeli CBS data, 464,000 "Jews and others" and 228,000 Arabs live in Jerusalem, including East Jerusalem. CBS, The Population of Israel (released April 25, 2004), at http://www.cbs.gov.il/hodaot2004/01_04_98e.htm#_ftnref2. According to the Palestinian Bureau of Statistics, 249,270 Palestinians lived in Israeli-annexed Jerusalem in 2003. PASSIA, Palestine Facts (2003) at http://www.passia.org/palestine_facts/pdf/pdf2003/sections1/4-population.doc.

[13] According to MADA, 55% of Palestinians in Israel live in more than 100 villages and 8% live in over 40 unrecognized villages. Arab Center for Applied Social Research (MADA), The Palestinians in Israel, available at http://www.mada-research.org/about/palsinisrael.shtml (last visited April 3, 2005).

[14] Israeli Ministry of Foreign Affairs, Minority Communities (February 1, 2004) at http://www.mfa.gov.il/MFA/Facts+About+Israel/People/SOCIETY-%20Minority%20Communities.htm.

social and economic injustice, lack of property and land rights and overt discrimination by the state of Israel. The thousands of citizens living in unrecognized villages in the Negev and Galilee are denied basic services such as health clinics, land development plans, permanent homes and schools, roads, electricity and running water.

SECOND CLASS CITIZENSHIP STATUS OF THE ARAB COMMUNITY IN ISRAEL

Israeli Constitution Proposal and Arab Minority Rights

The lack of a constitution in the Israeli legal system has resulted in limited legislation protecting the civil rights of Palestinian Arab citizens, while public discourse on the constitution has tended to ignore the Arab community's role and its needs as a minority. Although Arabic is an official language in Israel, it is infrequently implemented in government and in public institutions. The Arab community also lacks equal allocation of symbolic, political and material public resources, equal employment opportunities and fair representation in decision-making bodies. Palestinian Arab citizens demand official recognition of their status by the state and inclusion in discussion and design of the constitution.

Socio-Economic Discrimination against Arab Palestinian Citizens

The Israeli government continues to implement policies that directly discriminate against its Palestinian Arab citizens. From 1999 to the present, the regular governmental budget has disproportionately allocated funds to its Jewish population. Despite representing 20% of the total population of Israel, Arab localities only received 5% of funds in the 2005 development budget and only 3% of funds in the regular governmental budget.

Palestinian Arabs are also underrepresented in the government offices with only 6% representation. Only 3.5% of land in Israel remains in Palestinian Arab citizens' ownership.

The Killing of Arab Palestinian Citizens

In October 2000, Israeli security forces killed 13 Palestinian Arab citizens. In half of these cases, police pursued, shot and killed the victims although they did not pose any immediate threat. In many instances, it is clear that those killed were innocent of any transgression. There are no such cases of Jewish suspects killed in a chase. Since October 2000, 22 more Arab citizens have been killed by Israeli security forces. These killings highlight the reality that in Israel, Arab citizens are often regarded as inherently suspect. Worse, many in the Arab community today feel they are viewed as enemies rather than citizens.

Hate Speech and Incitement to Violence

Race- and ethnic-based violence against Palestinian Arab citizens continues to be tolerated, and in some instances sanctioned and even propagated by the state. In 2003, former Minister of Finance, Benjamin Netanyahu, called Arab Palestinian citizens a "demographic problem." Avigdor Lieberman, now deputy prime minister and minister of strategic threats, has called for the execution of Arab Members of the Knesset and stands behind the idea of the forcible transfer of the Arab community. Public statements such as these tend to incite and ignite the Jewish majority, resulting in direct physical attacks against Arab citizens by Jewish citizens. As a feeling of insecurity rises among Arab citizens, these acts of hate speech will reinforce fundamentalism and separation.

House Demolitions in Bedouin Communities

As part of the government's "Negev Development Plan," the Bedouin citizens of Israel face legal and political discrimination on two counts: The Removal of Intruders Law (1981) and its Amendment (2005). The Removal of Intruders Law (1981) details the legal process for the removal of the inhabitants from "illegal" homes built on governmental land in Israel, i.e. anyone living on the "non-residential" land as defined by the National Planning and Land Act (1965). The 2005 Amendment to this law strengthens the law's enforcement mechanisms by consolidating the body that issues demolition orders and the body that implements them – a process which will unjustly target the existing 38 unrecognized and 7 newly recognized villages in the Negev and streamline efforts to build Jewish settlements in their place. This is particularly acute in light of the 2005 withdrawal from settlements in the Gaza Strip, as governmental representatives held discreet negotiations with some Jewish settlers to appropriate land in the Negev in exchange for the withdrawal; some of the Gaza settlers have already been settled in the Negev.

Denying citizenship to spouses of Arab citizens

One of the most pressing recent legislations that directly discriminates against Palestinian Arab citizens is The Nationality and Entry into Israel Law (Citizenship Law), passed in July 2003 as a temporary measure requiring annual approval, which it receives from the Knesset with minor changes being made to improve the law. The Citizenship Law retroactively prohibits citizenship and legal residency status to all West Bank and Gaza Palestinians married to Israeli citizens and residents, including Palestinians who live in East Jerusalem and who hold special residency status in Israel. According to the Ministry of the Interior, this law affects at least 21,298 families. The law both prevents newly married couples from being able to live together and affects long-married couples whose requests for residence permits are still pending. This law directly discriminates against Israeli citizens of Palestinian origin and their spouses, as Palestinian Arab citizens of Israel are almost exclusively the ones to marry West Bank and Gaza residents. It violates the rights of both Palestinian Arab citizens and residents of the West Bank and Gaza to marry, form a family and choose a place of residence. This legislation does not affect marriages between Israeli citizens and other foreign spouses, including Jewish settlers illegally residing in the Occupied Palestinian Territories. As a result, this law permits discrimination on grounds of ethnicity and national origin and violates international human rights law, treaties and domestic laws under which Israel is obligated.[15]

THE 2006 WAR IN LEBANON: A CASE STUDY IN DISCRIMINATION

The war in Lebanon that began in July 2006 made evident the general discrimination against the Arab community of Israel. Throughout the conflict, the Arab citizens of Israel remained largely overlooked and misunderstood by the authorities of the state of Israel, the Israeli public and media, and a great

---

[15] Petitions against the law to the Israeli High Court of Justice are pending, with no decision yet delivered by the Court. See Mossawa Center press releases on the issue from 2003-present at <http://www.mossawacenter.org>

part of the international community, and were subject to increased instances of racism, discrimination and violence.

The Arab Community during the War

The second Lebanon war came by surprise to most of the Israeli public, quite particularly to the Arab community. A new government had just been elected, and the people of Israel had expected the new government's agenda to focus on strengthening the internal social and economic agenda in Israel and the withdrawal from the West Bank. Instead, the country felt the effects of the large-scale conflict with Lebanon, the destruction of cities and the deaths of civilians. The war took a heavy toll on the Arab community – 18 Arab citizens were killed during the shelling of Northern Israel during the conflict, making up 46% of the total civilian casualties in Israel. Aside from suffering civilian losses, the Arab community was the subject of incitement and discrimination from the government, public figures, security forces, the media and the general public, despite its clear position in support of peace during the war.

Continuing discrimination and large discrepancies in public resource allocation have created significant economic, social and political gaps between the Jewish and Arab communities of Israel. These social injustices were only further exemplified in political behavior, decisions and legislation passed during wartime.

Lack of infrastructure and government services

• According to an interview in *Ha'aretz* with Sharon Azrieli, a local security leader of the Union of Local Authorities, almost 30% of Israel's residents are without bomb shelters, with the majority of these residents from the Arab community.[16] A survey of 67 Arab localities made by the Follow-Up Committee for Arab Education in 2003 revealed that 38 lacked bomb shelters for their schools.[17] Many of the deaths that occurred in the Arab community were a direct result of the lack of an available shelter in which to take cover during air raids.

---

[16] Eli Ashkenazi, "Though officials were warned 5 years ago, bomb shelters weren't ready," *Haaretz* – Israel News Online, 29 Aug. 2006, 4 Sep. 2006, <http://www.haaretz.com/hasen/spages/755890.html>.

[17] *The Mossawa Center. Israeli Government Ignores Arab Citizens in Preparation for Iraq War*. Haifa: The Mossawa Center, 2003.

In fact, many of the Arab villages completely lacked an alarm system; people in these villages depended upon hearing the sirens from other nearby towns. The Arab village of Shagor, for example, had only three shelters and experienced four civilian casualties, while the neighboring towns of Tiberius, with 8,000 fewer inhabitants, had 633 shelters and no casualties (see Table below).[18] Although the Mossawa Center had petitioned for the construction of shelters and sirens for Arab villages through correspondence with various government bodies as early as 2003, no direct response was given to the issue of the lack of shelters in the Arab community in replies.[19]

Table: Gaps in protecting civilians in shelters in nearby localities

Cities	Civilian Casualties	Inhabitants in thousands	Shelters	Social economic level
Nazareth	2 killed	71.5	100	3
Nazareth Ilit	-	51.2	523	5
Cities	Civilian Casualties	Inhabitants in thousands	Shelters	Social economic level
Shagor	4	28	3	3
Tiberius	-	20.7	633	4
Carmiel	-	48.1	520	6
Cities	Civilian Casualties	Inhabitants in thousands	Shelters	Social economic level
Mughar	2	18.8	23	3
Misgav	-	18.2	350	6

Social economic levels according to the Israeli statistical data rank local councils from 1-10, 1 being the lowest.

---

[18] Mossawa Center, *Gaps in protecting civilians in shelters in nearby localities: Analysis of a database of the Union of Local Councils in Israel.* 31 Aug. 2006.
[19] Israeli Homefront Command. Letter to the Mossawa Center. 24 Mar. 2003.

- Following the bombing of an apartment building in the Arab neighborhood of Wadi Nisnas in Haifa on August 6, 2006, state and local governments failed to respond to the condition of the location and its tenants for three days. The tenants and families had no permanent housing, the rubble of their building was not cleaned up, and asbestos and broken sewage systems became an issue. The deputy mayor, however, had no difficulty using the site as a promotional stop for visiting diplomats and media coverage.[20]

- A report by the Ministry of Internal Affairs lists 59 of the 109 localities in the Galilee area as Arab.[21] During the war the Minister of Internal Affairs pledged over 120 million NIS to local councils in the Galilee for support during the war. According to an economic analysis by the Mossawa Center, only 29.9% of the 120 million NIS was allocated to Arab local councils, despite the fact that they make up over 50% of the localities.[22] About 40 of the Arab local councils report that they are currently unable to pay their staff members' salaries due to wartime costs, yet many requests to the ministry and government to assist in paying these salaries have been rejected.

- In yet another case of discrimination, the government created a national committee to address and plan solutions for the damage caused during the war. The committee did not include any Arab members even though a large percentage of war damage was incurred in the north, where, as mentioned above, a majority of the Arab population resides.[23]

- Other forms of discrimination have been indirect. Since the current government lacks a Ministry of Welfare, much of the aid given to the citizens of the Galilee area has come from local and international Jewish agencies. While it is not the intention of such aid agencies to discriminate against the Arab community, their priority is the Jewish community.

- In many cases, state assistance, benefits, housing options, loans and educational opportunities are contingent upon military service in Israel, which is not mandatory for Arab citizens. The MATI (Center for

---

20 Jehan Shahadi. Personal interview. 9 Aug. 2006.
21 Ministry of Internal Affairs. Internal Report on the amount of support given to local councils during the war. Unpublished. 15 Aug. 2006.
22 Union of Local Authorities. Damage from the war. Unpublished. 30 Aug. 2006.
23 "Olmert establishes a reconstruction committee for rebuilding the Galilee," *Haaretz* [Tel Aviv], 6 Aug. 2006.

Promoting Small Businesses) announced at the end of the war that it was offering special interest-free loans drawn from both private and state funds to help small businesses in the north. The loans, however, were made available only to Jewish citizens and former soldiers of the Israeli Defense Forces.[24] The Mossawa Center filed suit since these loans unfairly discriminate against the Arab community. Following the Mossawa criticism and intervention, MATI decided to stop the distribution of these funds completely rather than offering an equal distribution scheme.

Lack of Information in Arabic

With the bulk of major media sources in Israel being in the Hebrew language, and the lack of a significant and widely available Arabic media presence, information regarding the war during wartime was not always easily available to the Arab community, particularly in rural areas. The three major TV channels failed to transmit or translate important safety information in Arabic. Government brochures explaining responses to emergency situations were printed only in Hebrew, excluding the Arab community from vital, potentially life-saving information. Only during the last week of the war did they release an Arabic version of the pamphlet. The Israeli Homefront Command did not require the broadcasting companies to ensure that the Arab community be informed.[25]

Incitement and Violence

Israel is bound by both domestic and international law to protect its citizens against racism and discriminatory action based on race, ethnicity, color or national origin.[26] However, race-based violence against Arabs continues to be largely ignored by the government and law enforcement agencies. During the war, several instances of race-based incitement and violence against Arab citizens and political leaders were brought to the Mossawa Center's attention:

---

[24] Amiram Barkat, "Jewish Agency launches campaign to rehabilitate North," *Haaretz* [Tel Aviv], 16 Aug. 2006 <http://www.haaretz.com/hasen/pages/ShArtVty.jhtml?sw=small+business&iteNo=750950>.

[25] The Mossawa Center. Letter to the Prime Minister and Minster of Internal Affairs. 22 Aug. 2006.

[26] Israel Sentencing Law of 1977. 20 Nov. 2002; The UN Convention and the Elimination of All Form of Racial Discrimination ratified by Israel in 1979.

- A professor at an American university and a citizen of Israel as well as of Canada, was arrested for taking photos in a tourist area in Northern Israel. He was taken into custody and detained in Haifa for over three weeks, then released without further charges.[27]
- Several Arab MKs were ejected from a Knesset meeting while soldiers laughed and applauded "after heckling Defense Minister Amir Peretz and opposition leader Binyamin Netanyahu during their speeches on the war in Lebanon."[28] Jewish MKs called Arab MKs "representatives of Hezbollah in the Knesset"[29] and "a snake born to a snake," while another Arab MK received threats on his life in anonymous emails and phone calls.
- An Arab citizen was beaten by the police after he presented his ID card to them, simply because his name bore a resemblance to the last name of Hassan Nasrallah, leader of Hezbollah. A legal case has been filed by the Mossawa Center.[30]
- In several cases, demonstrators were arrested as well. Two staff members of the Mossawa Center were arrested by the police in a demonstration in Haifa on July 25. In Haifa, two civilians were arrested and forced to undress on a main street by the police, who claimed the civilians were planning to commit a suicide bombing. No bombs were found on their person or vehicles, yet they were detained for several days.[31]

Media Coverage

In many cases, media coverage was more discriminatory than actually causing incitement; the Arab perspective and position was often simply ignored by both the Hebrew and international media. However, in many cases, there was direct incitement against the Arab community; Arabs who did not support the war were labeled as Hezbollah supporters, and Arabs who blamed Israel's

---

[27] Carol Biliczky, "UA prof to stay in Israeli custody for week," *Akron Beacon Journal* [Ohio]. 18 Jul. 2006 <http://www.ohio.com/mld/ohio/news/15063076.htm>.

[28] "Three Arab MKs removed from Knesset session," *The Jerusalem Post*, 31 Jul. 2006 <http://www.jpost.com/servlet/Satellite?pagename=JPost%2FJPArticle%2FShowFull&cid=1153292040492>.

[29] "Arab MKs are taken from the Knesset and soldiers cheer." *Maariv* [Tel Aviv], 1 Aug. 2006: 7.

[30] The Mossawa Center. Letter to the Prime Minister and Minster of Internal Affairs. 22 Aug. 2006.

[31] Miran Rappaport, "Chief of Haifa Police arrests suspects on their way to attack," *Maariv* [Tel Aviv], 18 Aug. 2006: 16.

aggression for the deaths of family members were labeled extremists.[32]

RECOMMENDATIONS: THE LEBANON WAR AND BEYOND

Based upon the situation and ordeals confronting the Arab community during and following the recent war in Lebanon, the Mossawa Center proposes the following recommendations to the international community, including the Arab region:

1. **Ensure the participation of the Arab community in creating an atmosphere of peace and protecting their rights.** The unique status and accessibility of the Arab community should be utilized. The Israeli government should protect and ensure both the human and civil rights of this minority community and provide equal access to public resources and the legal system.

2. **Include UN international troops in the West Bank and Gaza.** The UN international troops that will secure the ceasefire in south Lebanon are an important step toward international protection of civilians in the region. The Mossawa Center calls the international community to create a similar force in the West Bank and Gaza Strip to ensure a ceasefire in these areas. The international community must remain aware and involved in the situation as it continues to unfold in the region.

3. **Create a UN international task force for peace negotiations.** The international community can play a key role as a mediator as it has in the past, helping promote peace agreements and fostering hostage exchanges.

4. **Increase the involvement of civil society.** A strong civil society has long been cited as a pillar of stability and an indicator of a thriving democracy.[33] By strengthening civil society throughout the region, we can hope to achieve a more solidly democratic system as well as an atmosphere of peace.

---

[32] Itamar Marcus and Barbara Cook. "Nasrallah Superman: An analysis of the war in Lebanon from the Palestinian perspective," *Palestinian Media Watch* Aug 2006, 30 Aug. 2006 <http://pmw.org.il/bulletins_aug2006.htm#b100806>.

[33] Michael Walzer, "The Civil Society Argument," *Dimensions of Radical Democracy: Pluralism, Citizenship, Community*, ed. Chantal Mouffe (London: Verso, 1992), 89-107.

5. **Encourage development in the region.** Although Israel was ranked number 22 out of 177 countries surveyed in the UN Human Development Index,[34] there are major development gaps not only between the Arab and Jewish citizens, but also between Israel and the rest of the Arab world as well. Poverty, low literacy rates, unemployment and lack of social services in Arab communities lead to discontented populations and further exacerbate the conflict in the region.[35] By building programs based on UN development reports, the international community will be able both to aid faltering communities and to help diffuse civil and political tensions.

6. **Strengthen democracy in the region.** As the Middle East undergoes political changes and the new elites struggle to share power with old, the international community has continued to attempt to intervene in the region on behalf of the ideals of democracy. Democracy in the region will be best strengthened by strengthening the voice of the people and encouraging democratic processes. The international community must support the demands of the people and not seek to force democracy through violence and military intervention.

---

[34] "Israel Fact Sheet," HDR 2005 – Country Fact Sheets. United Nations Development Programme (UNDP), 31 Aug. 2006 <http://hdr.undp.org/statistics/data/country_fact_sheets/cty_fs_ISR.html>.

[35] (2005). The Arab Human Development Report 2004. *Towards Freedom in the Arab World.* Z. J. Barbara Brewka, UNDP Regional Bureau for Arab States.

POLITICAL ANALYSIS
AND A VISION FOR PEACE

Ghassan Khatib

In spite of the difficult situation in which all Palestinians live today, the vast majority of the Palestinian people and leadership are still committed to the cause of peace. A true peace requires that the Palestinian people be treated with dignity and with respect. Such a peace would enable the Palestinian people to achieve their legitimate rights by ending the illegal Israeli Occupation that has lasted since 1967 in the West Bank, East Jerusalem, and the Gaza Strip. In spite of all the difficulties and in spite of all the suffering, the Palestinian people will continue to employ all possible means to stand against the continuation of this oppressive, illegal, inhumane Israeli occupation of the Palestinian Occupied Territories.

The last four or five years have probably been the most difficult for the Palestinian people since the beginning of the Israeli occupation. These years have witnessed not only an increase in both the level and means of injustice and oppression of the Palestinian people but also many dramatic changes in the internal and external contexts in which the Palestinian issue is perceived. Ten years ago, the Palestinians entered the peace process with optimism that it would enable us to live like the people of any normal nation. Independence and liberty and self-determination were the key terms in the aspirations and dreams of the Palestinian people. The international community assured the Palestinians that replacing violent means with political means on the basis of international law would enable us to achieve these legitimate objectives. And the Palestinian people entered into this peace process in a very serious and honest way.

Unfortunately, our experience of this peace process did not fulfill the promises that we were given in the beginning, and even more unfortunately, we found ourselves ten years after the beginning of the process even farther from realizing a genuine peace based on **international law** than we were at the beginning. Certain unfortunate developments can illustrate that failure. The first and probably most important is that Israel continued, throughout the period of the peace process, to expand the illegal Jewish settlements in all the occupied Palestinian Territories. For Palestinians, the peace process is about ending the occupation in return for peace, whereas the settlement expansion process, in our perception and in reality, is about consolidating the occupation. Palestinian people have difficulty understanding how the two processes could go together.

We have little difficulty understanding the Israeli motives behind their attempts to undermine the peace process by the expansion of the settlements. However, we have serious difficulty understanding how the international community, particularly the sponsors of this peace process, including the United States, at a certain point in time, and the Quartet, at a later point in time, would tolerate the continuous Israeli attempts to sabotage not only the foundations of the peace process and the notion on which this peace process is based, the two state solution, but even the future possibilities and potential of reaching peace. It is obvious that expanding the settlements creates facts on the ground which prejudice and diminish the possibility of establishing a Palestinian state in the West Bank, East Jerusalem and Gaza. The expansion of these facts on the ground precludes the possibility of making peace because peace is possible only if the Palestinian people can enjoy their right of self-determination within at least the small area which constitutes 22% of historical Palestine. The Palestinian people had already moved a long way in agreeing to accept the establishment of their independent state on only 22% of historical Palestine in return for Israel's ending its occupation of the West Bank and Gaza Strip.

The second major development, which is increasingly evident recently but which has been building up over the last few years, is the economic deterioration of the Palestinian people and the deterioration of their living conditions. The concern here is not only the humanitarian crisis and its expanding consequences, but also its effect on the attitude and perspective of the Palestinian people toward the peace-making process. Studies conducted by Palestinians or, in many cases by non-Palestinian academics, show very significant statistical correlations between the trends of deterioration of the standard of living, particularly the increase in unemployment and poverty, and the radicalization of the political and ideological mood of the Palestinian people. That is not a unique case for Palestine. It is a typical formula that scholars and researchers have found in many Third World countries.

In addition to these concerns, the last few years have witnessed a complete closure of political prospects for a peaceful settlement. The period that started with the leadership of Ariel Sharon in Israel has witnessed a complete shifting of Israeli strategy towards what was later called "unilateralism." Unilateralism is an Israeli strategy different from a tactic based on simply neglecting the existence of the "other side" as a partner for peace with Israel. It means taking unilateral steps, often by force, to determine the nature of the situation on the Palestinian side and the nature of the relations between Israel and Palestine. Such steps are usually designed in ways that take into consideration Israeli interests, needs and requirements at the expense of the Palestinian needs and interests. The way Israel has conducted its unilateral actions has contributed significantly to convincing a growing number of the Palestinian people that it is impossible to achieve our legitimate objective of ending the occupation by peaceful means.

The case of the unilateral withdrawal of the settlers and the military from Gaza is an example. If Israel had wanted to serve the cause of peace by the withdrawal from Gaza, it should and could have done that in the context of the peace process through dialogue and negotiations with the Palestinians under the leadership of President Mahmoud Abbas, who is known by everybody to be extremely committed to the cause of peace. Such an approach of ending Israeli control over Gaza through peaceful arrangements with the Palestinian leadership could have strengthened the Palestinian peace camp and increased the number of the Palestinian people who are convinced that the negotiations can bring us nearer to ending the Israeli occupation of the Palestinian Territories.

Instead, Israel decided to take a completely different approach. Israel chose to act completely unilaterally in a way that not only marginalized the Palestinian leadership and peace camp in Palestine but, in a way, enabled the opposition to the peace process in Palestine, led by Hamas, to claim that this Israeli withdrawal was an outcome of the resistance to the occupation in the Gaza Strip. Anybody examining the details of the Hamas election campaign in January 2006 will see clearly that this point was at the core of the campaign. Hamas managed to convince the majority of the public that the approach of

Mahmoud Abbas toward ending of the occupation had little chance of success because of Israeli policies and practices on the ground. Thus, many of the Palestinian people felt that the only possible alternative to help them reach an end to the Israeli occupation was that offered by Hamas and other political and religious movements which had been saying all along that Israel is not really interested in peace. Such groups also argued that Israel is only interested in finding different ways of maintaining its hegemony and control over the Palestinian Occupied Territories and that the language of peace is not a language that Israel is willing to respect and honor. Thus, they conclude that resistance and violence are the only alternatives left to the Palestinian people.

These are some of the major local factors which led not only to changing the political context of the conflict but also to changing the mood of the Palestinian people. This radicalization within the Palestinian public was illustrated, finally, in the results of the election held in January 2006, which ended in the failure of the political groups that campaigned on the basis of achieving Palestinian legitimate objectives by peaceful means and the victory of these groups that campaigned for achieving the same general objectives but by different means.

Of course, there is another factor which plays into the radicalization within Palestinian public opinion, and that is the regional context. There has been a clear radicalization, sometimes called Islamization, in the region in general. We must be clear in this regard because, in my analysis, if free and democratic elections like the one held in Palestine took place in any of the other Arab countries, with few exceptions, we would be likely to have more or less the same results that we had in Palestine. This reality should not be left to the superficial approach of President Bush. There is more at stake than security and a political way of understanding this phenomenon. There are very serious socioeconomic and cultural aspects and factors that need to be studied, understood and dealt with.

This region has been subject to different kinds of injustices. The world, the international community, has dealt with this region via double standards on more than one occasion, producing very deep negative effects upon the people of the entire region. This area has been witnessing economic deterioration and a widening of the gap in all aspects of life in the region as compared to those of the more advanced or industrialized parts of the world. This increasing gap is probably one of the primary root causes for the tension and for the radicalization evident today. The phenomenon of globalization has been really good at producing certain kinds of cultural hegemonies that also produce a negative effect on the mood and the opinion and the psychology of the people in this region. This negative effect in turn creates a fertile atmosphere for extreme forces seeking to take advantage of it. Therefore, when looking into the Palestinian case, in addition to examining the special characteristics of the Palestinian situation, analysts must take into consideration the regional context. In this regard, my view is that violence and political means are insufficient to deal with the issues we have. Non-politicians must have a share in trying to understand and contribute to solutions by examining the socioeconomic and cultural situations.

Another factor that has played into the regional context is the lack of democracy. I would also say that the dominant international superpowers have been responsible for that, because as all of us know, the least democratic regimes in the region, which are in some cases the most fundamentalist regimes as well as the least successful regimes in terms of development in the region, have received the maximum level of support from the major Western countries, especially the United States. If examples are needed, Saudi Arabia is an example for the first category, and the regime in Egypt is an example of the failure of the course of development. These regimes have been supported all along in all ways by the United States and other nations, simply because this has been a way of maintaining control and economic exploitation, including control of oil and other resources. There has always been a tradeoff in the American Middle East policy. The United States' policy in the Middle East for the last several decades has included sacrificing the need for democratization and development in this part of the world in order to maintain the existent political control of regimes by the United States. Unfortunately, that policy has not proved useful by any means, and part of the radicalization that we see in the region is a result, among other causes, of this lack of democracy and development in the region in general.

To return to the Palestinian situation, I must allude to the recent difficult situations and crises following the election of the Hamas government in Palestine. The international community decided to impose an embargo, essentially stopping aid to the Palestinian people; unfortunately the policy has backfired because the economic situation was already one of the factors in the radicalization process. The recent decision by the international community to further reduce aid to the Palestinian people has reinforced the economic crisis and played out negatively rather than achieving their objectives. At the same time, the last few years have witnessed an increase in the Israeli restrictions on the movement of the Palestinian people and commodities, as officially substantiated by published reports from the World Bank and U.N. agencies. This Israeli policy is primarily responsible for severe economic deterioration and for an unprecedented increase in unemployment, which, especially in Gaza, has reached at least 70%, leaving about 2/3 of the population below the poverty level. So, if Israel and the international community are trying to reverse Palestinian public opinion and to shift the balance of power in Palestinian politics and society by increasing Israeli restrictions on the Palestinian people, by increasing the hardships under which the Palestinians live, and by punishing the Palestinian Authority by reducing international aid, they are making serious mistakes. They are pushing things in exactly the opposite direction and reinforcing the same trends of radicalization that we have been witnessing.

What, then, is the way out of this vicious cycle? On the Palestinian side, the position which enabled Hamas to win the election was that the peace process had not been working because the peace process only enabled Israel to increase its settlements and consequently to consolidate the occupation. The Israeli argument is that the only way to fight radicalism and violence within the Palestinian community is to increase the restrictions and to increase the Israeli violence which characterizes the occupation. Thus, we are in a vicious circle which is useful only to the enemies both in Israel and in Palestine. My major recommendation for getting out of this vicious circle is an **active third party role** because one of the characteristics of the last four or five years is an international abandonment of the Palestinian/Israeli conflict. The United States has largely withdrawn, particularly since President Bush adopted the strategy of abandoning direct diplomatic activities related to the Palestinian/Israeli conflict. Maximum efforts were to come from the Road Map, but unfortunately, no political weight was invested in it by the United States. In other words, the American strategy was to leave the Israeli leadership, particularly Sharon, to handle this issue. That decision was disastrous, as we all know.

The first recommendation, then, in order to get out of this vicious circle is that the international community must pay more attention to the conflict because leaving the Israelis and Palestinians on their own only leads to deterioration of the situation, simply because of the great imbalance of powers between the two sides. Israel immediately realized that this was the time to take advantage of their military superiority but the Palestinians, as experience shows, will never give in to force and will keep refusing to submit. Thus, the whole deteriorating vicious circle continues.

The second recommendation for breaking the vicious circle is that the parties have to go back to the negotiation table on the basis of **international law**, and negotiations must include the international community and not only the governments and the Quartet and the U.N. People who have a general commitment to the cause of peace internationally as well as within the Palestinian conflict must take a side, and I don't mean the Palestinian side or the Israeli side. I mean that there is a set of resolutions of the United Nations General Assembly and in the Security Council that stipulates what is wrong and what is right in this conflict. There is also an **international law** that is applicable everywhere, including this part of the world. I urge everybody who wants to make a difference to take the side of international law and to work hard and speak out loudly against any party or individual or group which violates international law vis a vis this conflict. At the same time, the international community must show sympathy toward and must support, encourage and empower any individual or group who is promoting a solution based on the international law, whether that is the Palestinians, some of the Palestinians, the Israelis or some of the Israelis.

Third, the Palestinians should not be left in their current state of unemployment and poverty, not only because of the humanitarian aspect, which I do not underestimate, but also because the economic deterioration is not conducive for peacemaking. Economic deterioration and unemployment, especially among the younger generation, which statistically has the highest level of unemployment, are conditions conducive only for extremism, for hatred, for violence, for terrorism. We must try to help the Palestinians to help themselves in this regard by trying to alleviate their economic suffering. In this regard, the reduction of international aid to the Palestinians after the election of Hamas has been counter-productive. Of course aid does not only have to come through governmental means. There are all kinds of possibilities and channels that can take care of any legal sensitivity or any ethical sensitivity, but the question here is that the Palestinian people must receive more attention while the international community seeks to bring a political solution to this conflict. As long as the international community, led by the United States government, is refusing to pressure Israel to end this occupation, knowing that that is the only way to achieve peace, then the international community has to fulfill its commitment to respond to the Palestinian economic and political needs.

Finally, cultural exchange is extremely necessary at this point of time between Western people and the Arabs in general and the Palestinian people in particular. This exchange is vital because the part of the current crisis that manifests itself in a political manner is coming not from the political and economic factors mentioned earlier, but from cultural misunderstandings that seem to be growing rapidly just now. That is why gatherings like the Sabeel International Conference are extremely useful and provide a pioneering example that needs to be followed by people from different faiths and professions. We must not leave cultural exchange to politicians alone, but we must allow people to have their say, not only to understand these difficult situations and relations but also to contribute to reducing the wide gap in all aspects of life whether economic or political or cultural.

NOTES TOWARD AN ECONOMIC STRATEGY FOR LIBERATION FROM OCCUPATION

Yousef Nasser

He that would make his own liberty secure, must guard even his enemy from oppression; for if he violates this duty, he establishes a precedent which will reach to himself. (Thomas Paine [1737-1809], Dissertation on First Principles of Government, 1795)

The history of liberty is a history of resistance. The history of liberty is a history of limitations of governmental power, not the increase of it. (Woodrow Wilson Speech in New York, September 9, 1912)

With the signing of the Oslo Peace agreement between Israel and the PLO, many assumed wrongly that the military occupation and in particular the Israeli mechanisms of controlling every aspect of Palestinian life came to an end. They did not; Israeli control over the Palestinian territories occupied in 1967 and over the Palestinian people has intensified and has become more brutal and oppressive. Former US President Jimmy Carter has recently written a book *Palestine: Peace, Not Apartheid* in which he states:

> Israel's current policy in the territories is a system of Apartheid, with two peoples occupying the same land but completely separated from each other, with Israelis totally dominant and suppressing violence by depriving Palestinians of their basic human rights. Israel's continued control and colonization of Palestinian land have been the primary obstacles to a comprehensive peace agreement in the Holy Land. (215)

The first part of this paper will show the continuation of the occupation and the forms of oppression and hardship it produces. It will address the ongoing land theft, the settlement of Jewish populations among Palestinian communities, the building of the Wall to contain Palestinian communities and the checkpoints which control movement. The following section will address the economic impact of the occupation. The next section will address the failure of Palestinian economic policy. The final section will attempt to identify an economic model for liberation. These are initial thoughts requiring more rigorous formulation, but they can be utilized for the purpose of informing an economic strategy for liberation.

THE INTENSIFICATION OF THE OCCUPATION

The 1967 Occupation of the West Bank and the Gaza Strip brought the economic organization of these territories and the indigenous Palestinian population under the control of the oppressive and exploitive colonial settler regime of Israel. Between 1967 and 1980, Israel controlled the Palestinian territories through direct military rule. In 1980-81, it introduced the facade of a civil administration which in turn operated under military command. The 1994 Oslo Accords introduced a Palestinian Authority (PA) and allowed it limited autonomy over a limited territory. In Area A, which equals 3% of Palestinian territory, the PA has control over administrative and security issues; in Area B, which equals 24% of the land, the PA has civil responsibilities only; and in Area C, Israel has full control over land, security, and people.[1] All other powers remained ultimately under the control of the Israeli military forces. Rather than being a step towards liberation and freedom, the opposite occurred. The present conditions under which Palestinians live have never been so grave and full of hardship.

Today the forceful military occupation of the Palestinian territories continues, albeit under a cynical historical pretense of a stalled "peace process." Throughout the occupation and more so since the historical Palestinian compromise of recognizing Israel and renouncing an armed struggle, Israel

---

[1] J. Isaac and M. Rizik. *"Israel's land colonization policy and the viability of the Palestinian State"*, (Applied Research Institute-Jerusalem), http://www.arij.org

has continued to steal Palestinian land and water resources,[2] settle Jewish immigrants amongst the Palestinian communities, and most recently to build walls around Palestinian communities so that a Jewish majority can be maintained and not exposed to the indigenous population. In addition to the Wall, the placement of roadblocks throughout the West Bank has transformed the area into village-stans, town-stans and city-stans, much like the Bantustans of apartheid South Africa. This has severely restricted and in some cases prohibited the movement and access of people and goods between what I would venture to label the **Palestans**.

In 1985 it was estimated that over 52 percent of the land of the West Bank was under Israeli control.[3] Today about 60 percent remains under full Israeli control. However, recently the building of the Wall not only has confiscated large tracts of land but also has reinforced and solidified the Palestanization of the West Bank. The Wall has been built mainly on Palestinian land occupied in 1967. For example on September 5th and 12th 2006, the Israeli occupation authority issued two military orders for the Wall building process: number 69/06/T to confiscate 152 dunums (one dunum = 0.24 acre) in Al Khader and Beit Fajjar and number T/77/06 to confiscate 102 dunums of land in Al Khader and Artas villages west of Bethlehem near Road 60.[4] This barrier will eventually run for almost 700 kilometers (437 miles), of which over 400 kilometers (252 miles) have already been built. Confiscation of land not only takes place for the purpose of building the Wall but also for expanding existing settlements and starting new ones. One of the most insulting confiscations of land for the expansion of settlements took place in the Ramallah district only three months after the signing of the Oslo "peace accords." Since 1994 land confiscation has proceeded at an accelerated pace. Recently it was reported that a secret study conducted by the Israeli military showed that "…rampant illegal construction in dozens of settlements and in many cases involving privately owned Palestinian properties" continues unabated.[5]

---

[2] Attorney General Menachem Mazuz has defined the establishment of settlements on private Palestinian land as "land theft." See *Ha'aretz*, "Some 2,000 Palestinians banned from entering Jordan Valley" 14/03/2006

[3] M. Benvenisti. "1986 REPORT: Demographic, Economic, Legal, Social and Political Developments in the West Bank", (Jerusalem, West Bank Data Project, 1986), p.25.

[4] See ARIJ Website at http://www.arij.org/paleye/monthley/September_2006/index.htm

[5] *Ha'aretz*, "Settlements grow on Arab land, despite promises made to U.S." 24/10/2006, http://www.haaretz.com/hasen/spages/778767.html.

Furthermore, 107 outposts have been created since the Oslo Accords but that is small change compared to the construction in the older settlements which has been ongoing for years, in blatant violation of the law and in disregard of the peace commitments signed by numerous Israeli governments agreeing to stop such activity.

Additionally, Palestinian freedom of movement is severely controlled and restricted mainly by means of roadblocks and checkpoints. The U.N. agency, OCHA, recently reported that it has seen an increase of nearly 40 percent in the number of army checkpoints and physical barriers in the West Bank, from 376 in August 2005 to 528 in September of 2006. The number of checkpoints is now greater than the total number of Palestinian cities, towns and villages. In other words, there is more than one checkpoint for each Palestinian community. People are not allowed to cross many of these checkpoints without a permit issued by the military authorities. Other checkpoints do not require permits but the time and humiliation suffered by people is most often extreme, making travel between towns and cities a major hardship. The West Bank is today divided and separated into four major **stans**: the northern, central and southern **stans** and of course Gaza-**stan**. And within each block, local communities are further isolated from each other by more roadblocks and road closures into village-**stans** and town-**stans**.

THE IMPACT OF OCCUPATION ON THE ECONOMY

The structure of the Palestinian economy today is distorted as a result of both the past and present policies of the occupation authority and of the historical forced interaction between a capital intensive Israeli economy and a traditional labor intensive Palestinian economy. The main distortion is found in the employment, trade and production sectors. During the pre-Oslo period, a significant segment of Palestinian labor found employment in Israel (mainly unskilled and manual labor), and another found employment in the Diaspora (brain drain). Within the Palestinian economy very few new employment opportunities were created. For example, between 1967 and 1987, domestic employment in the West Bank remained constant. Remittances from employment outside the economy led to an increase in aggregate demand, which in turn was mainly supplied by imports from Israel and not by an increase in domestic productive capacity.

Throughout this period occupation authority policies blocked the creation and expansion of Palestinian productive capacity. occupation policy dictated licensing and permits for each stage of business initiatives, and these were rarely granted.[6] In addition, military occupation authorities imposed effective administrative barriers to Palestinian exports. Another important factor contributing to non-investment in productive capacity is the high risk associated with political instability and uncertainty deriving from occupation.

Some observers have had the audacity to claim that the Palestinians have benefited from exposure to the Israeli economy. Basically differing interpretations and conclusions have been reached about the outcome of this encounter with settler colonialism. However, there is agreement that the consequences of the occupation on the economies of the Occupied Territories have been profound and far-reaching. It would be difficult to challenge an observation, made as early as 1977, that although there was no

...Israeli master-plan for changing the external economic relationships of the two occupied territories [West Bank and Gaza Strip] or a long-range vision of a preferred economic future for them ... what happened after 1967 was more complex and no less profound than if such a master-plan actually existed.[7]

Eighteen years after occupation, an Israeli observer reached a similar conclusion. He noted that after his examination of the facts, Israel's economic policy seems to be clear and consistent, aimed at

...freezing the economic development of the Palestinian sector...economic stagnation at the communal level; discouraging independent economic development that would enter into competition with the Israeli economy, and prevention of independent economic development that could enable Palestinian political forces to establish power bases, and eventually a Palestinian state.[8]

---

6 A. Aronon, et al. "The Palestinian Economy: Between Imposed Integration and Voluntary Separation" (Leiden,Brill, 1997), p. 233.

7 B. Van Arkadie. "Benefits and Burdens: A Report on the West Bank and Gaza Strip Economies Since 1967" (New York, Carnegie Endowment For International Peace, 1977), p.37.

8 M. Benvenisti, et al. "The West Bank Handbook: A Political Lexicon", (Jerusalem, West Bank Data Project, 1986), p.67.

Economic relations since 1993 in general, and since the Protocol on Economic Relations negotiated and signed in Paris on April 29, 1994 (hereafter the Economic Protocol) have led only to cosmetic change. The basic economic relations between Israel, the rest of the world and the Palestinian economy remain the same. The Protocol preserved the imposed captivity of the Palestinian economy that existed between 1967 and 1994, with only minor peripheral modifications.

The terms of trade between Palestinians, Israel and the rest of the world remain *a de facto* customs union with Israel. Israeli customs policy, rules and regulations apply to trade between Palestine and Israel and between Palestine and the rest of the world. The Economic Protocol granted the Palestinians a few crumbs, such as the mandate to independently determine "…the rates of customs, purchase tax, levies, excises and other charges, the regulation of licensing requirements and procedures and of standard requirements"[9] on three lists of goods. List A1 includes goods produced in Jordan and in Egypt in particular, while List A2 includes goods from the Arab, Islamic and other counties. List B consists of food items and other goods for the Palestinian economic development plan. Goods on these lists have no strategic significance for Palestinian development, and to add insult to injury, the quotas on the quantities were fixed, and could not be increased without approval of the Joint Economic Committee (JEC), such increase to be based on an estimate of the Palestinian market need. This committee was set up by Article II of the Economic Protocol and can only reach a decision by agreement (Article II, paragraph 4). So if the Israeli side does not agree, no change can take place. Again the Israeli occupation authority continues to rule.

Other concessions made by the occupation authority involved the financial sector. Arab and Palestinian banks were allowed to open, and a Palestinian Monetary Authority recognized; however, the banks were subjected to the rules and regulations of the Israeli Central Bank as is the Monetary Authority. The Palestinian Authority was also allowed two additional concessions: to determine and collect their income taxes, and to import vehicles free of tariffs. In short the terms of economic activity between Israel and Palestine, and Palestine and the rest of the world did not change. Only minor and insignificant mandates were allotted to Palestinian decision making.

---

[9] *PROTOCOL ON ECONOMIC RELATIONS between the Government of the State of Israel and the P.L.O., representing the Palestinian people*, Paris, April 29, 1994. in Aronon, A. et al., 1997, pp.239-268.

Today the economic, social and political conditions prevailing in the **Palestans** are disastrous. The unemployment rate is over 40 percent; almost 80 percent of the population in **Gaza-stan** is living below the poverty line, and over 50 percent live under the poverty line in the **West Bank-stans**. As of November 2006, over 150,000 PA employees had not received salaries for over six months, and today many businesses are near bankruptcy. Economic developments have been and continue to be determined mainly by the occupation authority and by other external factors. The Israeli authorities owe the PA almost one billion U.S. dollars in taxes they collected and did not transfer. The Western and other donors have imposed a boycott on development funding to the PA. It is often asked in amazement how the Palestinian population has held up. The only response is an educated guess, with an evaluation that they have had the ability to adjust their behavior according to circumstances. How long they can survive is anyone's guess.

However, it can be seen that on the social level the society is reverting to its tribal heritage and affiliations. This is the institution that seems to be providing a form of personal and economic security and protection. Politically rather than confronting the evil occupation, Palestinians are pre-occupied with blaming and accusing each other for these Israeli-imposed problems, and more recently we have witnessed sporadic and bloody gun battles among Palestinians, mainly in **Gaza**-stan.

THE FAILURE OF POST-OSLO ECONOMIC POLICY

As shown above, a close reading of the Economic Protocol indicates that the basic economic links with Israel and their impact on the structure of the Palestinian economy remained relatively unchanged. The major change since Oslo has been the initially gradual restriction and then abrupt ending of Palestinian employment in Israel.

Donor funding aimed at building the Palestinian state somewhat compensated for the major loss of income from employment in Israel. However, a significant portion of this capital was wasted on technical assistance (training and consultants), and siphoned into private accounts by corrupt officials. The workers who lost their jobs in Israel were not compensated and had to compete for limited jobs created by donor-financed infrastructure projects at much lower wages. Unwisely, the Palestinian Authority made a small dent in unemployment by hiring over one hundred twenty thousand into the civil service and security sectors. Today there are around one hundred fifty thousand government employees, whereas in 1993 there were fewer than thirty thousand. The thirty thousand were more or less providing the same level of services provided today by the one hundred fifty thousand.

Palestinian government expenditure policy has also been a disappointment. Resources were allocated to non-productive and wasteful activity. Government spending (fiscal policy) and hiring policy were determined by political and social imperatives rather than by economic logic. Today the public sector is well-known for its over-employment. Over 60 percent of the recurrent budget is for wages and salaries of employees. At a time when the developing world was reducing the size of the public sector, the Palestinian Authority was doing the opposite. Not only were they over-hiring but they were hiring under-qualified and mediocre performers. Hiring practices were rife with nepotism, political cronyism and favoritism.

The allocation of the budget to different sectors was and continues to be inappropriate for the needs of liberation from occupation. The lion's share of the budget goes to security forces (police and a host of other military and para-military apparatuses) which have proven to be ineffective in confronting the occupation forces. On the other hand the share of the budget allocated to strategic sectors, such as health, education and social services is insignificant. Consequently the major economic developments have been the birth and growth of monopolies, concessions, capital flight, and the differentiation of society into a few super rich, a large impoverished class, and a dwindling middle class. These classes do not have a common interest that can bind them together to confront the oppressive occupation. What has happened is the concentration of capital and wealth in a few hands, i.e. monopolies (Paltel and Jawal), whose main interest is to maximize profits regardless of the consequences, and who, on top of this, export their profits for investment in more lucrative opportunities (Latin America and the Gulf States) outside of Palestine.

In addition we see collusion and price fixing (concrete producers, steel merchants and cement merchants) among the major businesses supplying strategic inputs to production. In the early PA years, we saw the flight of over two billion dollars of capital out of the country during the first two years of bank operation. We see the production of shoddy and low quality goods and the import of cheap, low quality goods that compete with local producers: textiles and furniture from China and the Far East, olive oil from Europe and

Turkey and so on. In short, we see among many producers no competition although that is supposedly the hallmark of free market systems. In one case it was found that one major producer managed to acquire an exclusive right to sell products that directly compete with his own goods. When asked why, he said, "If I did not get it, someone else would and would compete with me." Eventually this producer reduced his production lines significantly, and now is a merchant selling the products of a foreign producer. Unfortunately this guarantees him his profits, but reduces the value added to the Palestinian economy, in addition to decreasing the employment of Palestinian workers.

An alternative economic model for liberation

A major decision taken by the Palestinian leadership during the initial days of the Palestinian Authority was to adapt the free market model for Palestinian economic activity. The hypothesis to be addressed in these preliminary notes is that the free market system of economic organization is inappropriate for liberation in general and from occupation in particular. Two reasons stand out for why this is so in the Palestinian case. The first is that the prevailing economic environment and the legal structure are not conducive to or appropriate for the operation of a free market system, and the second is that the purpose of a free market system is to serve the interest of the individual (consumer or firm), and not the community purpose of liberation.

Free market economics is based on the rational actor model of human behavior. Behavior is explained as that effort of individuals which maximizes, satisfies or optimizes self-interest. It is claimed that the individual, by pursuing his/her self-interest, will serve and optimize the interest of the community at large. Furthermore it is claimed that impersonal markets produce the optimum or most efficient allocation of resources. How, you may ask? There is no logical answer to this question. The celebrated answer is that it is achieved "…as if by an invisible hand." Basically it is an article of faith. However, history has shown that when the market mechanism is allowed to operate freely, it can produce mayhem in the economy and hardship in the society. The Depression of the 1930's, pollution, global warming, and mad-cow disease are just a few examples. Once market failure hit western capitalist countries and society suffered often prolonged economic hardships, the leaders of these countries realized that markets had to be managed. Consequently laws and regulations were introduced, such as the Antitrust Act of 1890 in the U.S.A., which regulated and prohibited specific behavior of individual firms to form cartels, fix prices, and rig bids. When the system nearly collapsed in the 1930's, it was recognized that the markets might stabilize (come to a state of equilibrium) at levels far below full employment and that these levels were well below what was socially acceptable. Thus it was proposed and then accepted that the market economy needed to be managed, i.e. raise interest rates and reduce government spending when the economy is over-heating and vice-versa when it is in a recession. Today the market economies of the west are highly regulated by consumer protection laws, minimum wage laws, environmental protection laws, bankruptcy laws, business disclosure laws, etc. The point is this: if free markets worked perfectly, all these laws and regulations to protect the individual consumer would not be necessary.

The laws and regulations controlling the market mechanism are mainly aimed to protect the interest of the very same individual that the free market mechanism is supposedly meant to serve and benefit (the individual consumer). It is accepted that the purpose of the free market mechanism is to serve the interest of the individual consumer, just the same as western democracy serves the individual rights and protects the liberty of each individual citizen. However, the market mechanism can only achieve this if it is regulated and directed to do so.

In the Palestinian case, when our leaders adapted the free market system, the laws and regulations in operation were and continue to be lacking or to be inappropriate for such a system. In addition, the institutions necessary for the operation of a market system were simply not there. Among these are financial institutions, legal institutions, consumer protection agencies and institutions, enforcement institutions, and public protection institutions. The laws and regulations existing and in operation were developed to serve the interest of empires (Ottoman) or colonizers (British) or caretaker governments (Egyptian and Jordanian) or settler colonialists (military orders). They were aimed at strengthening the power of the central government and weakening local communities. What is mind-boggling is that after ten years or more of Palestinian legislative power, the laws, rules and regulations in determining economic factors are those of the past regimes. For example, rental laws enforced in the West Bank are the Jordanian Law dating from the 1950s and are anti-free market. The contraband regulations are based on Israeli military orders. And the list goes on.

One of the fundamental issues addressed in the political economy is the purpose of economic activity. As discussed above, the purpose of the free market system is to serve and benefit individual consumers. In other cases the purpose may be to empower a social class, an ethnic group, or a religious denomination. Or it may be to maximize national power. In the Palestinian context, I propose that the purpose of economic activity should be liberation from occupation and from Zionist Settler Colonialism in particular.

Given this goal, an attempt will be made to put forth initial ideas and proposals for a political economic strategy of national liberation. The material economic and political conditions under which Palestinians live have been briefly touched upon above but need further evaluation so that appropriate and concrete mechanisms for liberation can be proposed. An economic model for the purpose of liberation needs to be developed, and a strategy based on such a model formulated. Below is an attempt to put forth rough preliminary ideas on what such a model may look like, and what the strategy is most likely to entail.

First of all, the purpose of economic activity in the economic model to be developed is liberation from colonial occupation and from oppression and exploitation. To be realistic, this model cannot ignore the role of markets in the daily life of production and reproduction of Palestinian society. The market has a role to play because in daily transactions, the individual knows why, how and where his best interest and benefits lie. However, the markets must be regulated to protect the individual from unfair competition, from monopolies, from price setting and from occupation policy. The market must also be regulated and managed to protect local producers from cheap and shoddy imports. The purpose of economic activity and of the model is to serve the liberation of Palestine, not the individual consumer, nor a sector of society, nor a privileged class. Economic policy must protect both the individual Palestinian consumer and the individual producer and direct them to allocate resources to those productive activities that enhance Palestinian society's capacity to resist occupation and to achieve liberation. The maximization of individual self-interest contradicts social interest and contradicts the task of national liberation. Liberation is by definition a community effort. Resources must be allocated to those sectors which maximize the benefit to community for the purpose of liberation. Where the market mechanism can contribute to our purpose, it must be allowed to function, but where it does not, it must be restricted and other mechanisms identified and deployed.

THE BASIC AND PRELIMINARY STRATEGY

The strategy appropriate for achieving the purpose of liberation in regards to macroeconomic factors includes several components: reallocation of the Palestinian Authority budget; government insurance on loans to small scale investors who generate employment and domestic production; a concerted boycott campaign; an efficient social welfare system based on Palestinian needs and not on imported models.

The share of the budget allocated to security must be reduced, and the share going to health, education and social welfare increased. It does not make sense that one of our major and most important resources (human capital) receives less than 20 percent of the national expenditure budget for its maintenance and development. This is especially pressing given that the student population makes up more than 35 percent of the total population. (There are over 1.2 million students enrolled in primary, middle and high schools.) The more educated a population and the higher the quality of education, the more productive the population is. In today's world the importance in terms of the linkages and contribution of knowledge to economic activity is well-recognized. The knowledge-based economy will not only be a means to by-pass Israeli trade restrictions and sanctions but will equip the population with non-military and more effective means and tools for confronting the occupation.

The health sector is grossly under-financed, as well as being inefficient. Having only nine percent of the budget going to health care in a country where few can afford private health care is a gross misallocation of resources. The priorities need to be overhauled and restructured. On paper, preventive medicine is given priority; however, tertiary medicine consumes the lion's share of the budget. It has been proposed and indicated in a number of studies that with a significant decrease in the latter and a corresponding marginal increase in the primary health sector, the health service demands of the nation will fall significantly in the tertiary sector. Furthermore, the healthier the population, the more productive that population is. It is recognized that education services and health care are means by which society can pull its people out of the poverty trap or at least not let more fall into the poverty trap.

Job creation for this educated and healthy population is another aspect of the strategy that must be considered. When Israel directly ruled over Palestinian economic activity, they prohibited any growth and development.

Historically the increased income and therefore rising aggregate demand from employment in Israel was channeled to imports from Israel. Even today, with no employment in Israel, demand for goods is met by imports from Israel. A major component of the strategy for liberation is a boycott campaign of Israeli goods which have Palestinian substitutes during the initial phase, coupled with incentives for investment in extended and expanded productive capacity. Eventually investment should be directed towards production that allows us to expand the list of boycotted goods coming from Israel. At the same time Palestinian producers must be regulated to prohibit them from making windfall profits, producing low quality goods, or even re-packaging and labeling imported Israeli goods as Palestinian produced goods, as happened during the first Intifada.

A successful Palestinian boycott campaign will strengthen the international campaign to boycott Israeli products, an effort which is presently going through its initial and partially successful stage. The boycott of Israeli goods will provide a push and incentive for investment in expanding Palestinian productive capacity.

Production activity that utilizes local raw material inputs and local labor, as well as a local market for output, should be given priority in terms of its support. In addition to this, production of products that substitute for Israeli goods needs to be given priority. Locating production in local communities will also reduce the power of the occupation to impact economic activity via their roadblocks, checkpoints, and trade barriers. It will also reduce the transactions cost of production and marketing output. Since the segregation of the Palestinian territory by the Wall and the checkpoints, transport cost alone has risen by over 200 percent. These small scale producers may face a capital constraint for investment, and this is where the PA comes in to provide insurance on loan defaults from commercial banks. The major obstacle banks face in granting loans to businesses is the absence of adequate collateral. Government insurance of some type or other can remove this obstacle.

The tax system in the PA needs to be reevaluated and redesigned to meet the purpose of the liberation strategy. The bulk of PA revenues come from the value added tax (VAT). This system of taxation disproportionately taxes the poor more than it taxes the rich. The rich pay fewer taxes than do the poor, yet the poor spend more of their income on basic goods. The rich save in banks, and the banks transfer this capital to the global market. It is an unequal tax; however, it is imposed upon us by the Economic Protocol. It cannot be revoked, yet the Protocol gave the PA the right to increase it or decrease it by two percent from the Israeli rate. So today one can reduce it to 13.5 percent (given the Israeli rate of 15.5 percent), and the PA can more than make up for this loss in revenue by increasing income tax on corporations which have been making windfall profits from their monopoly positions.

Furthermore taxes collected by the PA must be ploughed back into the local communities, mainly to strengthen the only consistent form of government serving the Palestinian population and existing independently of Oslo and the occupation. This government is that of the local authorities (Municipal Councils, Village Councils), which must expand their capacity to develop policy and serve their inhabitants by providing them with infrastructure development funding. Other innovative tax options can be introduced that aim to serve the liberation purpose.

CONCLUSION

This has been a brief discussion of the continuity of the occupation, despite the existence of the PA., in addition to some of the problems arising from improper PA economic policies. The hypothesis is that a free market mechanism is inappropriate for economic strategies of liberation. The free market concept must be incorporated and brought to serve an economic system conducive to liberation. Some initial elements of an economic strategy for liberation have been presented. However, these need to be further analyzed and fine tuned. Basically they are intended to initiate a dialogue or discussion on the subject of economic strategies for liberation. Further rigorous research is needed to develop a more comprehensive model and strategy. Economic strategy is only one factor that needs to be implemented for achievement of liberation. There are other elements that need to be incorporated, as one Palestinian patriot recently commented: the Palestinian people need to invest in their unity, social trust, collective work and human resources for confronting the occupation and achieving liberation.

STRATEGIES TO END
THE OCCUPATION AT THE GRASSROOTS

Terry Boullata

The majority of the Palestinian people have reached the point of thinking that nobody cares about their situation, but international presence and attention restore hope that many people do care. This support is vital as we consider the role of grassroots efforts in Palestine to end the occupation.

First let me say the occupation will end. No occupation has lasted forever, and the Israeli occupation will not be an exception. When it will end depends on lots of things, certainly including the role of the Palestinian grassroots movement in resisting the occupation.

HISTORY OF THE GRASSROOTS MOVEMENT IN PALESTINE

The history of the Palestinian grassroots movement starts at the beginning of the last century when Palestinians realized that their country was about to be colonized by the Zionist movement with the help of the British, who occupied Palestine at the time. The revolts of the 1920's and 30's were early markers for the successes of organized grassroots movements.

In the 1980's, with the outbreak of the first Intifada, the Palestinian grassroots movement reached its peak. It was very well-organized, included every sector and covered every aspect of life within the Palestinian society. Teachers, farmers, medical professionals, women, youth, and the collective unity among all the sectors gave the Israeli occupation more than it could handle. It was totally active non-violent resistance, collective and on many occasions, spontaneous. When Israel closed our schools, sports fields and backyards became the schools. When Israel blocked shipments of food into the Occupied Territories, every person became a farmer and we ate from the land. We called for strike days and we ended the strikes when we wanted. The Palestinian people were in control and that happened without firing a single bullet. The struggle of the grassroots movement in the eighties put the Palestinian issue on the map, brought Palestine into the headlines, exposed the ugly face of the occupation and led to the beginning of the peace process.

The second Intifada is different; it became very violent because the grassroots movement was sidelined from the beginning. Young armed groups were frustrated by the lack of progress in the peace process after ten years of negotiations with Israel had produced no change in the life and collective aspirations of the Palestinian people.

The second Intifada produced a devastating impact on the grassroots. The majority of the Palestinian people were sidelined in their efforts to resist the occupation and they were used as a punching bag by the Israeli army in revenge for some of the acts of the young Palestinian militants. The lack of a clear collective vision and the lack of leadership at the grassroots level left the grassroots movement in despair.

In 2002 when Israel started constructing the Wall, the grassroots movement started showing signs of life again. The Palestinian grassroots Anti-Apartheid Wall Campaign was established in October 2002 under the name Palestinian Environmental NGOs Network (PENGON). The aim of the campaign was to establish popular committees that mobilize and coordinate efforts on local, national and international levels. Since its inception, the Campaign has been the main national grassroots body mobilizing and organizing resistance against the Wall. It presently coordinates the work of 54 popular committees in communities which are being or will be destroyed by the Wall. The committees form the space where people can meet, organize, strategize and mobilize.

In some areas, mobilization efforts have been very successful as in the example of Bil'in, where the people of the village gather every Friday to defend their lands and confront the occupation forces non-violently. They have also managed to attract peace and human rights activists from the Israeli peace camp and from around the world. The people of Bil'in are still resisting, and they deserve the respect and the admiration of all peace-loving people.

In 2004, some individual efforts led to the establishment of the Palestinian Campaign for Freedom and Peace. The first act in the campaign was to bring to Palestine Dr. Arun Gandhi, the grandson of the great Mahatma, in order to promote a Palestinian campaign of non-violent resistance against the occupation. The tour and the visit were very successful as they brought thousands of Palestinians to rally in Ramallah, the largest rally ever held in the history of that city. Abu Dis and Bethlehem rallies with Dr. Gandhi also showed the Palestinians' acceptance of non-violent resistance.

WHAT CAN BE DONE?

In order to determine and point out what can be done, one must be honest and list the obstacles to the grassroots movement struggle. In brief, these include:

- Lack of collective vision at the grassroots level
- Lack of leadership
- Non-governmental organizations losing touch with the pulse of the street and becoming fat cats defending their own interests and achievements
- Lack of support for the grassroots movement by the top level leadership, including the President, Prime Minister and the PLC
- The brutality of the occupation in dealing with the grassroots movement as in Bi'lin, for example
- Lack of positive media coverage of the grassroots non-violent activities
- Lack of hope among the Palestinian people emerging from the feeling that nothing will change as long as the American government remains adamant in denying Palestinians' rights and freedom.

The reality we live in may be depressing, but I don't want to leave you with the impression that things are dead. We still witness the people of Bil'in demonstrating every Friday. We still have courageous individuals like Hani Abu Haikal, of the Tel Rumeida area in Hebron city, resisting the settlers and their daily intimidation on his own. And as history shows, no occupation lasts forever.

SO WHAT SHOULD BE DONE?

There are many positive steps we can and should take:

- Open a serious and healthy debate among Palestinians so that at the end of the day, we will produce a common vision for the country to unite our efforts. There has never been a people living under occupation who did not go through such a stage, and we must re-organize our vision.
- A new and young leadership must emerge and must be encouraged and nurtured.
- NGOs need to come down from their high horses and start including the grassroots within their projects, resources, budgets and staff.
- Top leadership needs to encourage the grassroots movement by addressing them directly, participating in their events and providing them both moral and financial support
- The methods, the tactics and the ugly face of the brutal occupation must be exposed, and that is where the role of the international community comes in.
- Positive media coverage of the grassroots non-violent activities is crucial, but convincing CNN to report the truth is very difficult and at times seems impossible.

Finally, let me remind you that there is a birth for every nation and for every birth there is labor and for every labor there is pain. We are witnessing and feeling the pains of the birth of the Palestinian state.

STRATEGIES TO END
THE ISRAELI OCCUPATION

Khalil Nakhleh

First, let me start with the assumption that you are reading this because you believe that injustice has been done against the Palestinian people, and you are committed to doing something about it.

To be fair to your commitment, and to help move the discussion forward, I shall focus in this presentation not on the analysis and dissection of the current political situation and why we are at this impassable point in our struggle but on elements of a strategy that could break this engulfing vicious cycle in which we find ourselves. Today, in the age of lightning-fast electronic communications and unhindered information, there is more and more accessible, reliable and critical data and more and more insightful and daring analysis to which one can turn. So you, as well as I, can easily retrieve that information, if interested.

However, the back side of the huge, readily available body of information and analysis lies in the difficulty of discernment and discrimination between real and fictitious, primary and secondary, marginal and essential, official and individual perspectives. We need constantly to remind ourselves of the core issue of the struggle, as if we have to keep peeling off the artificial layers that have been piled on it to meet the interests of the different parties.

THE MAIN ISSUE

The main issue of the struggle, as I see it, is that a colonial-settler movement – Zionism – has been embarking for nearly a century on ethnically cleansing the land of Palestine of its native population by various coercive and illegal means, combining military, economic, legal, psychological, and environmental ones. This has resulted in the forceful transformation of the native population of Palestine into several groups: dispersed refugees outside their land; internally displaced persons on their land; people who have been relegated to the status of second-class citizens or unwelcome foreigners in their home land (the Palestinian communities in Israel); and those who have been subjected to a prolonged and relentless military and economic occupation by Israel for forty years (the Palestinian communities in the West Bank of the Jordan River, East Jerusalem and Gaza). This comprehensive view ought to help us set the actual parameters of the struggle in which we have been engaged for over half a century and to develop strategies for how to proceed.

Thus, it should be emphasized that:

- This is not a religious struggle or a struggle between two religiously-based opposing ideologies;
- This is not a struggle between those who believe that Israeli citizens have a right to exist in an independent state, abiding by international conventions and agreements, free from oppression and persecution, and those who don't;
- This is not merely a struggle to find temporary arrangements for how to end military occupation or minimize its deleterious effects on the Palestinian population under the occupation which began in 1967;
- Contrary to public opinion and perception, this is not just a struggle to gain freedom for the Palestinians from Israeli occupation, however limited and truncated, and to achieve independent living, however curtailed, over limited areas of historical Palestine;
- **But this is, and ought to be, a struggle against the structure that allows and condones the occupation and suppression of the other; a structure whose basis is a system of apartheid and an ideology of exclusion; a structure that is nurtured by an insatiable ideology and practice of ethnic cleansing and population transfer, in order to achieve "Jewish purity" in the land of Palestine.**

ELEMENTS OF A STRATEGY

To respond to this grave and threatening challenge, I propose for your reflection and discussion what may be the elements of a strategy:

1. I am proposing the launching of a **people's strategy**. The purpose of this strategy is not merely to end the present military occupation of parts of Palestine, but to work against the prevalent structure of occupation, seeking the dismantlement of its apartheid, exclusionary ideology that is premised on ethnic cleansing and population transfer of non-Jews.

2. To achieve this goal, I see two levels of struggle: an internal level centered in the land of Palestine/Israel, and an external level centered in different locales in the rest of the world, focusing on areas where Jewish presence is high and politically involved in what happens in our region, and specifically, but not exclusively, in the USA. At this level, Americans who are opposed to the structure of Israeli occupation in Palestine are urged to coalesce with like-minded Jews in that country. These individuals and groups, then, become the external nucleus that spearheads the dismantlement of the apartheid structure of occupation.

3. The "internal level" is to set the tone of the struggle, and to reverse it from its current, inert, "reactive" mode to a genuine "proactive" mode. The internal level should set the agenda and its tone for the rest of the world. It should be the primary and critical level.

4. At the internal level, there ought to be a purposeful coalition of all internal forces that are committed to stand genuinely against the structure and ideology of occupation which are premised on ethnic cleansing and population transfer, and the abhorrent and racist "demographic formula."

5. This coalition should not be exclusionary; it should include all forces committed to this approach: Israeli Jews, Muslim Palestinians, Christian Palestinians, secular Israelis, secular Palestinians, etc.

6. The uniting platform of this coalition should have a clear and unambiguous commitment in opposition to the Israeli **structure and ideology of occupation**, and should work to dismantle it. This must be so, if we are seeking a just and sustained resolution to this historical conflict, irrespective of how politically unpopular these concepts are, or how unacceptable they sound to the ears of the so-called "international community," which has been usurped successfully by the US under the threat of brute power and economic sanctions.

7. I propose that this "coalition of the committed" should discard and reject the often repeated slogan of the two–state solution, which has become inane, redundant, unrealizable, and totally undermined by internationally-sanctioned Israeli apartheid policies. I propose, further, that this two-state objective should be rejected because it is unjust, unresponsive to people's need for freedom and independent living and to their right to unfettered development, and because it legitimizes historical and ongoing stealing of the lands of indigenous Palestinian communities.

8. I propose, furthermore, that the two-state solution should be discarded and rejected because it maintains existing racist and oppressive policies and is premised on the concepts of exclusion, population transfer, ethnic cleansing, ghettoization of local communities, and artificial separation of the people—all the people—in the land of Palestine/Israel.

9. I propose that this "coalition of the committed" should struggle to transform the present land of Palestine/Israel into a democratic, just domain where the people of the area—all the people—can live freely, independently and equally and are allowed to exercise all their rights. Then, the people themselves can choose what to call this domain. Once we achieve such a domain, we will have succeeded in liberating our minds!

IMPLICATIONS OF THIS STRATEGY

1. This is a people's strategy that defies current official positions on all sides, undermines them, and seeks to transform them in harmony with people's aspirations and needs.

2. This approach exposes the redundant, superfluous and hollow official claims and negotiation premises that have been circulating over the last 15 years, and it shows how barren and impractical they are.

3. A people's strategy can be, and likely would be, undermined, coerced and interrupted by adversary official power; therefore we should expect it to be a prolonged struggle with little, if any, immediate results. On the other hand, such a people's strategy can turn into a powerful driving force, coalescing people hitherto disconnected, and liberating their minds.

4. Such a people's strategy can generate new, innovative and sustainable lines of power and commitment.

Finally, your commitment to be involved in this difficult and protracted struggle to end occupation, apartheid, and injustice and to circumvent actions of illegal population transfer, displacement and ethnic cleansing—in short, the liberation of the mind and the land—is the essence of liberation theology. Thank you for being engaged.

The following photographs were taken during
the Sabeel Sixth International Conference

"The Forgotten Faithful"

held November 2-9, 2006.

Patriarch Theophilos III, Greek Orthodox Patriarch of Jerusalem and all the Holy Land and Jordan

Mgr. George Bakar, Patriarchal Vicar, Greek Catholic Patriarchal Exarchate; Patriarch Michel Sabbah, Latin Patriarch and Archbishop of Jerusalem; Father Humam Khzouz, Latin Patriarchate

Archbishop Aristarchos, Greek Orthodox Patriarchate; Archbishop Aris Shirvanian, Armenian Orthodox Patriarchate; Archbishop Mar Swerios Malki Murad, Syrian Orthodox Patriarchate; Father Afriem Elorashalimy, Coptic Orthodox Patriarchate, Bishop Alan Bartlett, Episcopal Church, USA; Rev. Dr. Naim Ateek, Sabeel Ecumenical Liberation Theology Center

Bishop Munib Younan, Evangelical Lutheran Church in Jordan and the Holy Land

Bishop Dr. Kenneth Cragg

Bishop Suheil Dawani, Episcopal Church of Jerusalem, and Archbishop Paul Sayah,
Maronite Patriarchal Exarchate

Celebration of Christianity at Notre Dame, Jerusalem

Plenary session, Bethlehem University, Bethlehem

Presentation in hall of Latin Church, Aboud with Rev. Ibrahim Nairouz, Episcopal Church

Worshipping with Greek Orthodox congregation in Ein 'Arik near Ramallah

Plenary session, Baptist Church, Nazareth

Yasmeen choir under the direction of Hania Soudah Sabbaara

Rev. Dr. Kenneth Bailey

Plenary session, Cultural Palace, Ramallah

Holy Communion, St. Peter's Primacy, by the Sea of Galilee